IN TRANSIT

IN TRANSIT
IN THE COMPANY OF STRANGERS

Photographs by Jonathan Moller

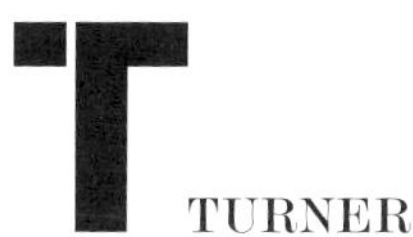

TURNER

CONTENTS

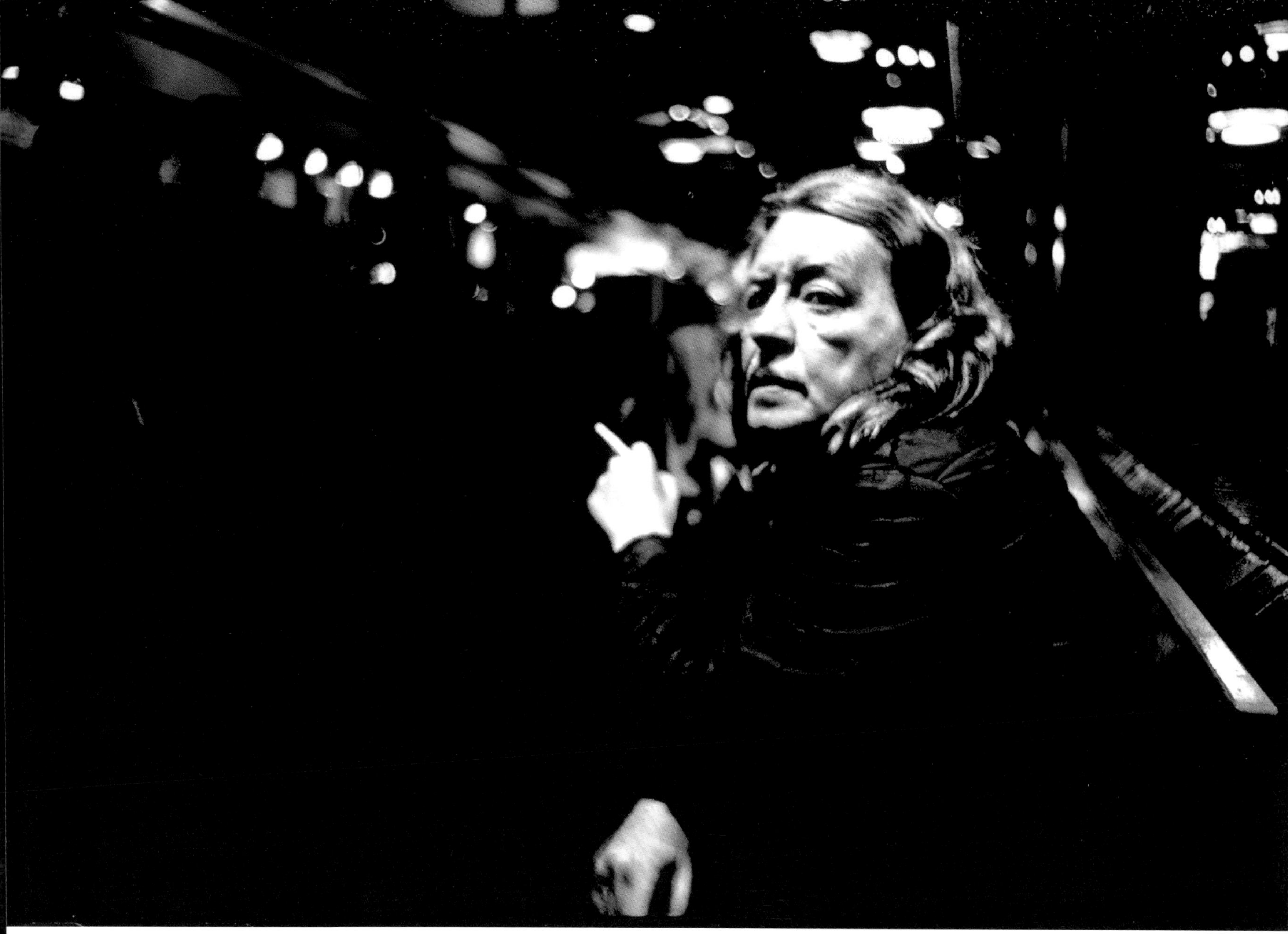

Boston Subway. Massachusetts, 1986

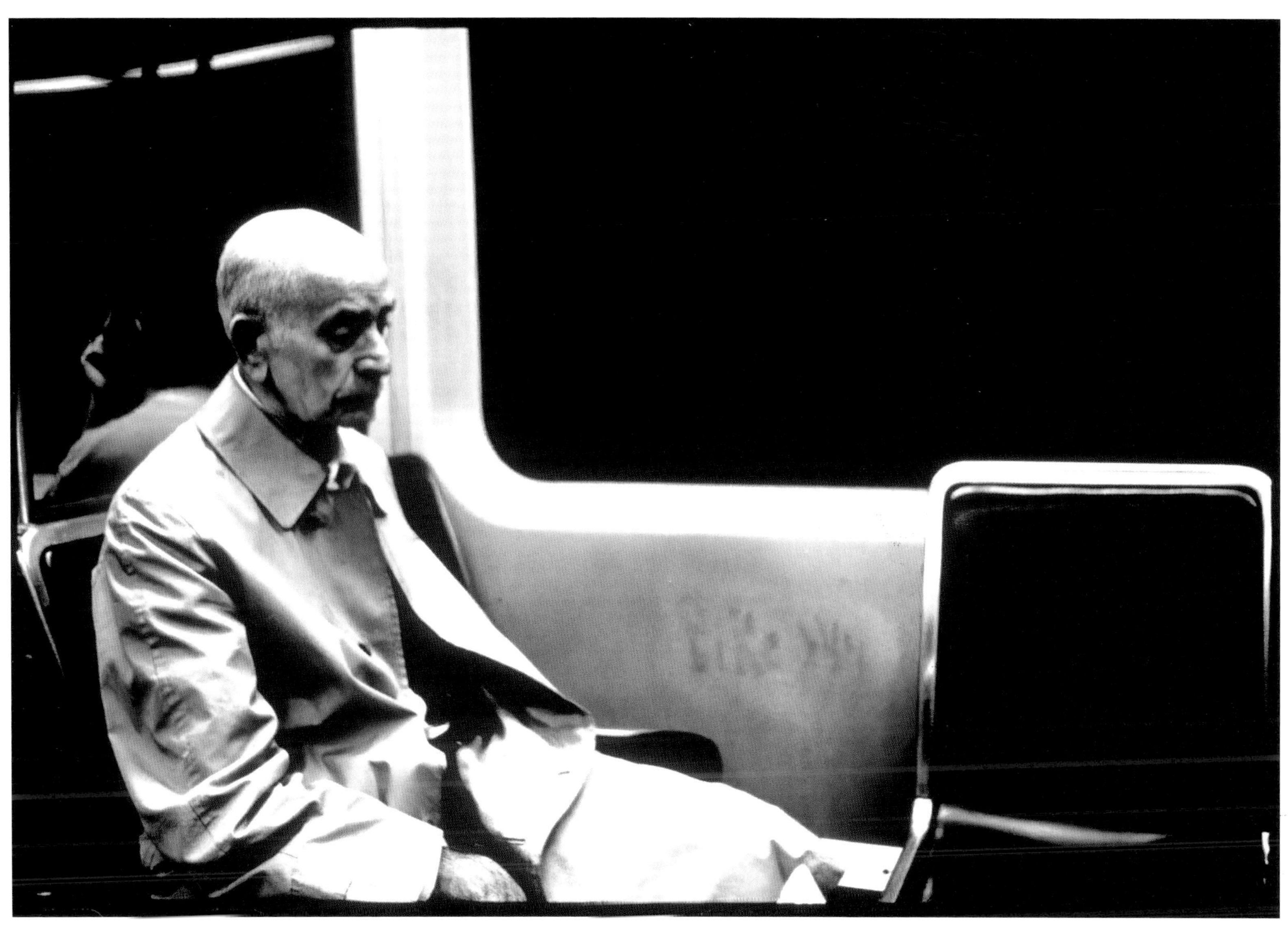

Boston Subway. Massachusetts, 1987

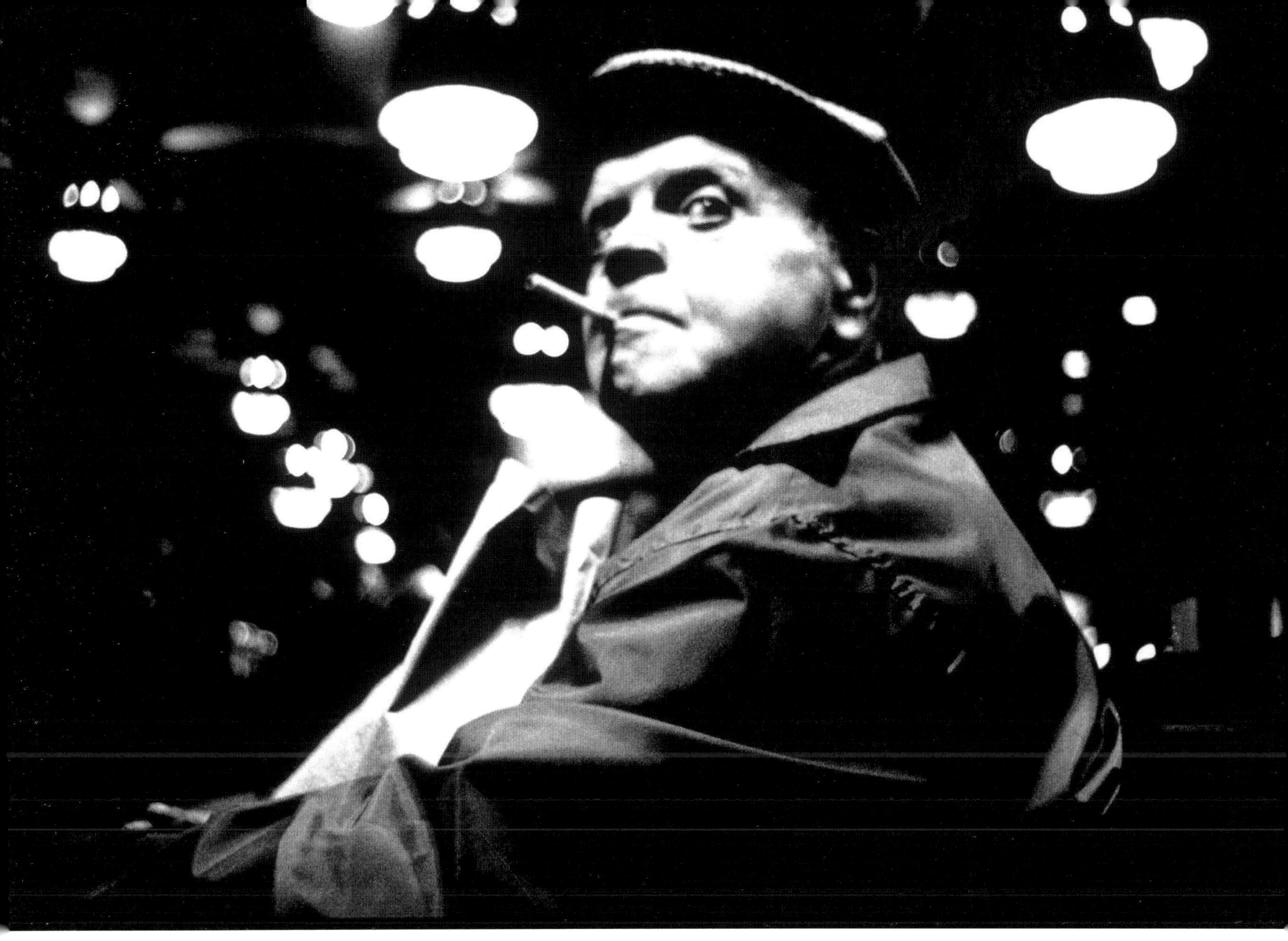

Boston Subway. Massachusetts, 1986

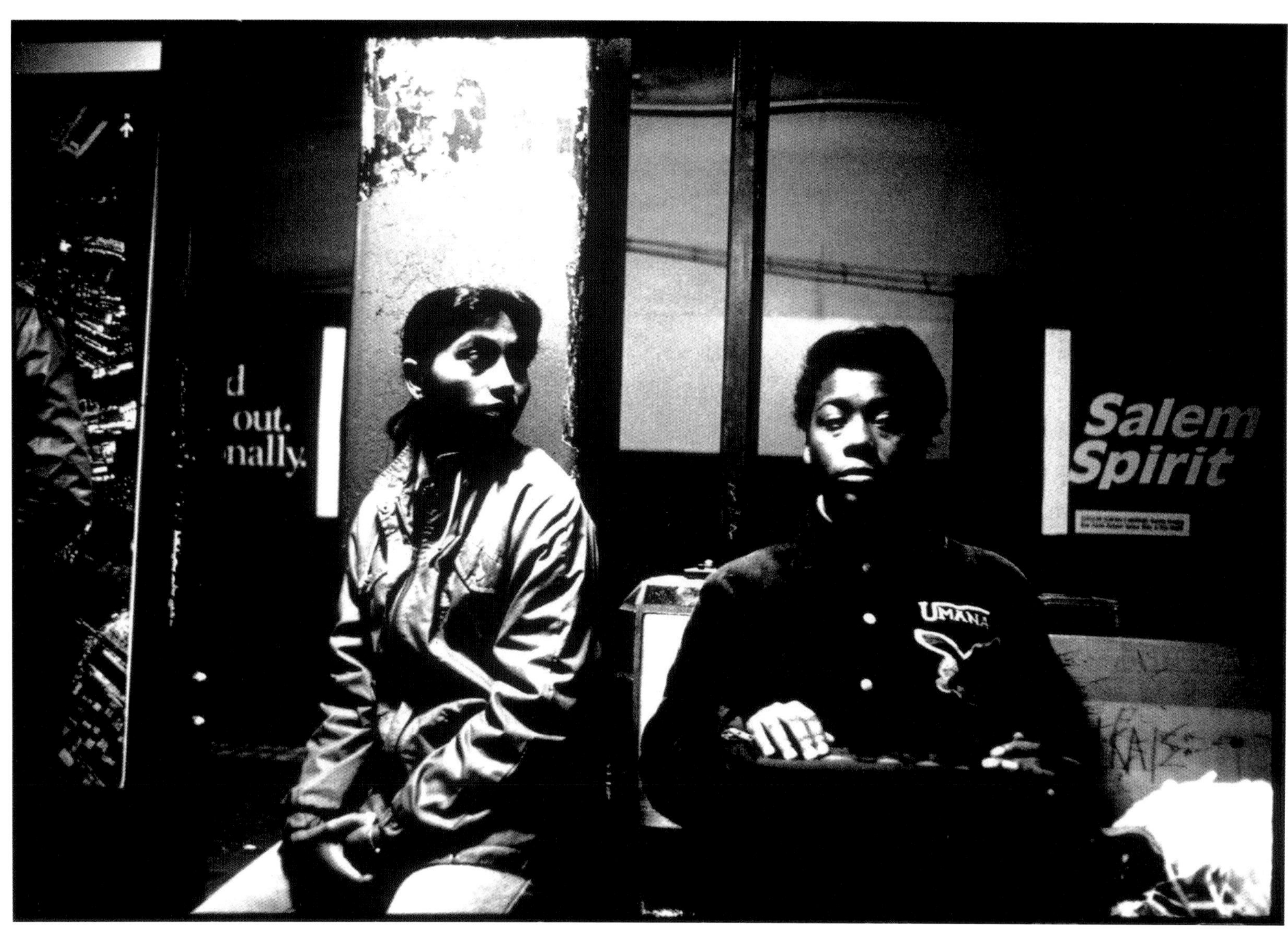

Boston Subway. Massachusetts, 1987

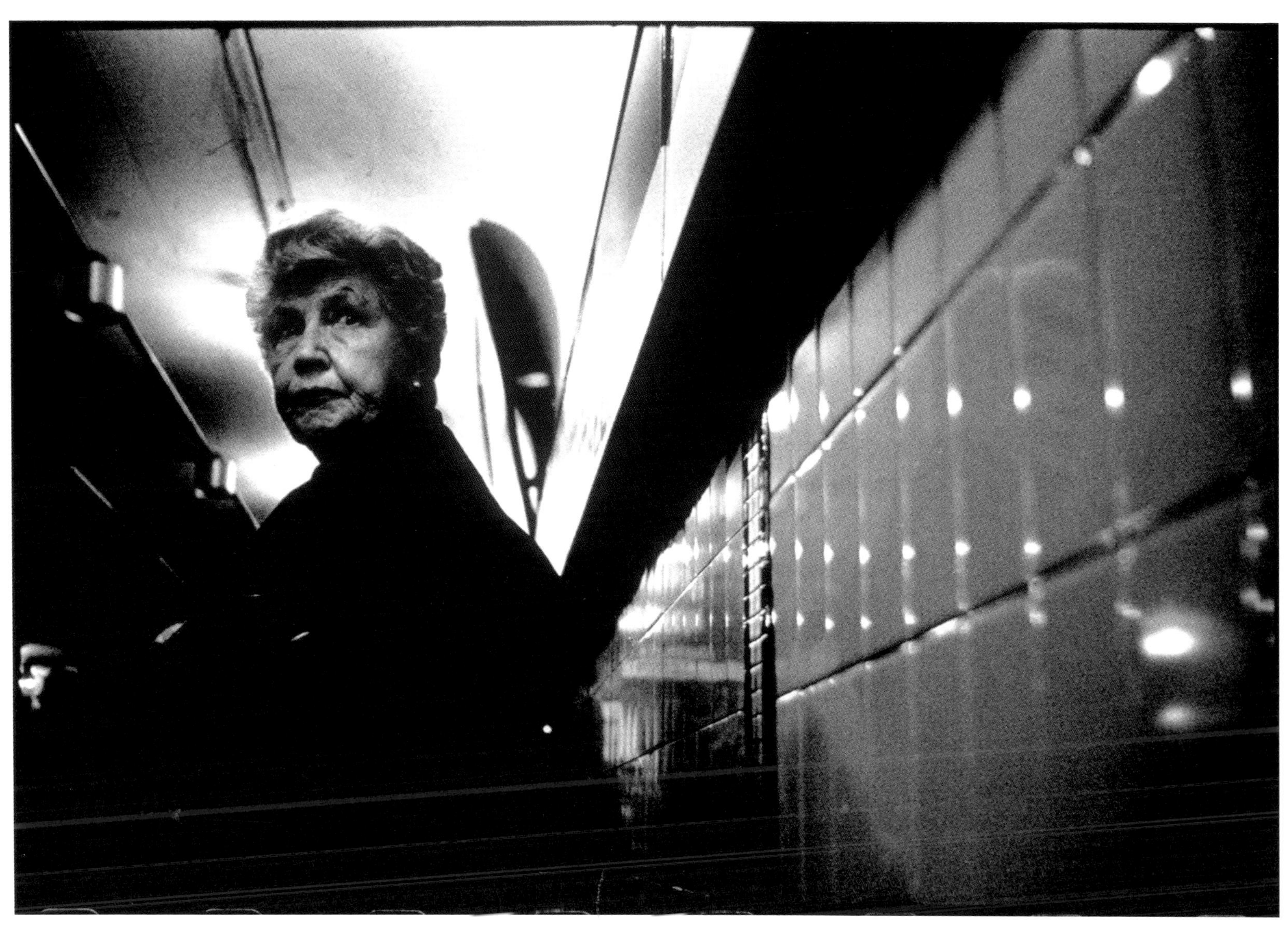

Boston Subway. Massachusetts, 1986

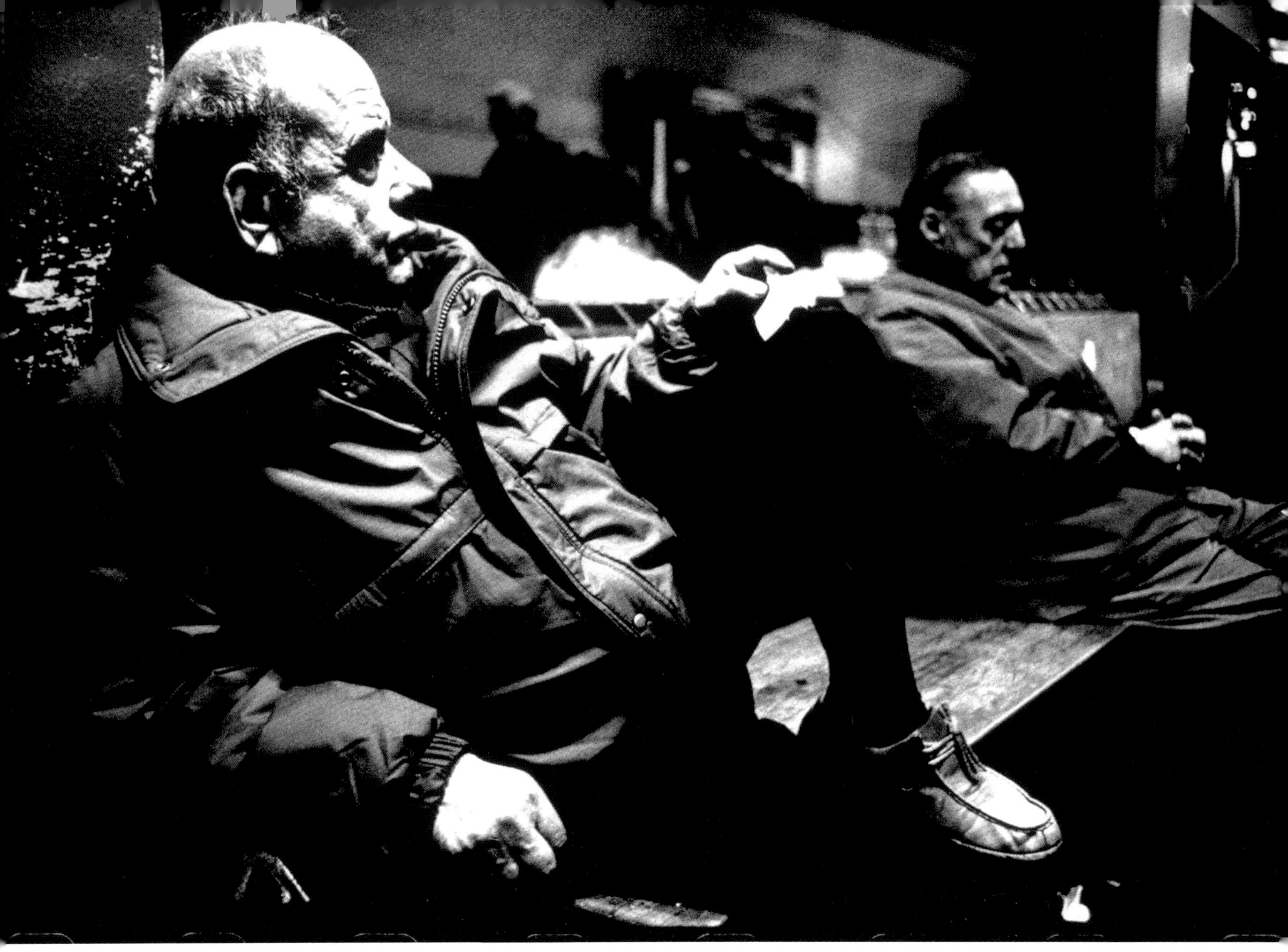

Boston Subway. Massachusetts, 1986

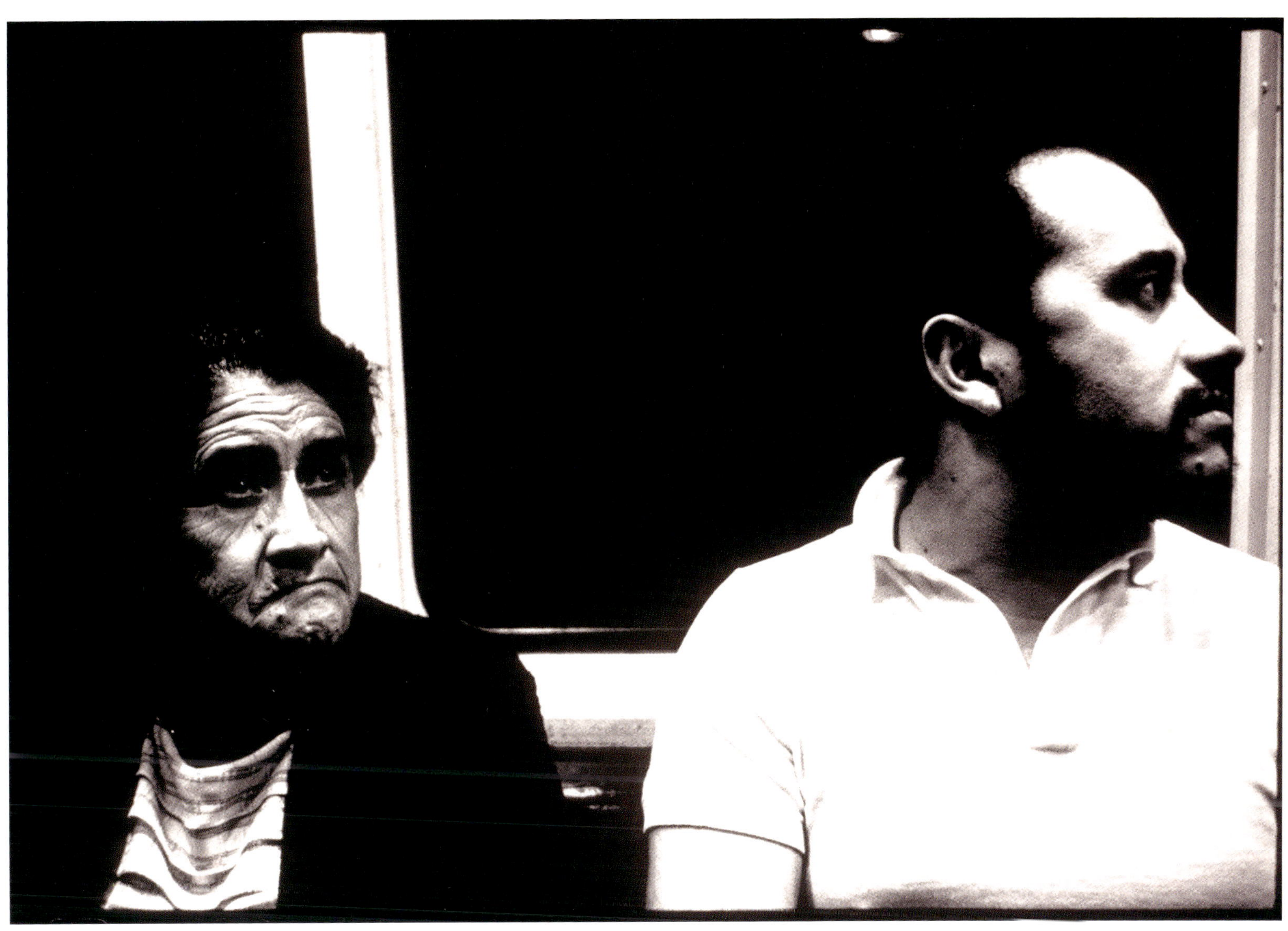

Boston Subway. Massachusetts, 1987

Traveling Alone in the Forest of Humanity

This collection of images spans many years—beginning from the mid 1980s in Massachusetts—up until a recent trip to Guatemala in 2022. This collection in a way represents a visual diary of my movements and travels over the years, including an extended time living and working in different countries in Latin America.

It started as a sporadic and largely unplanned series that little by little began to take shape. It began during my years in art school in Boston. As undefined and informal a project as it was in the beginning, it slowly developed into something quite personal. After all, I too was "in transit," searching for and beginning to define a personal vision as an artist-activist—while experimenting technically with the medium—and perhaps on a deeper level, discovering my feeling and thinking self. It was the beginning of an awakening, a lifelong journey.

In the 1980s while studying at the School of the Museum of Fine Arts in Boston, much of my work focused on stillness and solitude, and in that context, looking at the early (B&W) images that are in this book, I began to photograph people in transit: people temporarily in a suspended state; people in the close company of others yet in their own worlds; people often alone; people anonymous and isolated.

Then in 1991, I went to Nicaragua for five months to work with an archive of photographic negatives about the civil war in El Salvador. Sometimes I was shooting my own photographs, too. In early 1993, I traveled to El Salvador and from there to Guatemala, where I ended up spending over six years working in solidarity with uprooted indigenous populations while sporadically taking photographs—usually in the context of human rights work and sometimes of people in motion, in transit.

The B&W subway and ferry photographs in this book represent my early work. Even then, I was beginning a life-long exploration of solitude and connection, beauty and tragedy, anonymity and solidarity. This vision has imbued my work in the nearly forty years since those first shots were taken in the 80s. Whether my subjects have been landscapes, family portraits, or the often-political images of repressed and internally displaced indigenous campesinos in Guatemala or Peru, what I believe comes across—in mood and in look—in many of my photographs is a consistent personal thread. I have often thought that this thread is best expressed by a particular piece of graffiti written on the Berlin Wall: "We stand alone, as a tree, but in the brotherhood of the forest."

Although I began working with B&W film, in the mid 90s I also began to take color photographs, often in the context of multi-year projects in countries other than Guatemala—such as Peru and Cuba—or during trips to other places in Latin American or to Europe, for exhibitions and presentations or printings of my books in Spain, or simply during trips for pleasure.

Over the years, I have held on to my avid interest in people in transit and their struggles to move forward and at times to simply survive. Through my personal sense of connection, I too am in motion—passing through this world and my life—at times accompanying people on foot, or in boats, buses, cars, subways and airplanes in numerous countries around the world. This work is not just about people using different forms of transportation; it is also very much about the people themselves, their situations, and their lives. It is about our shared humanity.

Jonathan "Jonás" Moller

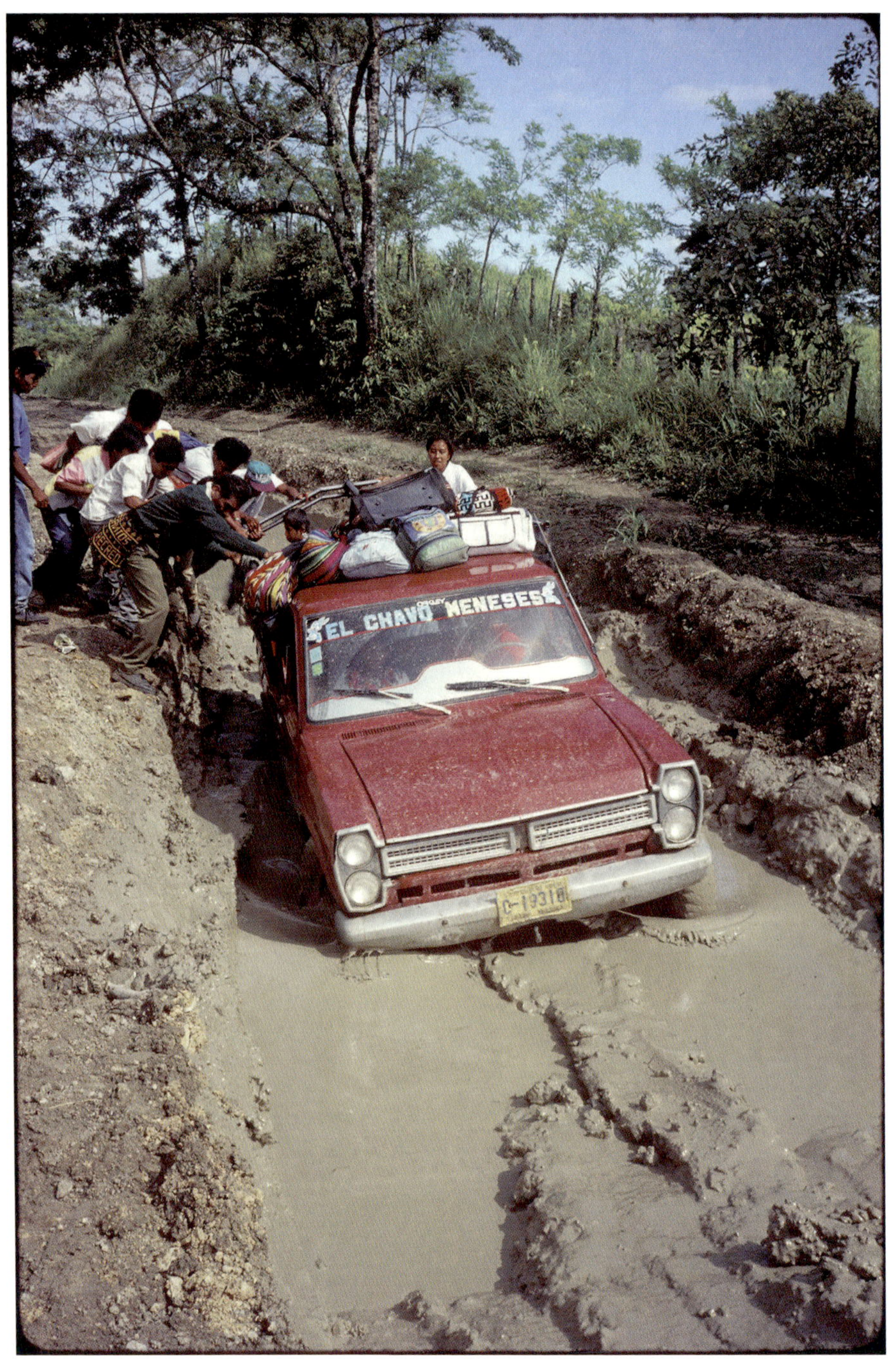

Public transport from Cobán, Alta Verapaz province to Cantabal
in the northern Ixcán region of Quiché province. Guatemala, 1994

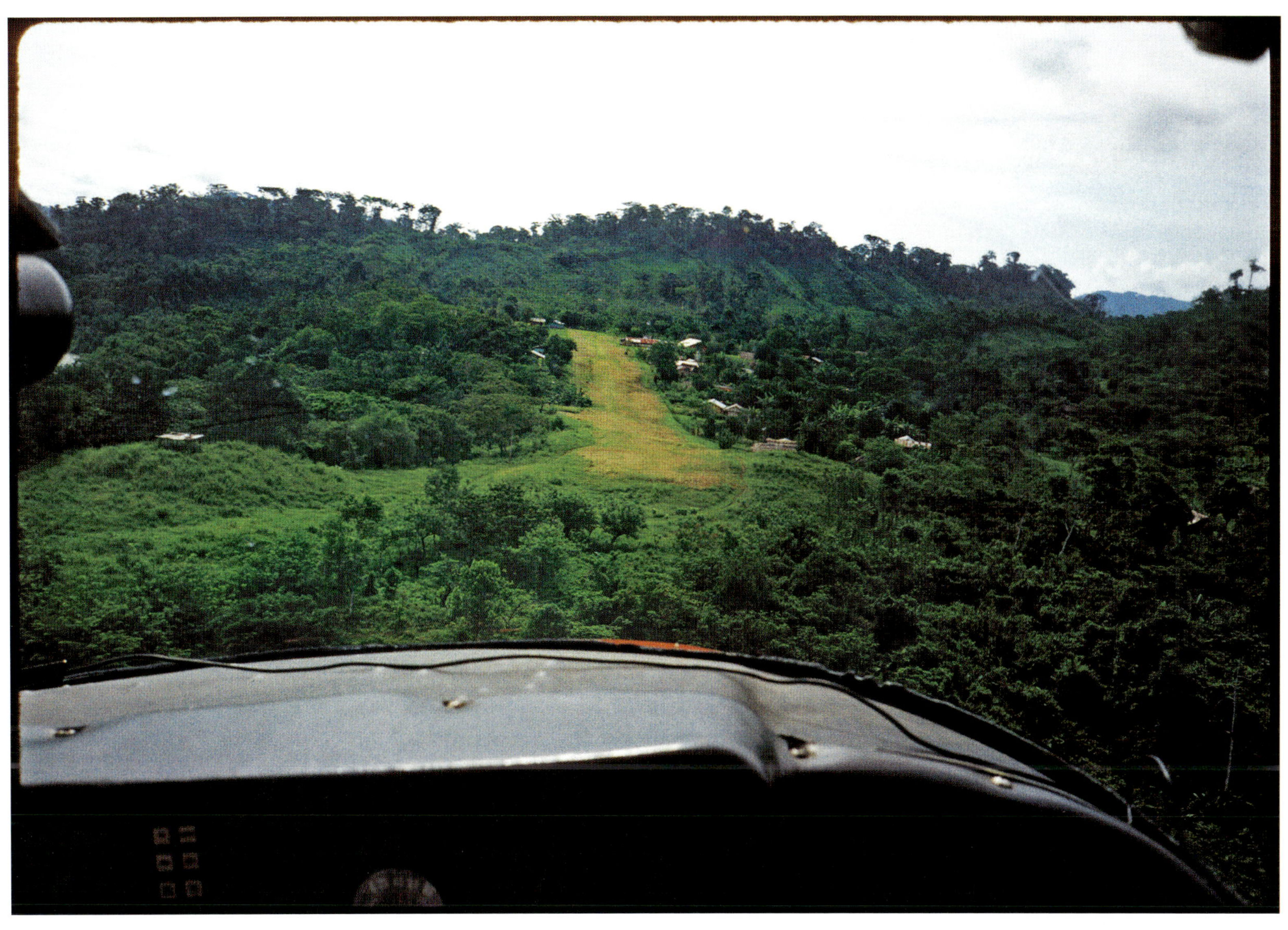

Landing in a small plane in the village of San Marcos in Quiché province, a community with no road access; from here, we went up the Chixoy River to the returned-refugee resettlement community of Copal AA La Esperanza. Guatemala, 1997

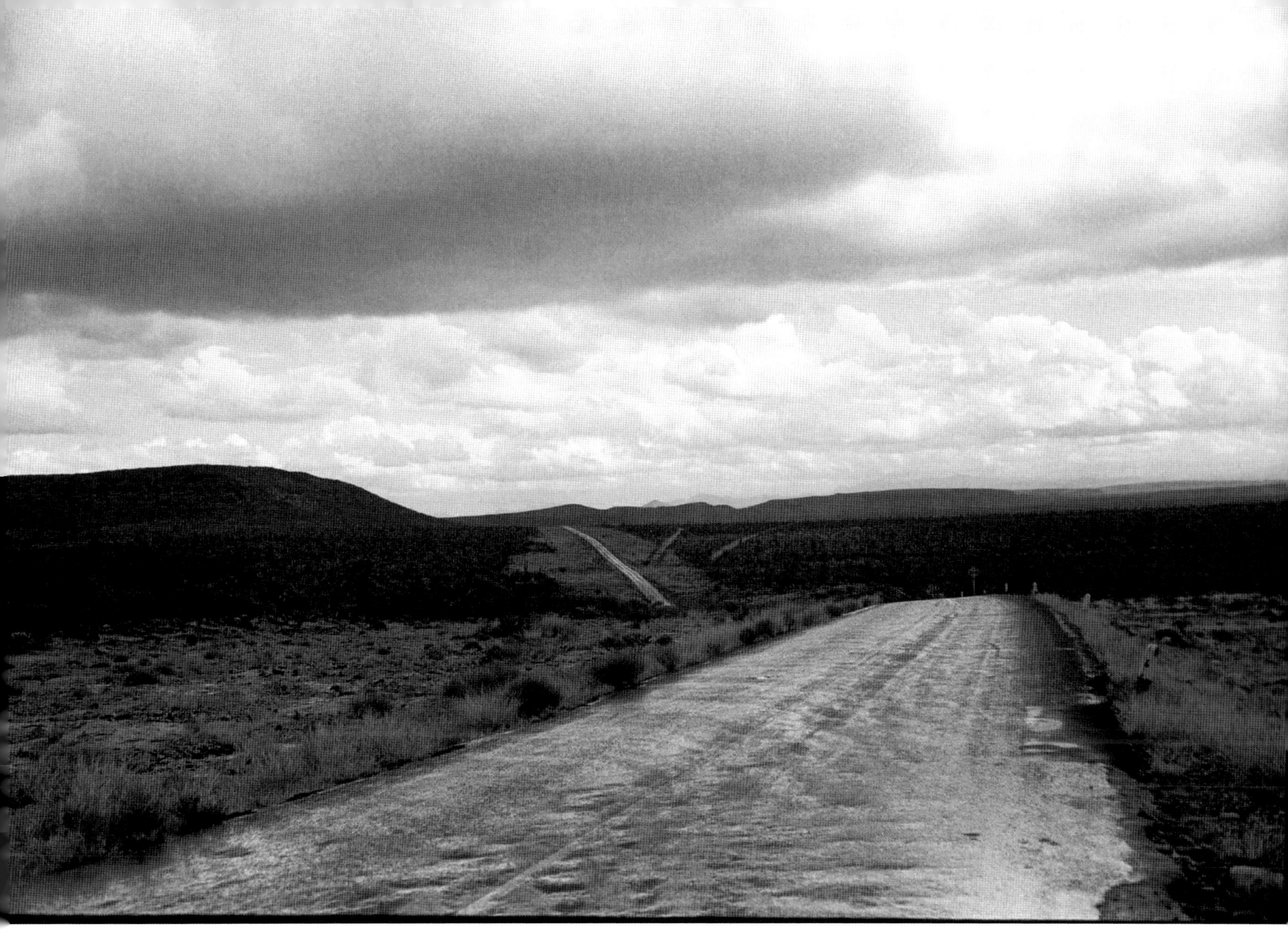

Driving from Tijuana, Baja California state, south to San José del Cabo,
Baja California Sur state. Mexico, 1984

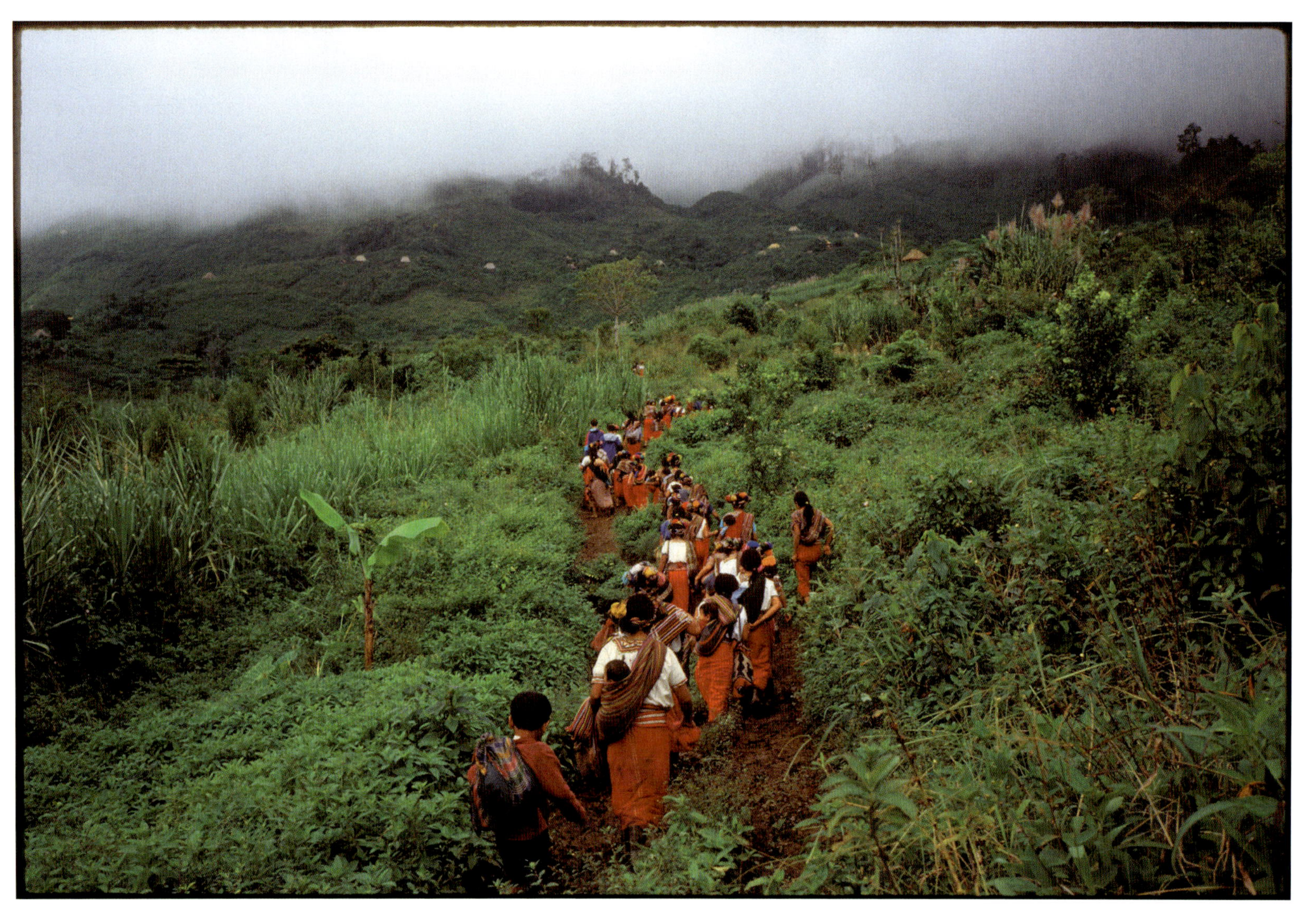

People of the Communities of Population in Resistance of the Sierra, walking from the small weekly open market in one settlement back to the settlements where they currently live. Guatemala, 1993

Right: Children on their way from the town of Paloma to another town on Ometepe Island. Lake Cocibolca, Nicaragua, 1991

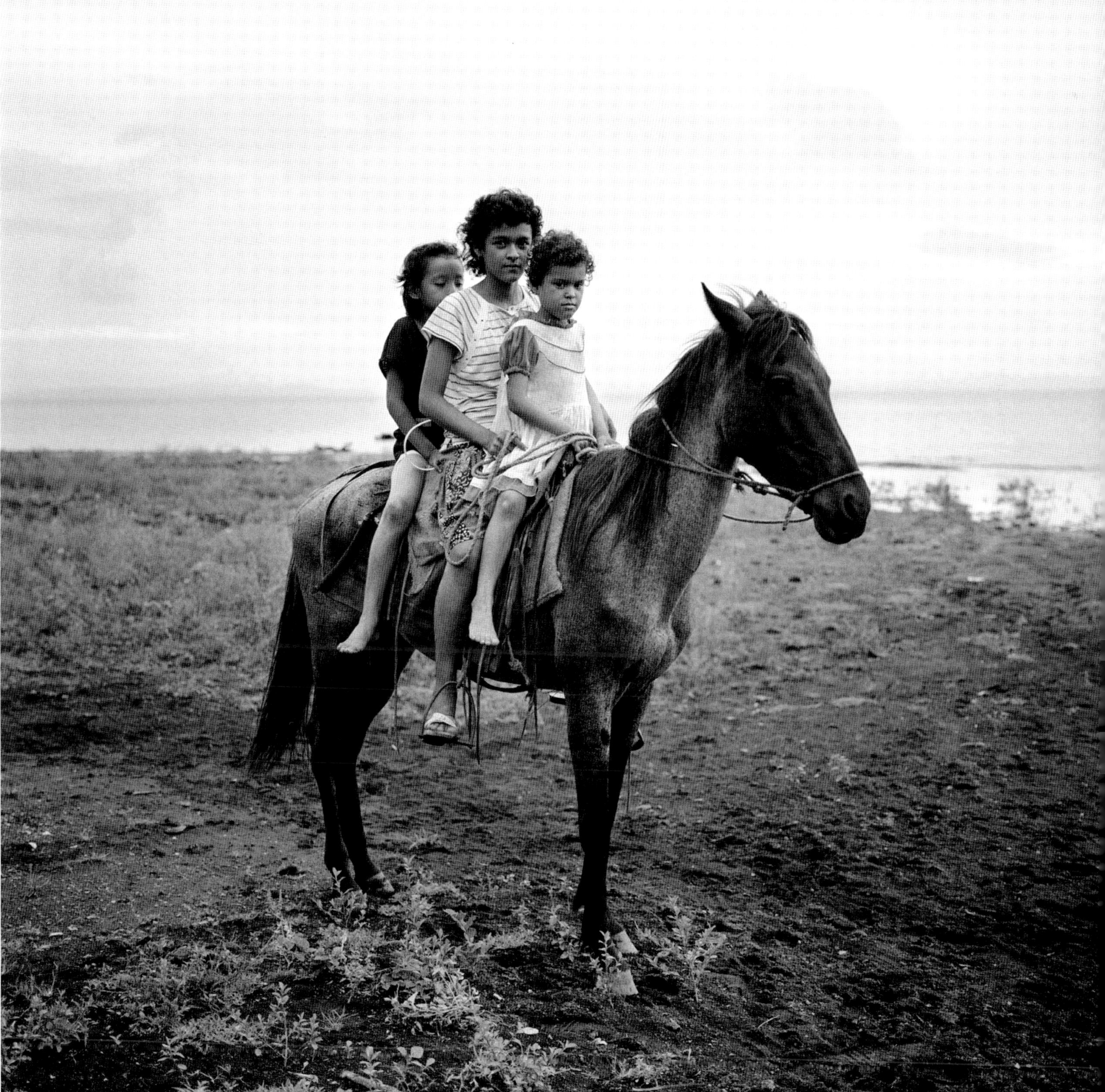

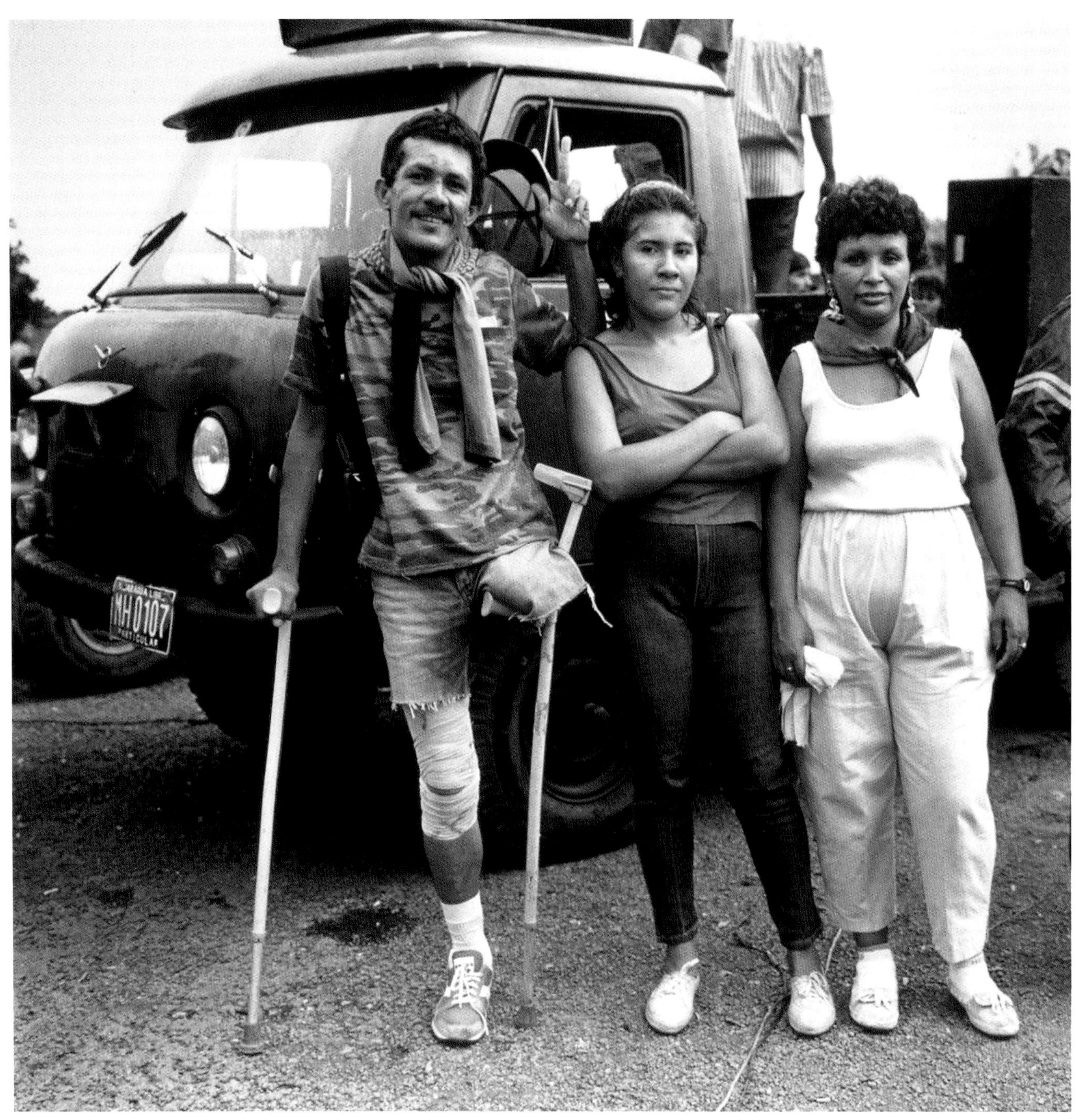

People about to leave Chinandega on a truck to go to a
protest in the city of León. Nicaragua, 1991

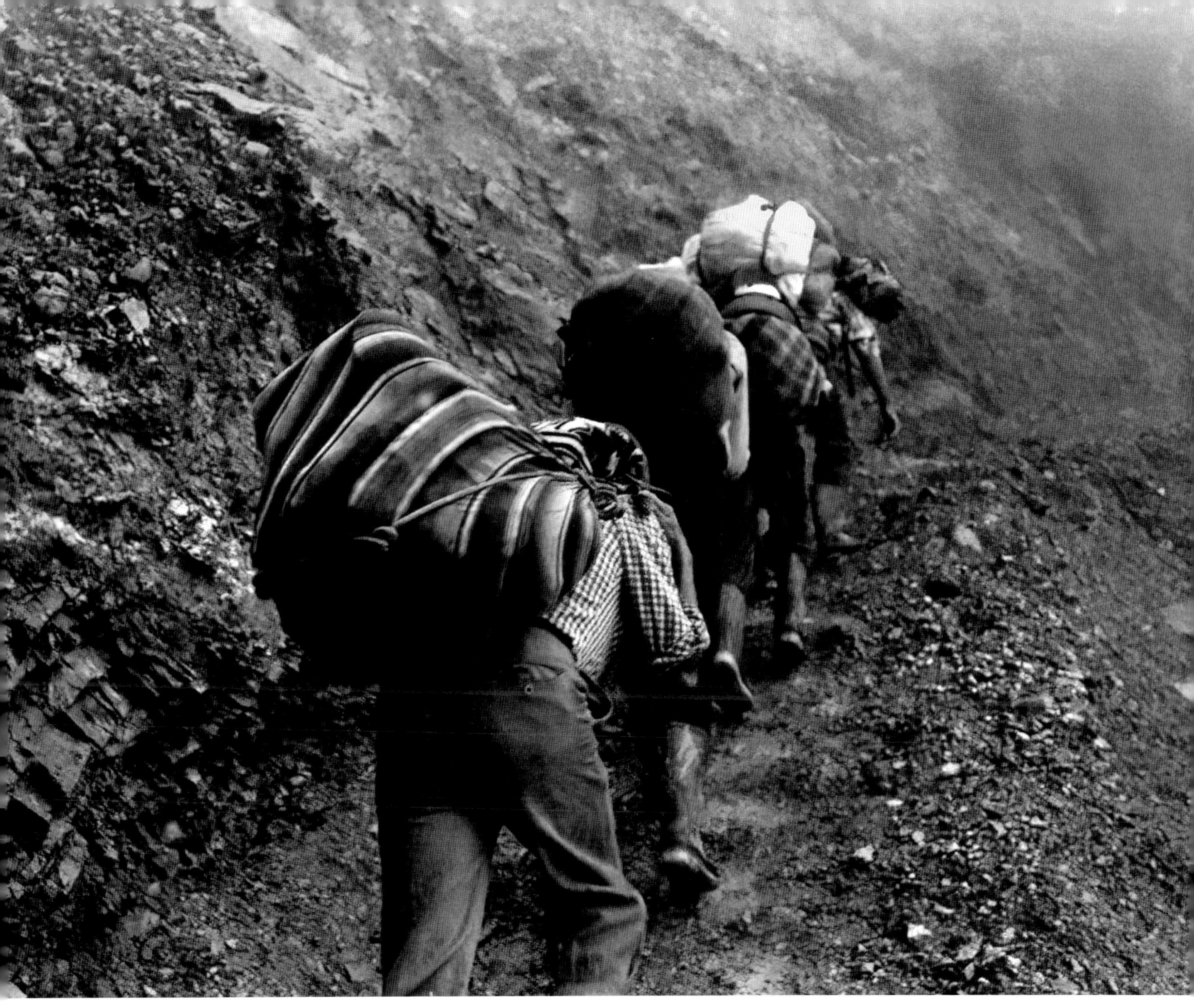

Men carrying rations and supplies into the mountains, to the Cabá region of the Communities of Population in Resistance of the Sierra; it's almost a two-day walk to where these internally displaced populations live. Guatemala, 1993

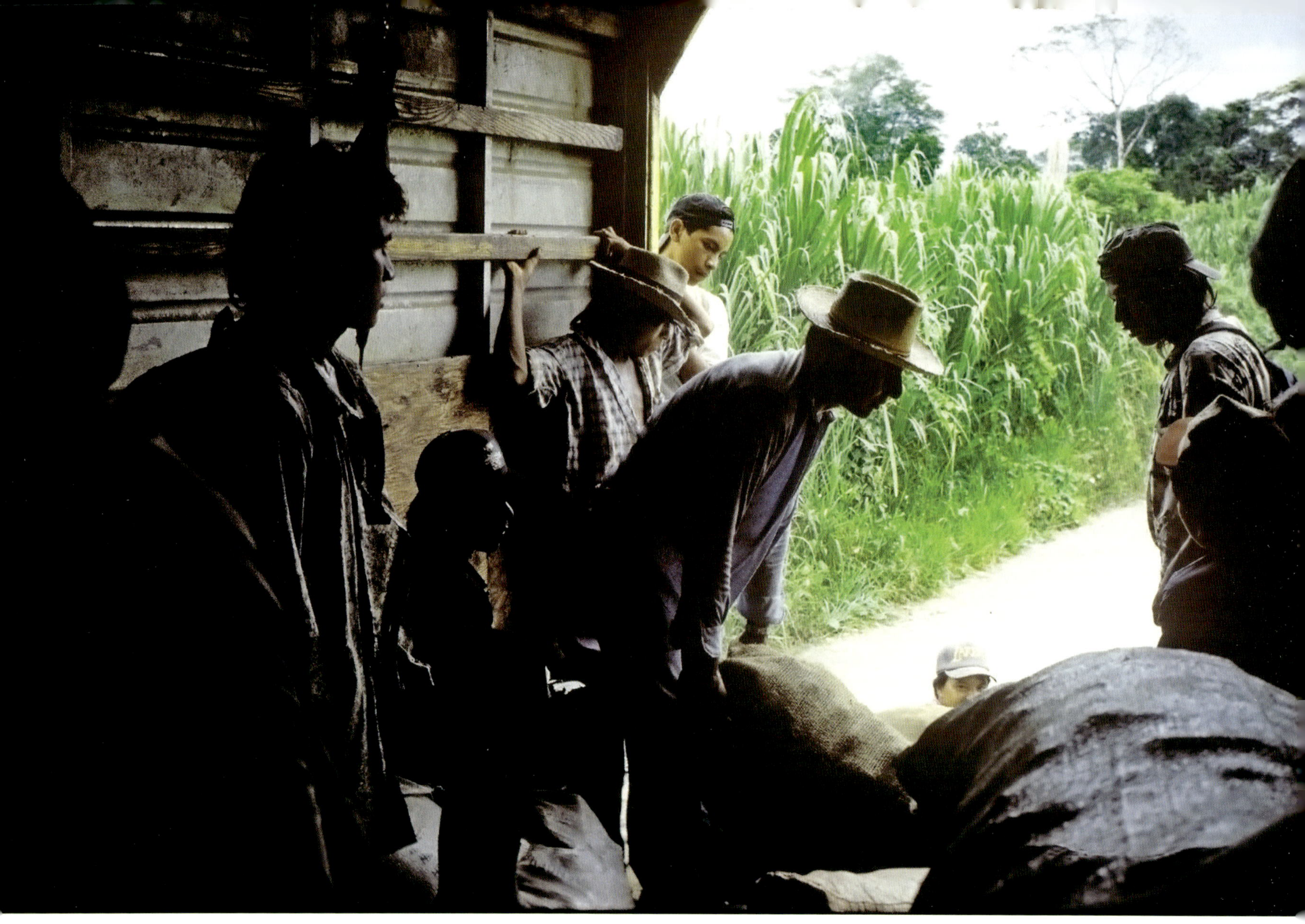

A truck transporting people and goods from Pueblo Nuevo to Cantabal,
in the Ixcán region of Quiché province. Guatemala, 1994

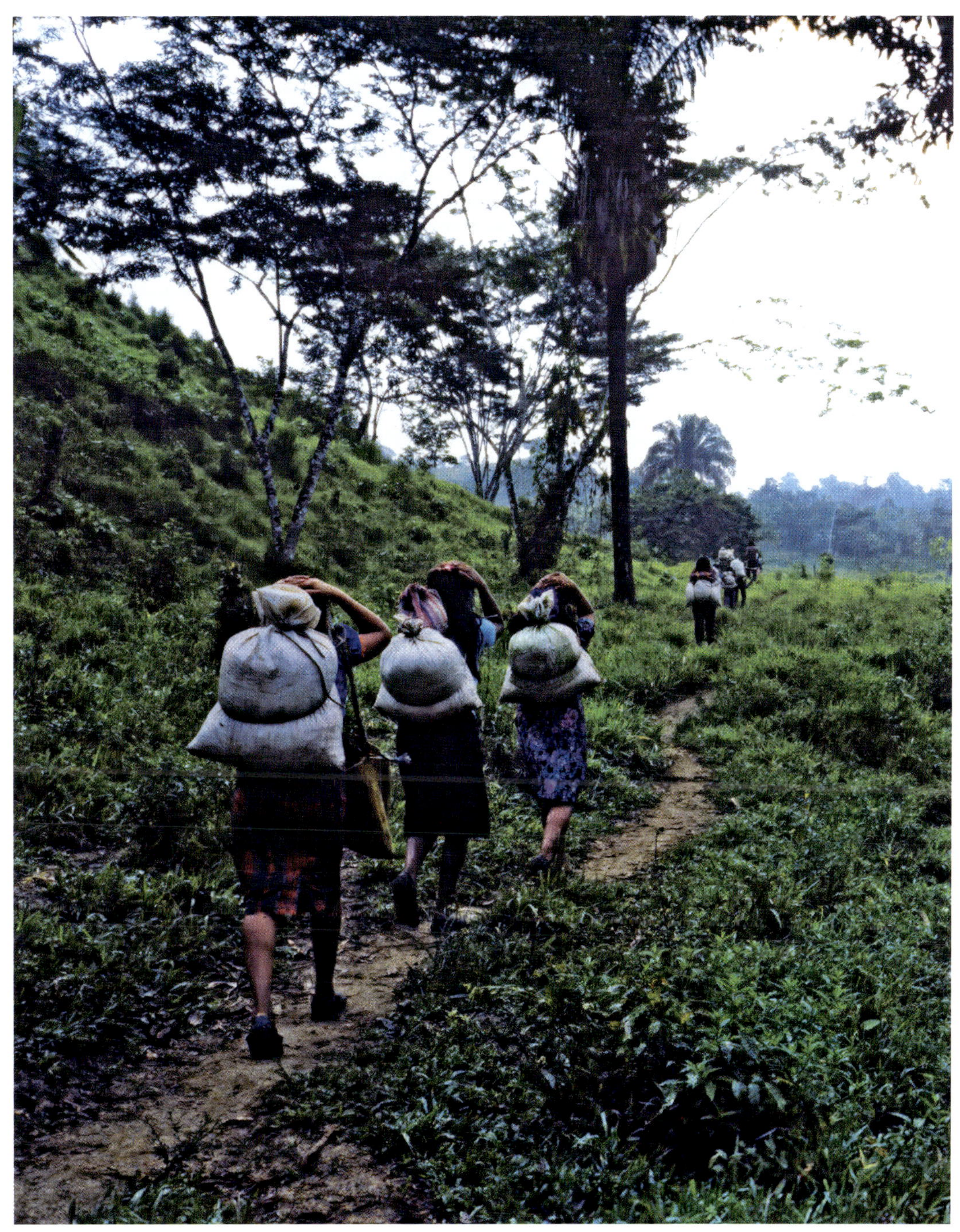

Members of the Communities of Population in Resistance of the Ixcán carry rations and goods
they got in Mexico back to their settlements in Guatemala. Puerto Rico farm, Ixcán, Chiapas, Mexico, 1994

For in the immediate world, everything is to be discerned for him who can discern it and centrally and simply, without either dissection into science, or digestion into art, but with the whole of consciousness, seeking to perceive it as it stands: so that the aspect of a street in sunlight can roar in the heart of itself as a symphony can, perhaps as no symphony can: and all of consciousness is shifted from the imagined, the revisive, to the effort to perceive simply the cruel radiance of what is.

James Agee
from *Let Us Now Praise Famous Men*,
first published in 1941

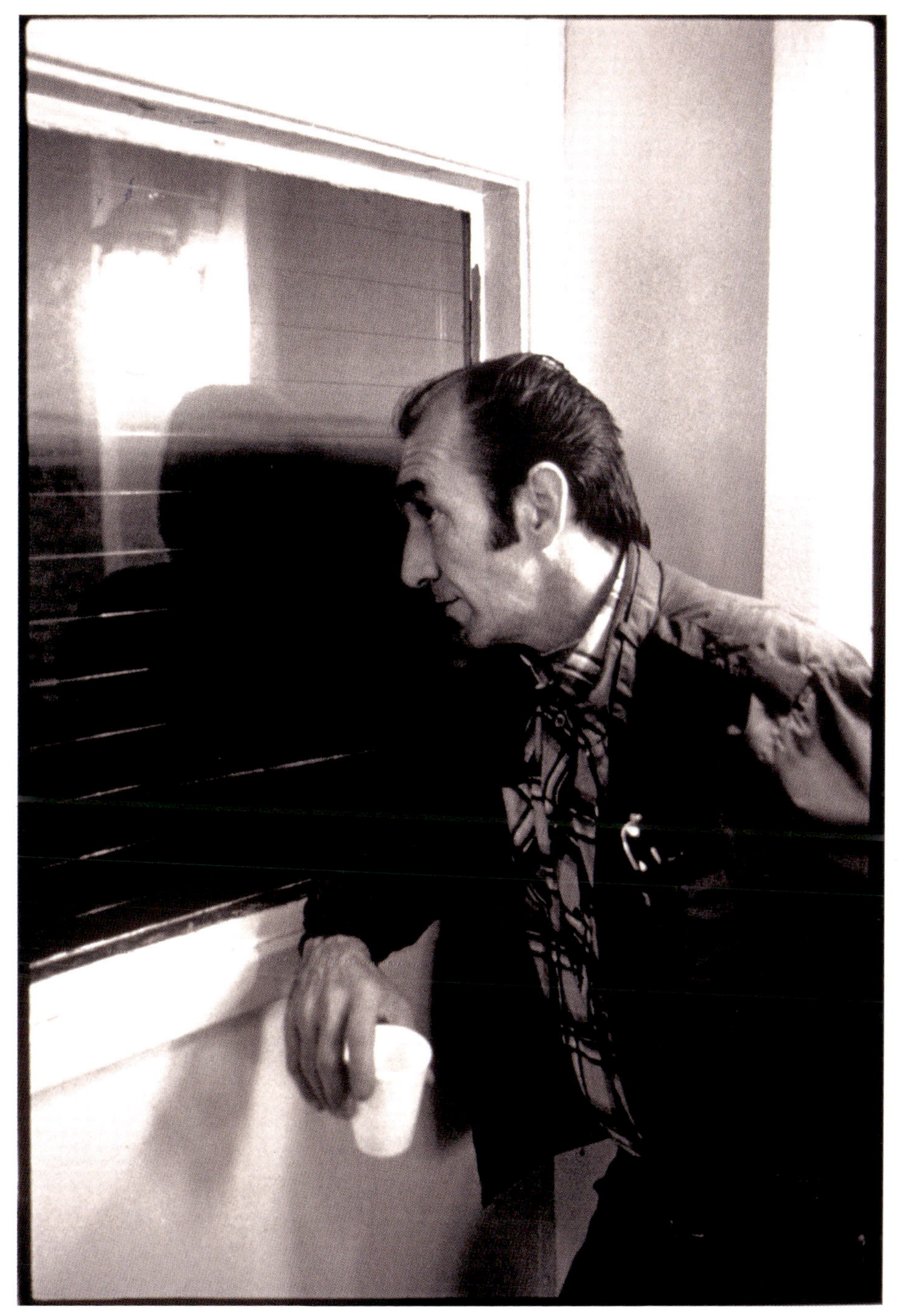

On the ferry from Woods Hole to Vineyard Haven.
Massachusetts, 1987

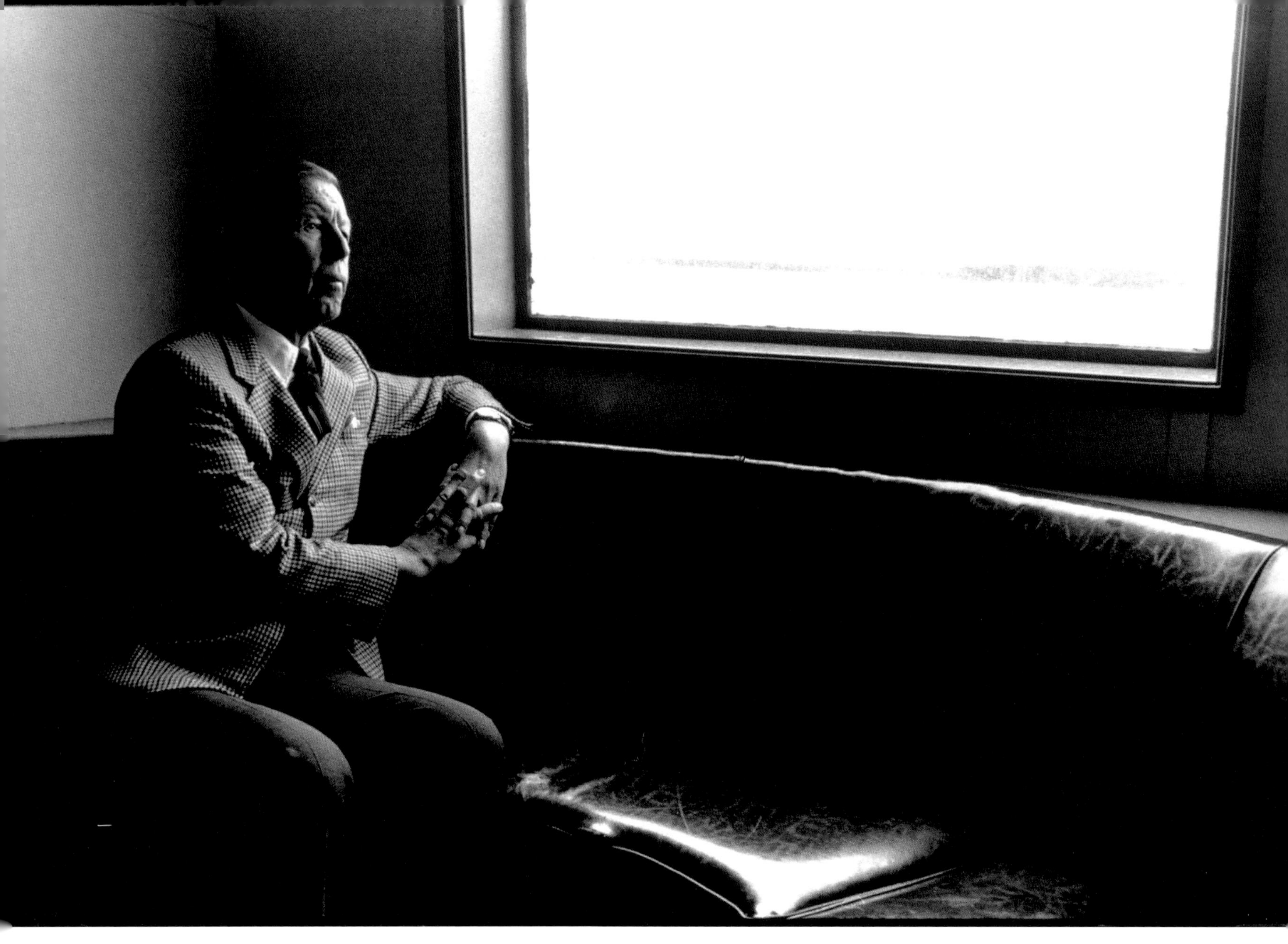

On the ferry from Woods Hole to Vineyard Haven.
Massachusetts, 1987

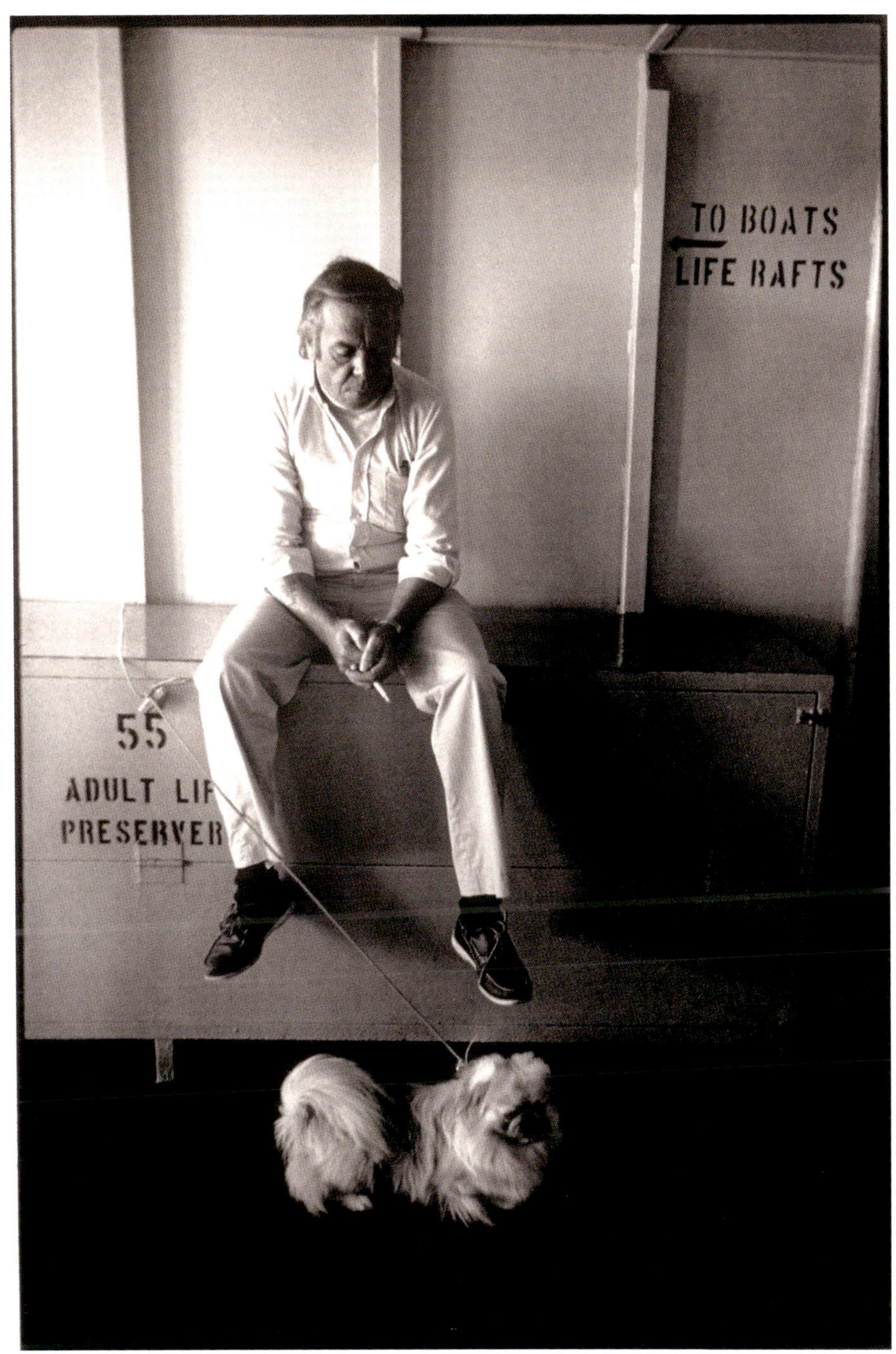

On the ferry from Woods Hole to Vineyard Haven.
Massachusetts, 1987

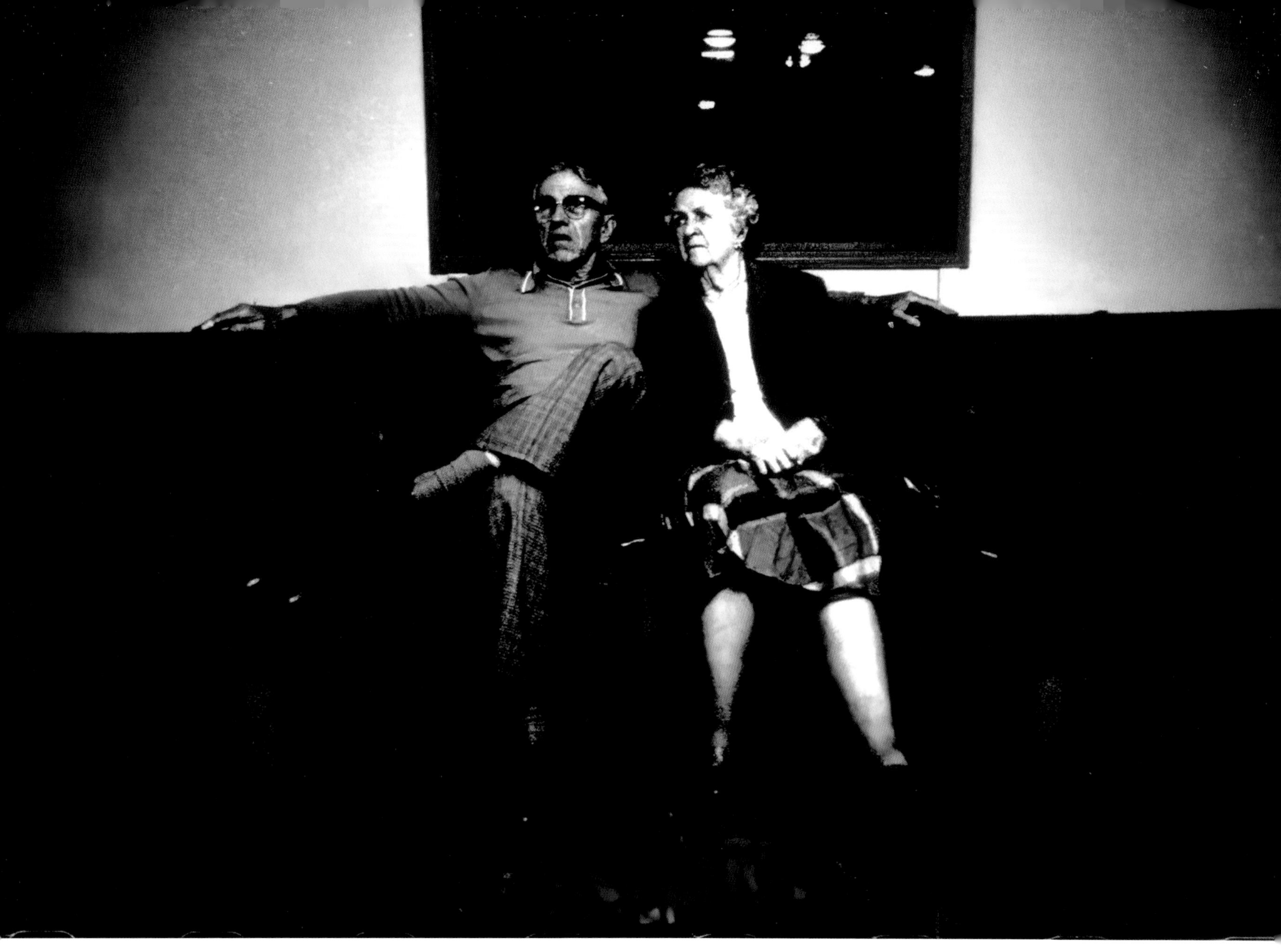

On the ferry from Woods Hole to Vineyard Haven.
Massachusetts, 1987

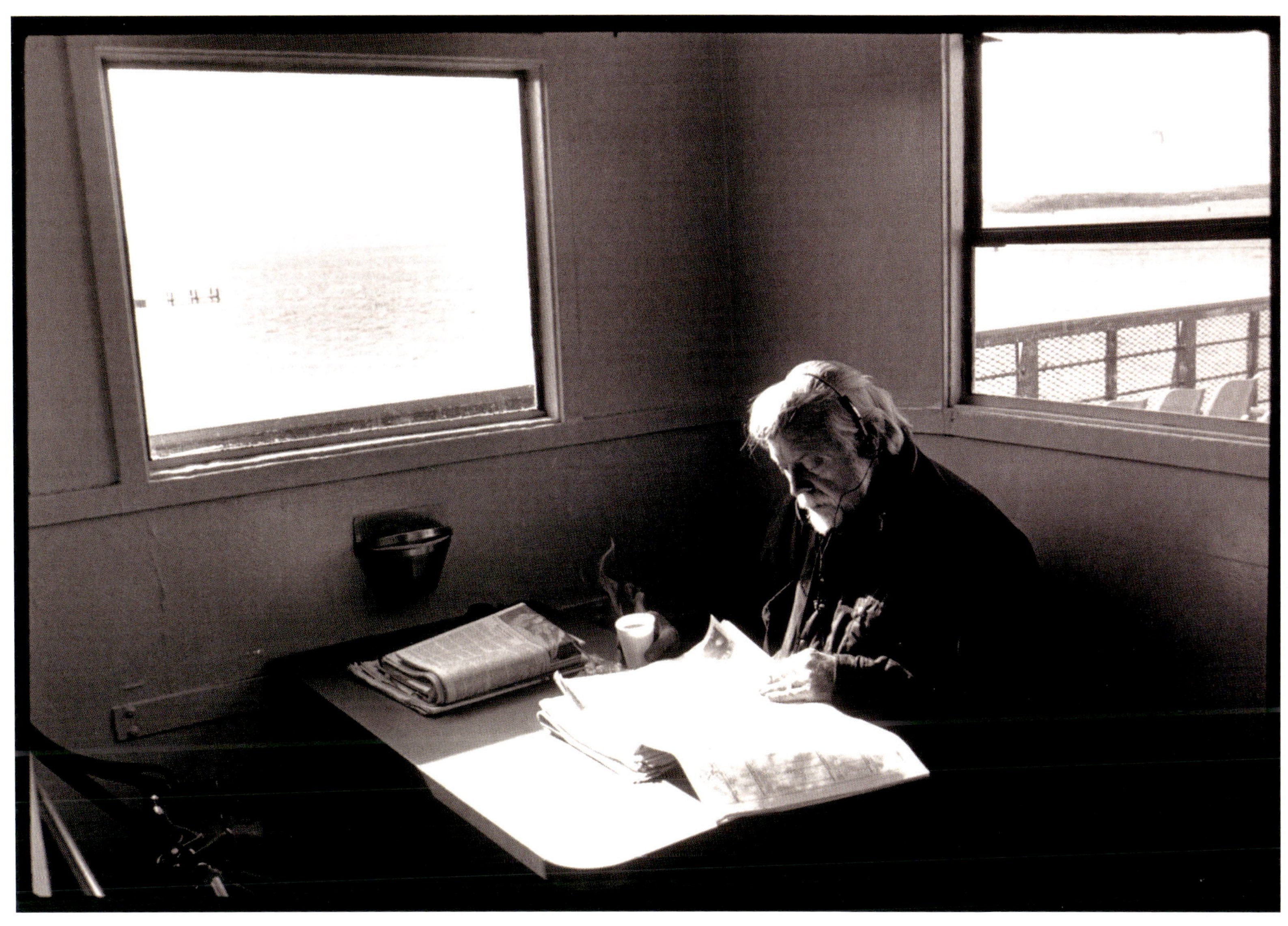

On the ferry from Woods Hole to Vineyard Haven.
Massachusetts, 1987

Rethinking Stasis

The thing about Jonathan Moller's photographs is that they appear to be about transit, travel, machinery, and people in motion. But they aren't really actually about that; such a simplified explanation is only about what can be seen on the surface. Sure, folks are on buses, trains, subways, boats, and other ways to move people about the planet, but once you remove the subjects from the form of transport, Moller's photographs are essentially about people—portraits, to be exact.

My read on Moller's work is that it's primarily about people and their plight. Their situations need not be dramatic; it could be something as commonplace as a daily commute to work. What informs Moller's strongest images are the gestures that evoke the sheer humanity and struggle to move forward. He describes himself as a documentary photographer and human rights activist, and it's an apt description. Sometimes in a photographer's work, the two are inextricably intertwined—exemplified by W. Eugene Smith whose images were often a call to action. Ironically, the photographers we celebrate the most for their impassioned work are often far from the "neutral observers" ideal that photojournalists are "supposed" to be.

So, which camp does Moller fall into? His photographs are empathetic to his subjects, while his activist aspect comes from the larger story the images create. He doesn't take cheap shots—his subjects are treated with respect, conveying a careful sense of their location, almost by precisely establishing the shot. Interestingly unlike *In Transit*, his *Black Lives Matter* project contains no people at all—the protest signage does the work of activism. It's also a documentary statement for the historical archives, since such temporary, extemporaneous signs of urgency tend to melt away and vanish with the next rain or windstorm, only to be replaced when the next controversy takes over the latest news cycle.

Moller's idea of capturing and preserving the transient is important. Similarly, one thing I'm enthralled by in the work of Eugène Atget, Charles Nègre, and other pioneering photographers, is to see the street signage, graffiti, and detritus. William Henry Fox-Talbot's image of *The Nelson Column, Trafalgar Square, London, Under Construction, 1843* shows how the column was built; it also includes the advertisements, handbills, and posters. Moller's *Black Lives Matter* images are a record showing the same, that unique takeover of spaces, poles, walls, and will be part of the archival canon long after we're gone.

At a recent Daguerreian Society Symposium, a colleague, Dr. Mike Robinson, discussed "tacit knowledge" as a research tool. So what exactly is "tacit knowledge" and why does Moller's work intersect with it? It represents what we might call the common knowledge of the day. Because such knowledge is rarely notated or preserved, the historical importance of documentary photography that includes it can't be overstated.

The wonderful thing about the single-minded documentation that Moller devotes himself to is that it helps to fill in and preserve the undocumented details of daily life. For example, looking at how Moller's travelers used technology to take advantage of interstitial time is valuable unto itself, as are all the myriad details his other photographs celebrate.

His projects aren't only a romantic look into the past either. For every photograph depicting a simpler time and place—such as his 2001 image of three women from Sacapulas, Guatemala, walking along the banks of the Chixoy River with baskets on their heads—there are scores of images showing people behind computer screens. He enjoys clever wordplay, images, words, and ironic signage whose humor underscores the documentary impulse.

One of my favorites of his lighthearted images—taken at the Marco Polo Airport, Venice, Italy, in 2018—is of a view looking down into an airport terminal, with a graphic of a smartly dressed shopper high on the glass above. The message of promised exclusivity available to the shopper versus the huddled seated masses below couldn't be more ironic or well executed. Almost a depiction of Alfred Stieglitz's *Steerage* for modern times, especially since the actual well-heeled shopping traveler is probably sitting in an airport club lounge sipping a drink, not crammed into a set of chairs at an airport gate. The irony between the perfectly coiffed mythical model, depicted as a high-class shopper, and the folks below, some of whom are surely waiting for their decidedly non-glamorous economy seats, is perfectly seen scathingly humorous commentary.

One way we measure documentary work is to assess how in-depth the commitment of the photographer, publisher, and distribution network is; his work shows that long-term engagement. Moller doesn't fly in for the day, make some images and depart; instead, his projects take time and patience, demonstrating a dedication to revealing the complexities at hand.

I'm not sure one book can do his work justice. I found myself poring through his different book projects, and each one revealed an antsy, eager mind at work. Documentary work that is influenced by activism seems inherently elegiac. The photographer, writer, editor, publisher, human rights worker, all know that they can only have a temporary impact, and that bad people doing bad things will continue, almost because of, instead of prevented by, their callous disregard or even the encouragement of malevolent intent. Inflamed by injustice, unintimidated by the contradictions of state-run infamy, Moller's work rarely describes a world in stasis, or at peace with itself; rather he shows people trying to adapt to an ever accelerating, exhausting, and bewildering rate of change, with few obvious benefits to show for all that motion.

Harris Fogel

Independent Writer and Curator, Springfield, PA
Former Professor of Photography, and Director/Curator,
Mednick Gallery of Photography, and Founder,
Gallery 1401 of Photography. The University of the Arts,
Philadelphia, PA

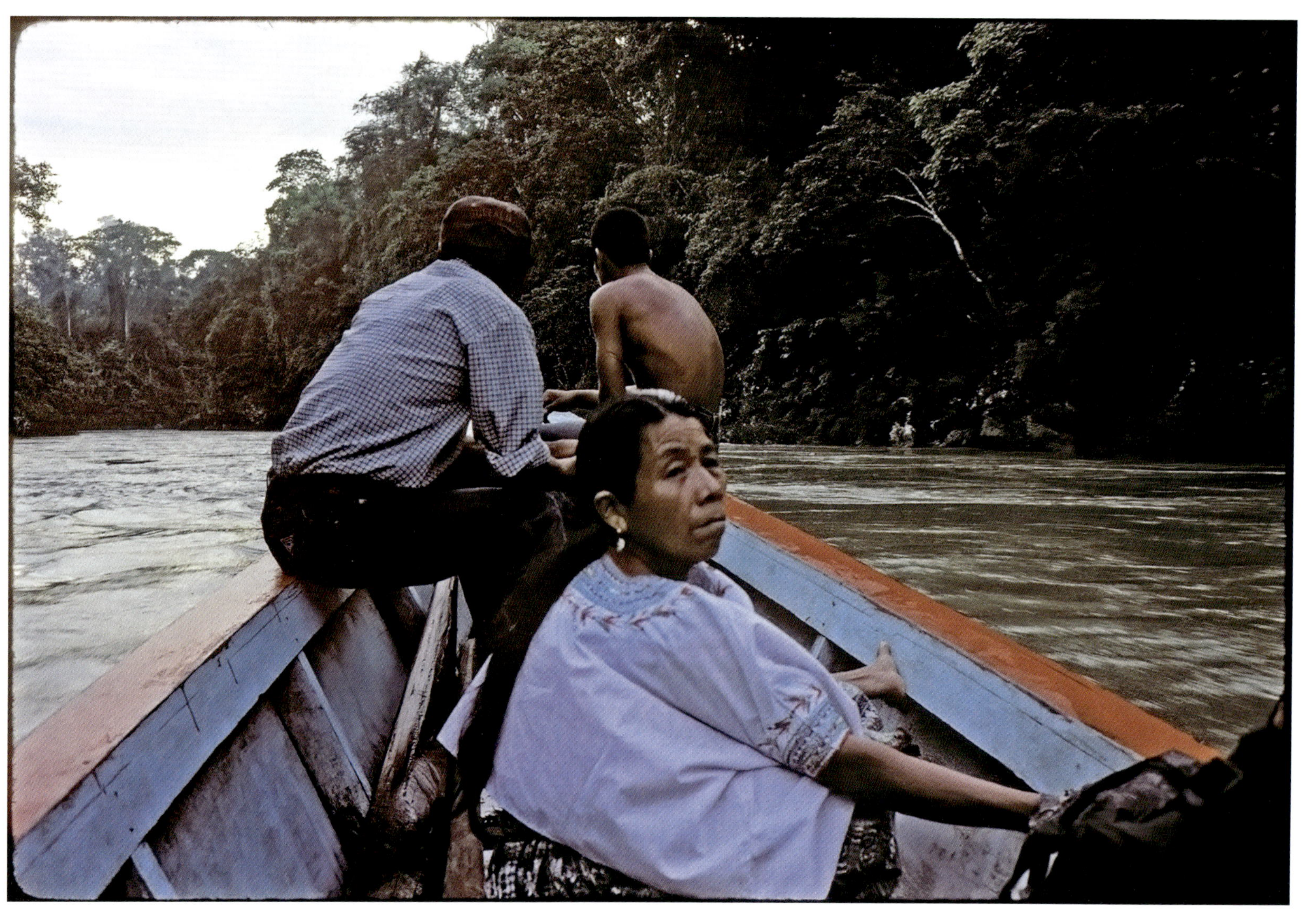

Transport by boat on the Chixoy River from the community of Primavera del Ixcán
to the main town of Cantabal. Quiché, Guatemala, 1996

Right: Primavera del Ixcán, a resettlement community for people of the Communities of Population in Resistance of the Ixcán;
at this time there was no road, so the only way to travel in or out was by boat along the Chixoy River. Guatemala, 1996

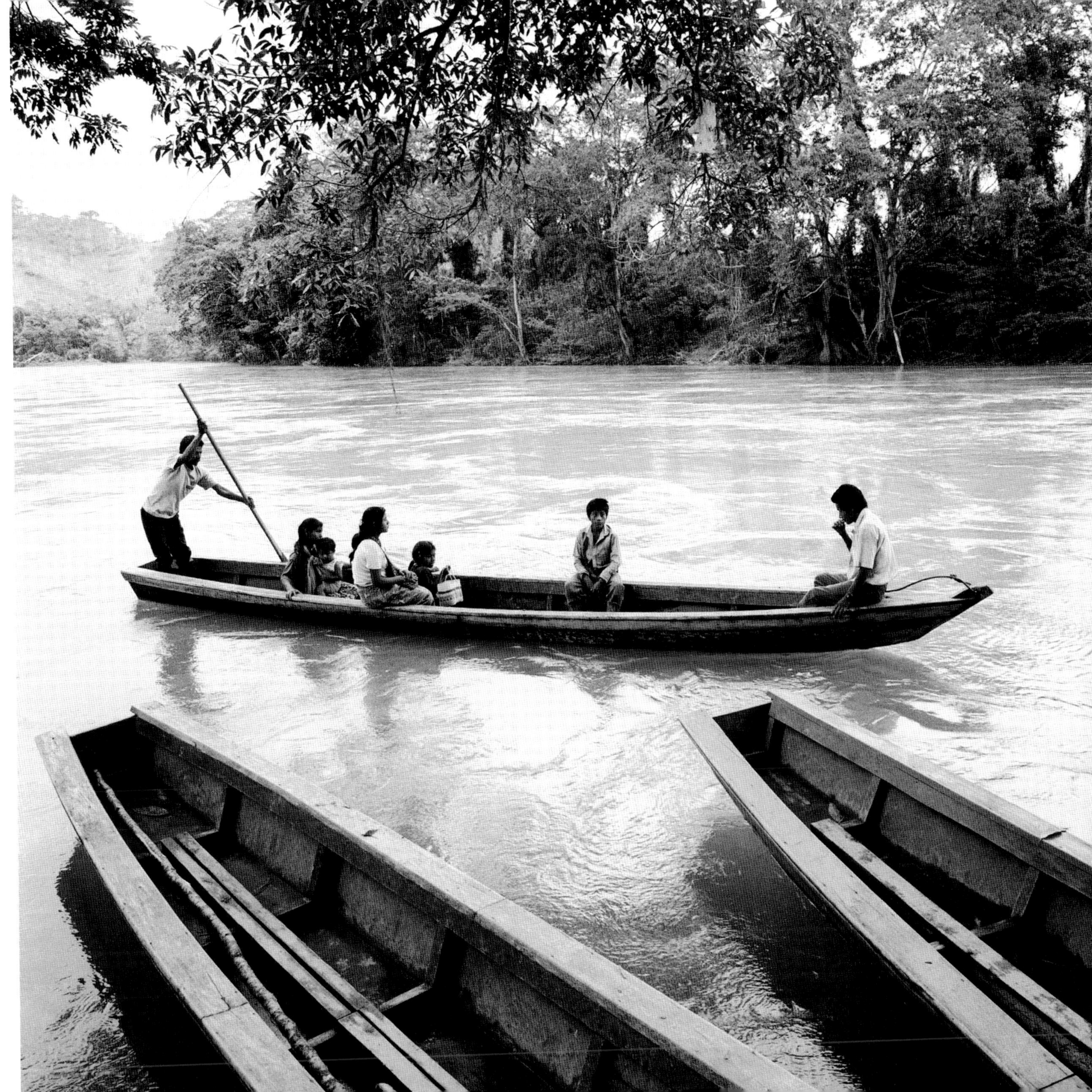

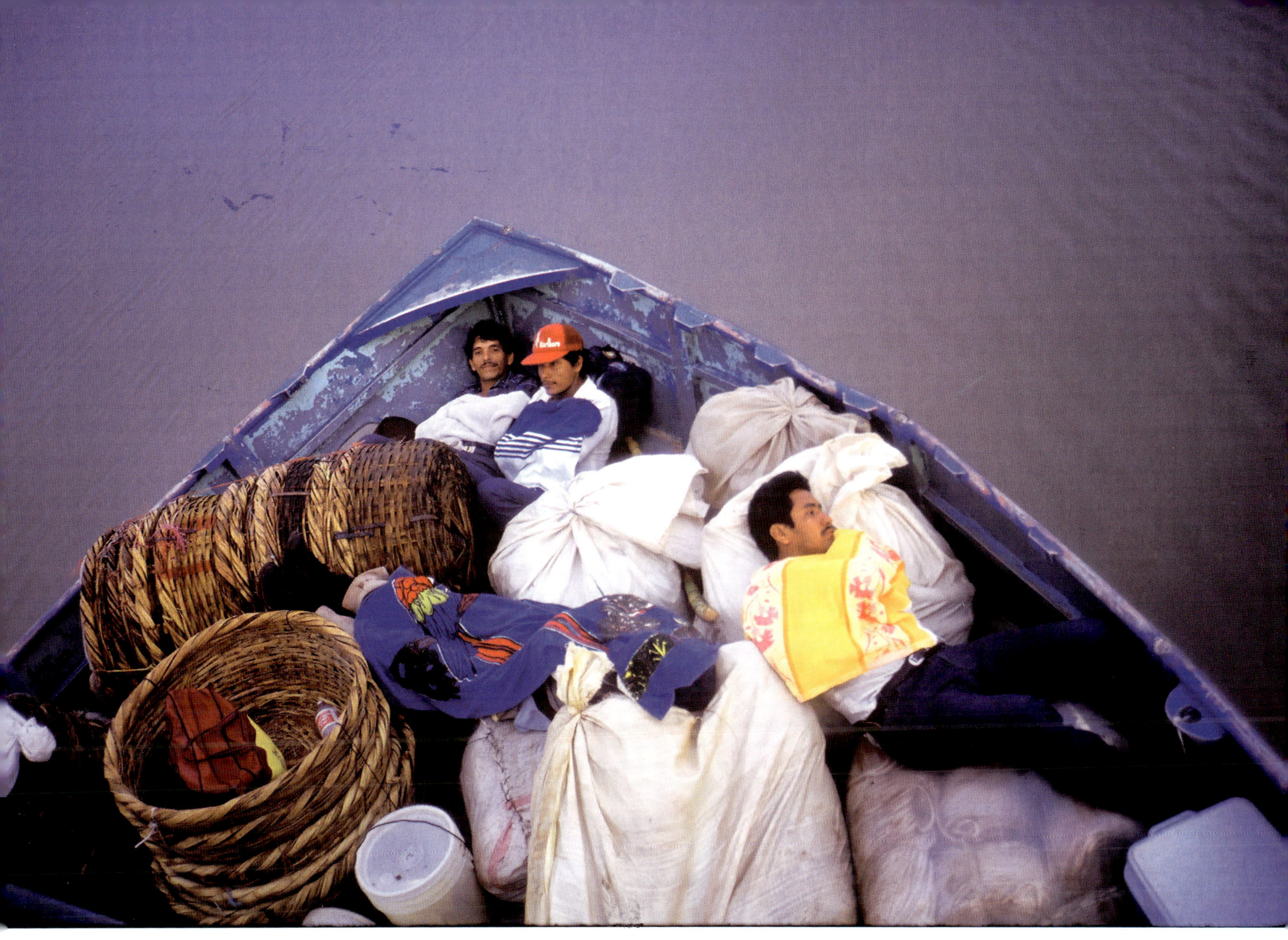

The overnight ferry along the Escondido River
from Rama to Bluefields on the Caribbean coast. Nicaragua, 1991

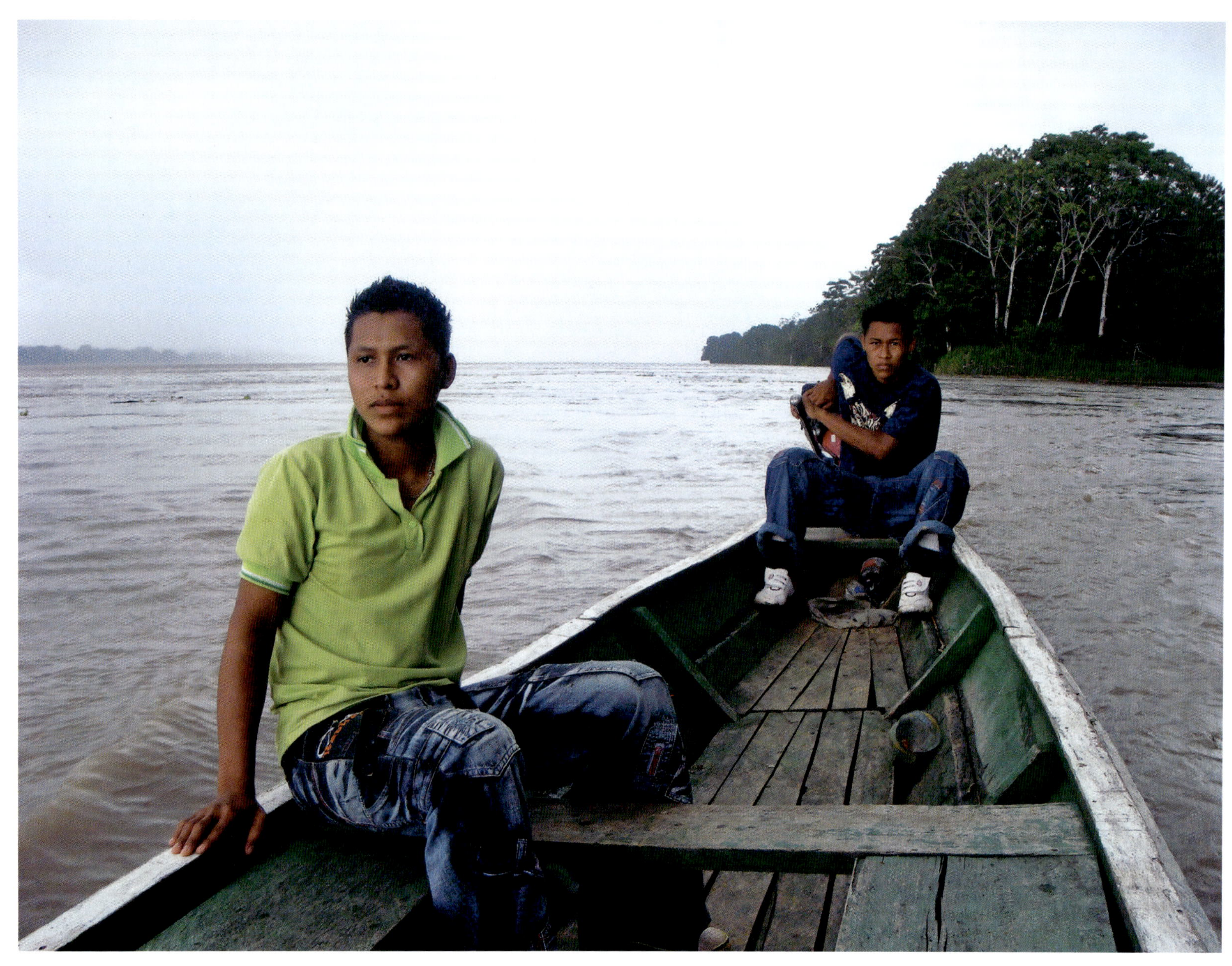

Transportation between communities on the shores of the Amazon River
along the coast across from Brazil. Colombia, 2010

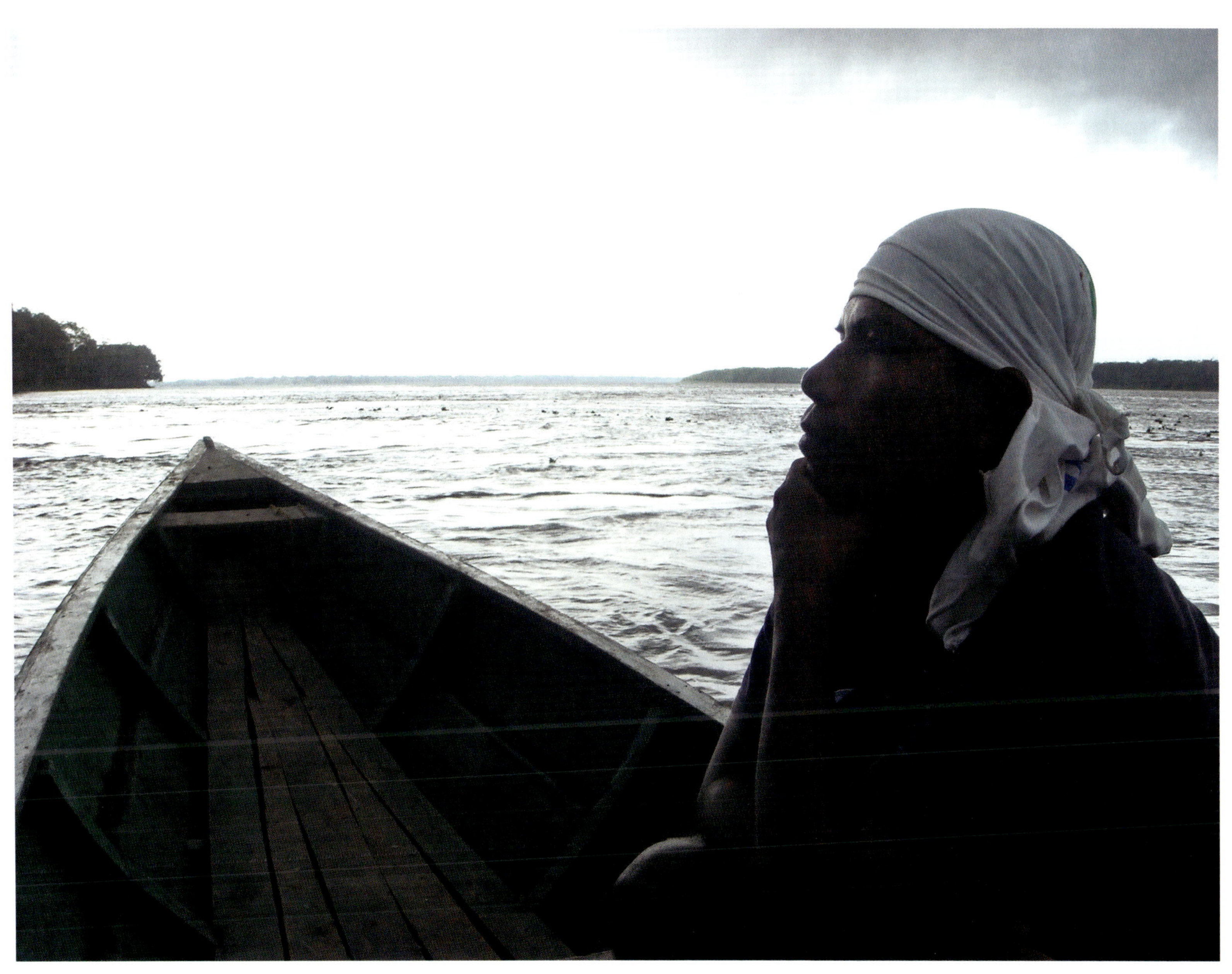

Transportation between communities on the shores of the Amazon River
along the coast across from Brazil. Colombia, 2010

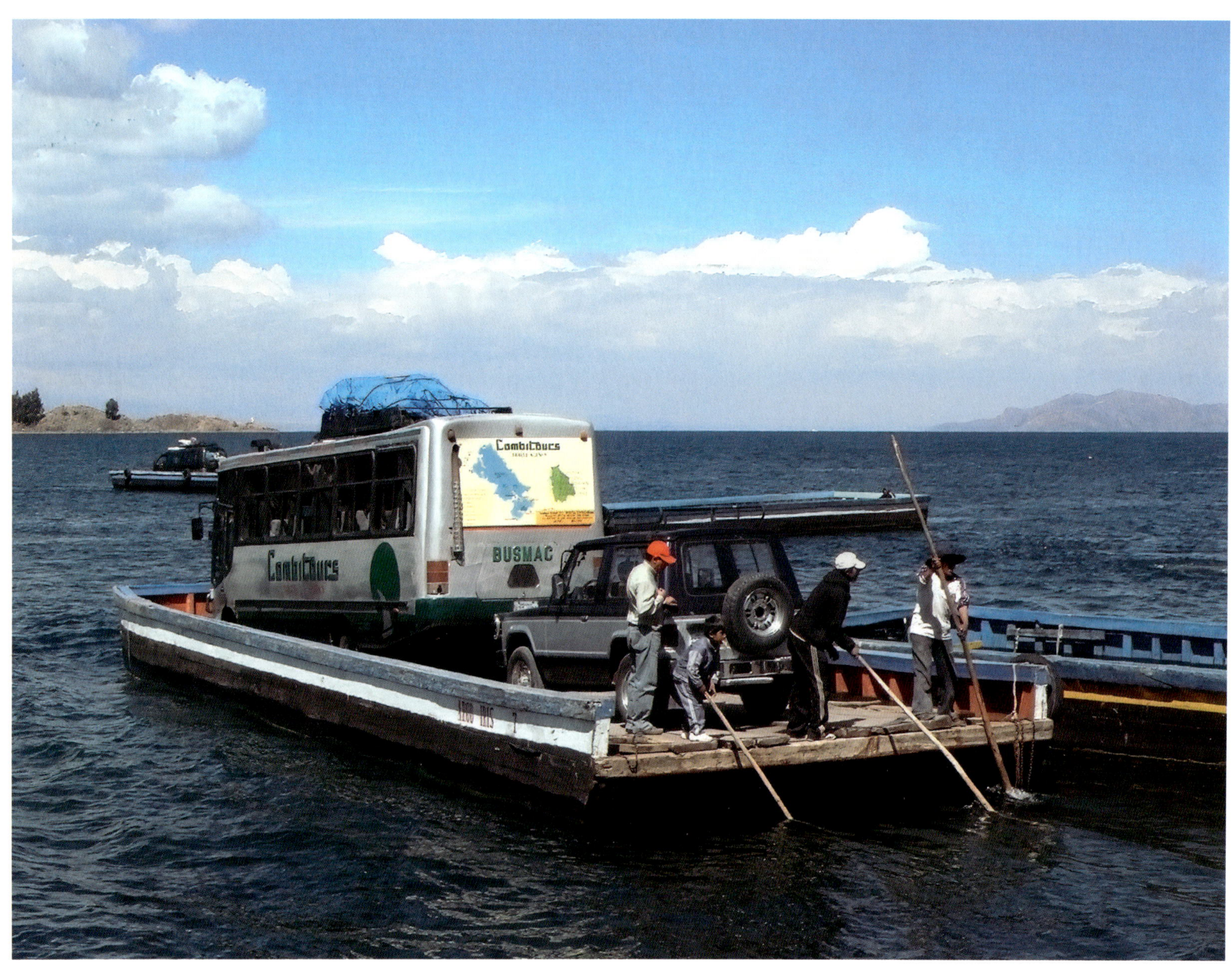

Lake Titicaca. Bolivia, 2007

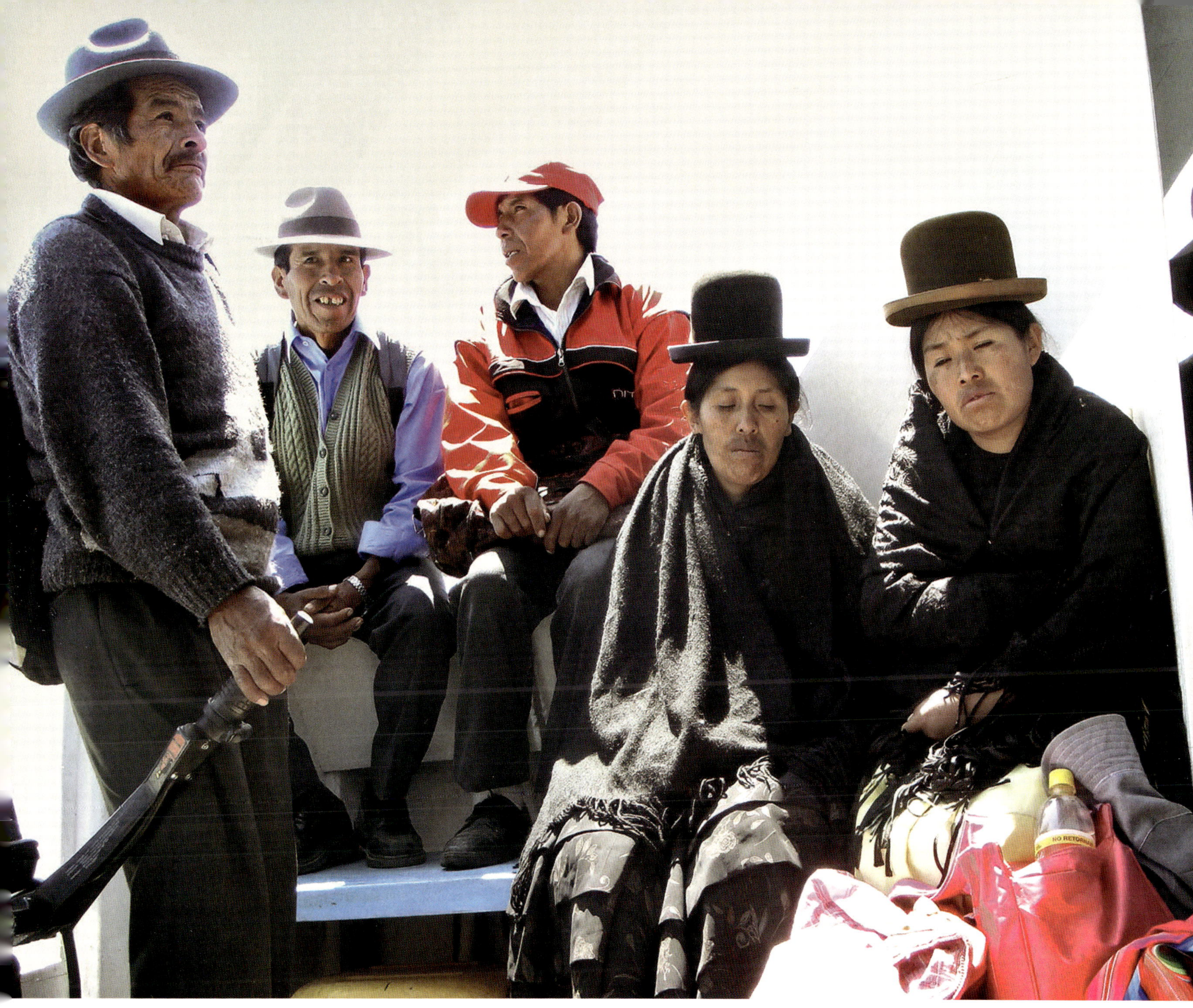

Lake Titicaca. Bolivia, 2007

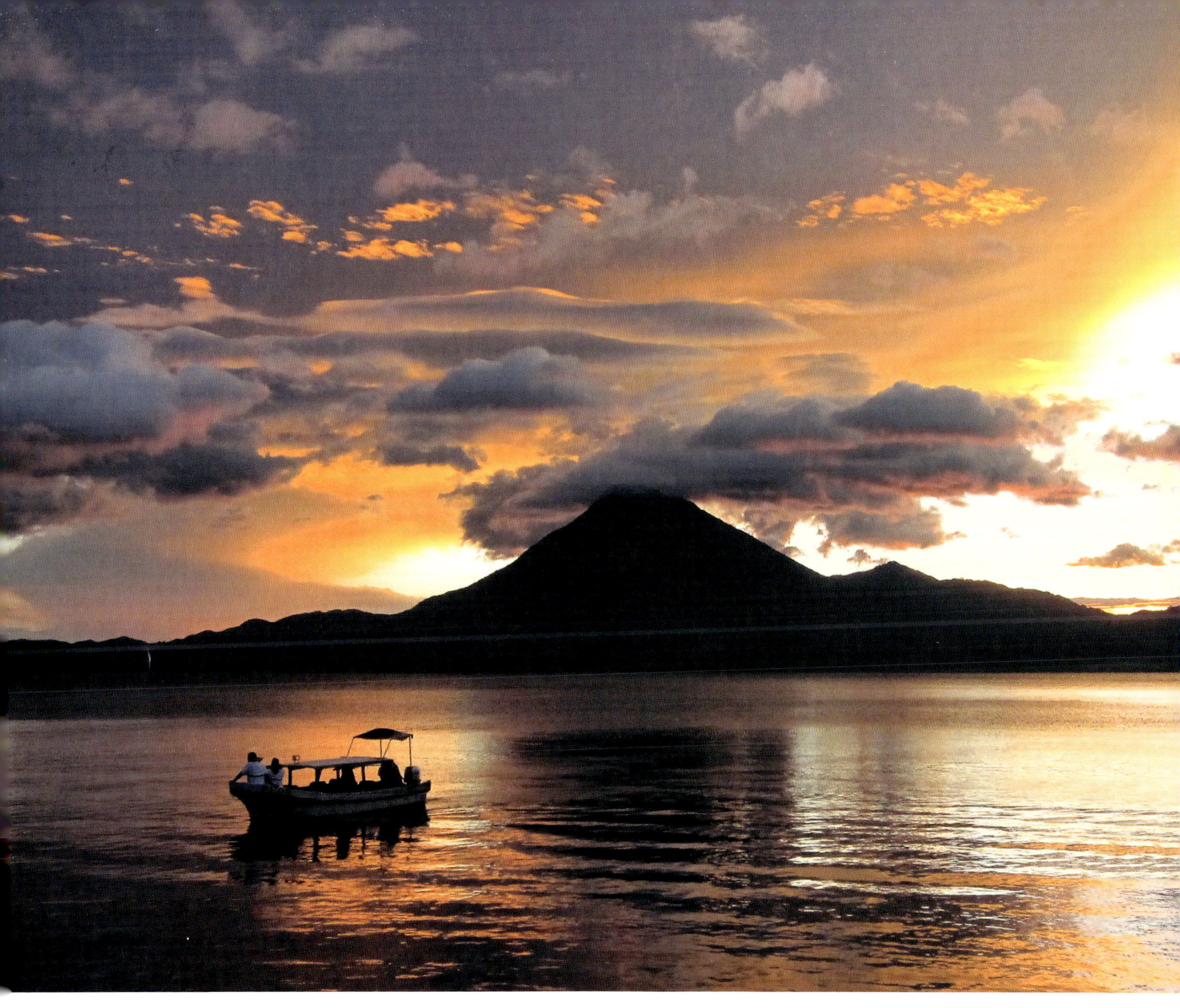

These types of boats take passengers between different towns on the shores
of Lake Atitlán. Sololá, Guatemala, 2013

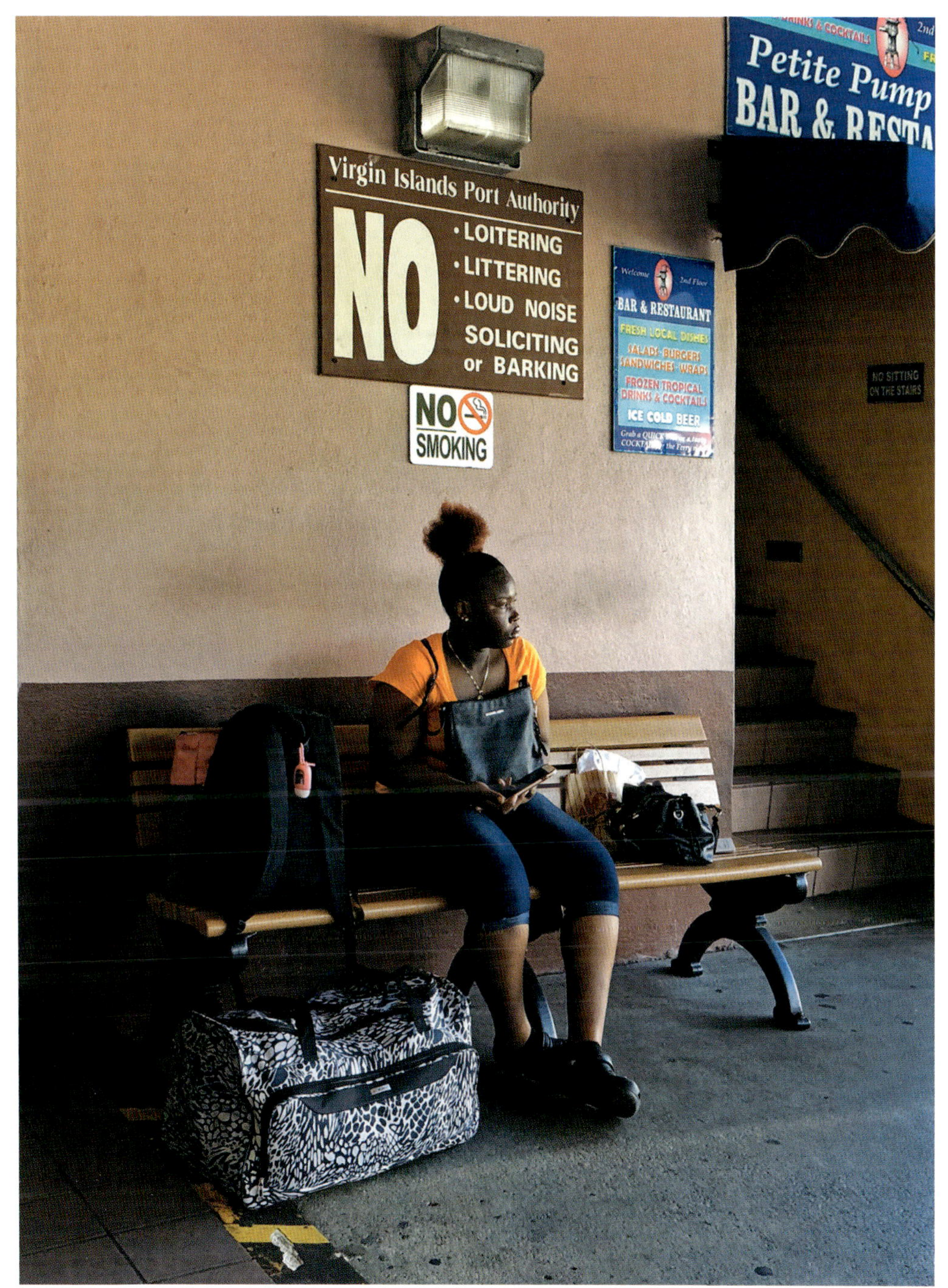

Ferry terminal. St. Thomas, US Virgin Islands, 2019

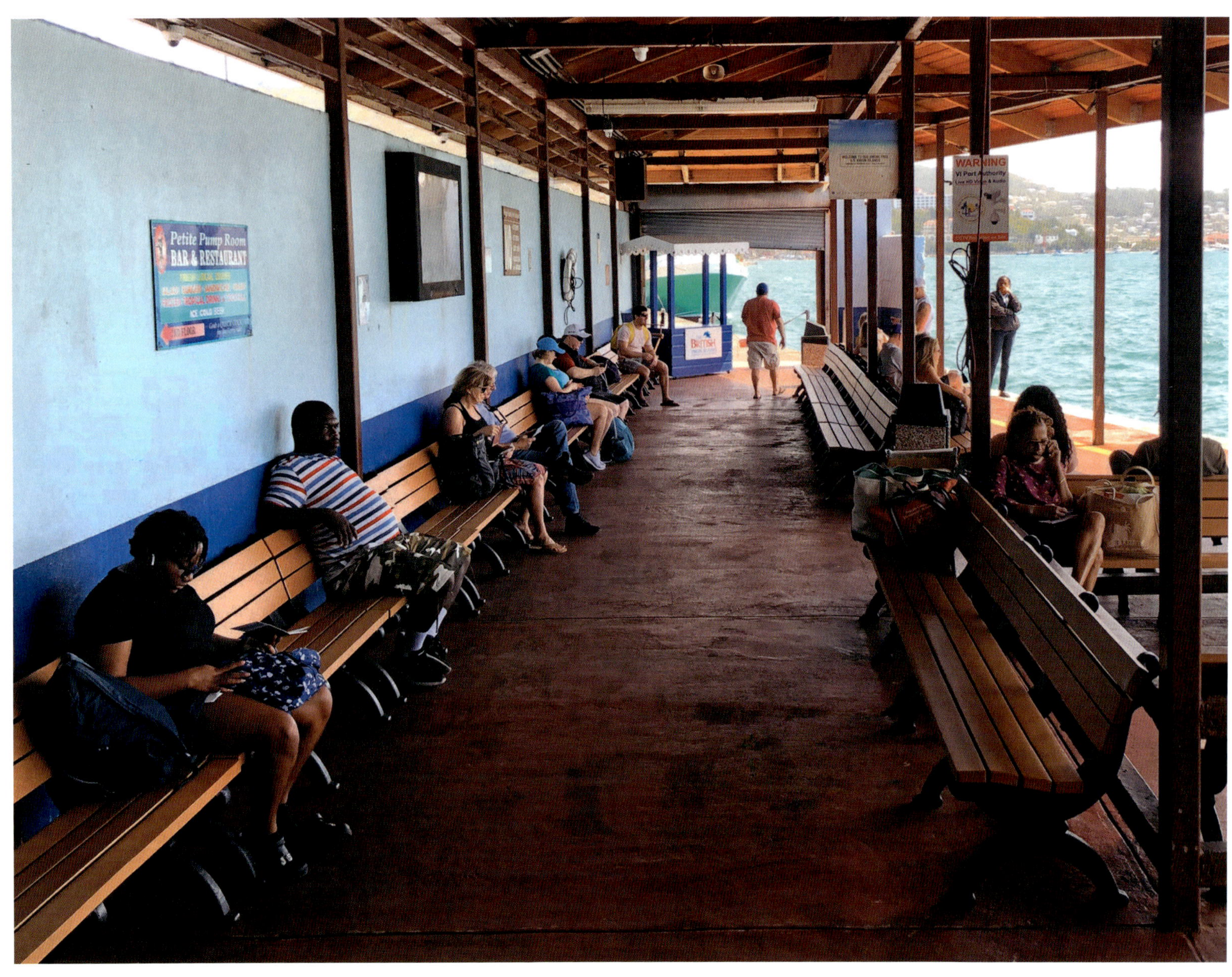

Ferry terminal. St. Thomas, US Virgin Islands, 2019

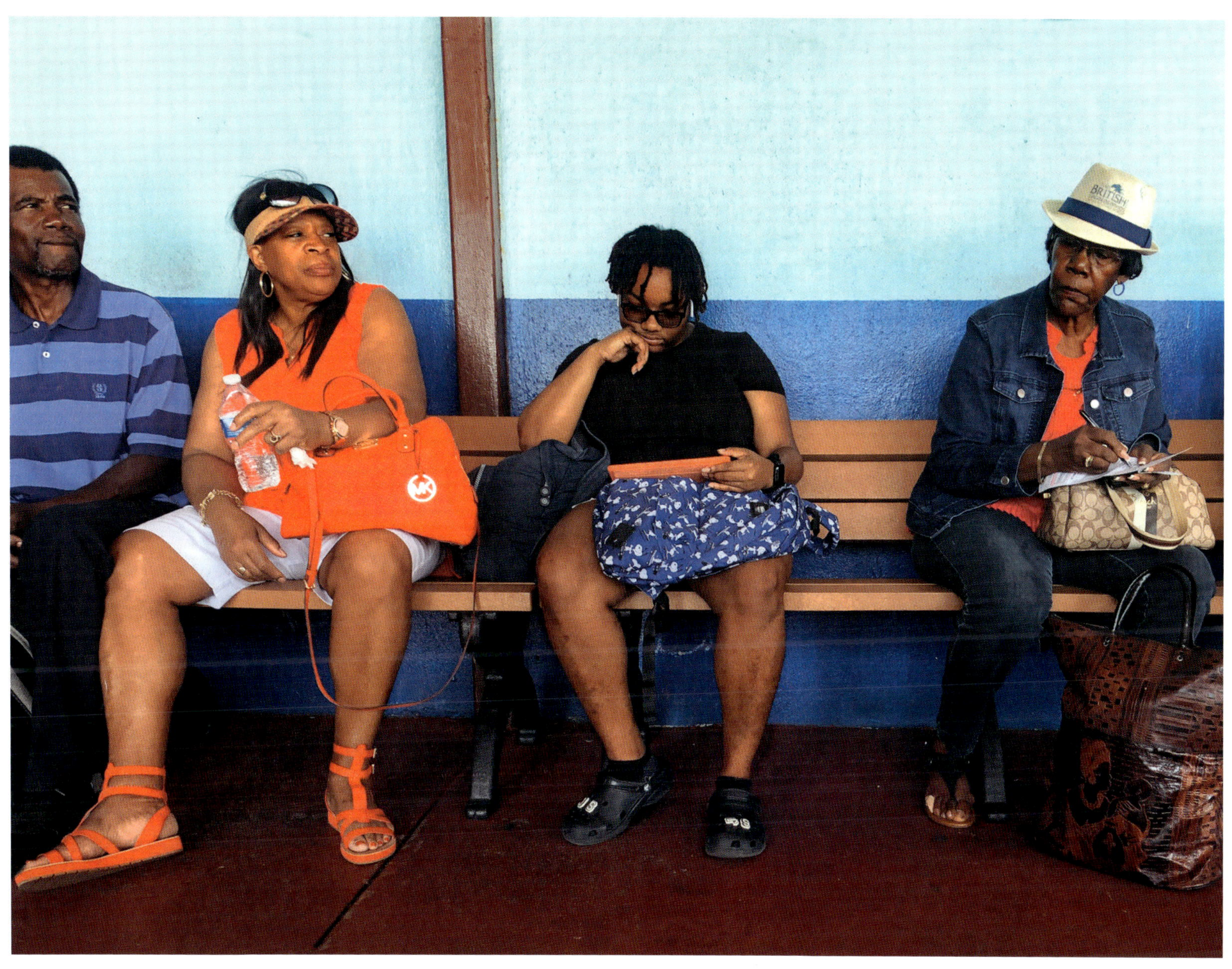

Ferry terminal. St. Thomas, US Virgin Islands, 2019

Moller Through Time

In true encounters, the boundaries
between times are erased
Jean Dubuffett

Through his magical photographic eye, Moller shares a new testimonial of the displacement of people—migrants, refugees, or simply locals on a walk—and also of images of chaotic cities full of bustle in contrast with moments of joy, sadness, melancholy, traditions, or syncretism. In all, moments of time.

As opposed to some who reflect scenes of nature and panoramic views, Moller's personal experience comes from his immersion in the societies that make up *In Transit*. Through his lived experience, he holds up evidence of universal human value. Whether by portraying the basic struggle for survival or in depicting the eternal search for an ephemeral dream pervading our collective existence and the history of humanity.

Everything in life is a cycle. That everything, that cycle, has been part of our history and our behavior since origins of images of ourselves as human beings. Everything is repeated continuously, only in different contexts. It is part of our human nature. We are the eloquent sum of our own evolution through the past, the present, and into the future. Just so, the images in this book will remain etched in our collective memory through time.

Rudy Cotton
Director
Museo Nacional de Arte Moderno "Carlos Mérida"
Guatemala

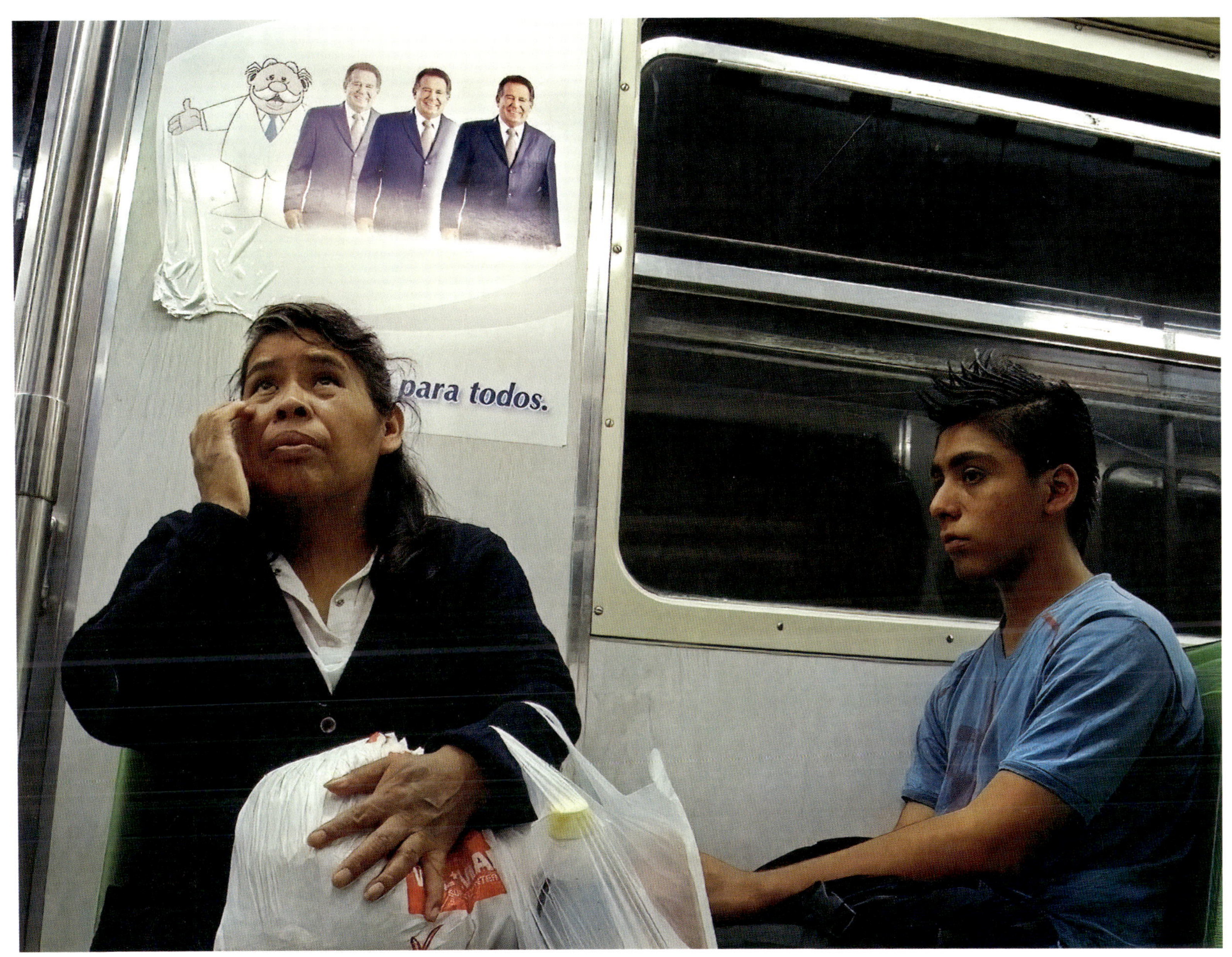

Mexico Cily, 2005

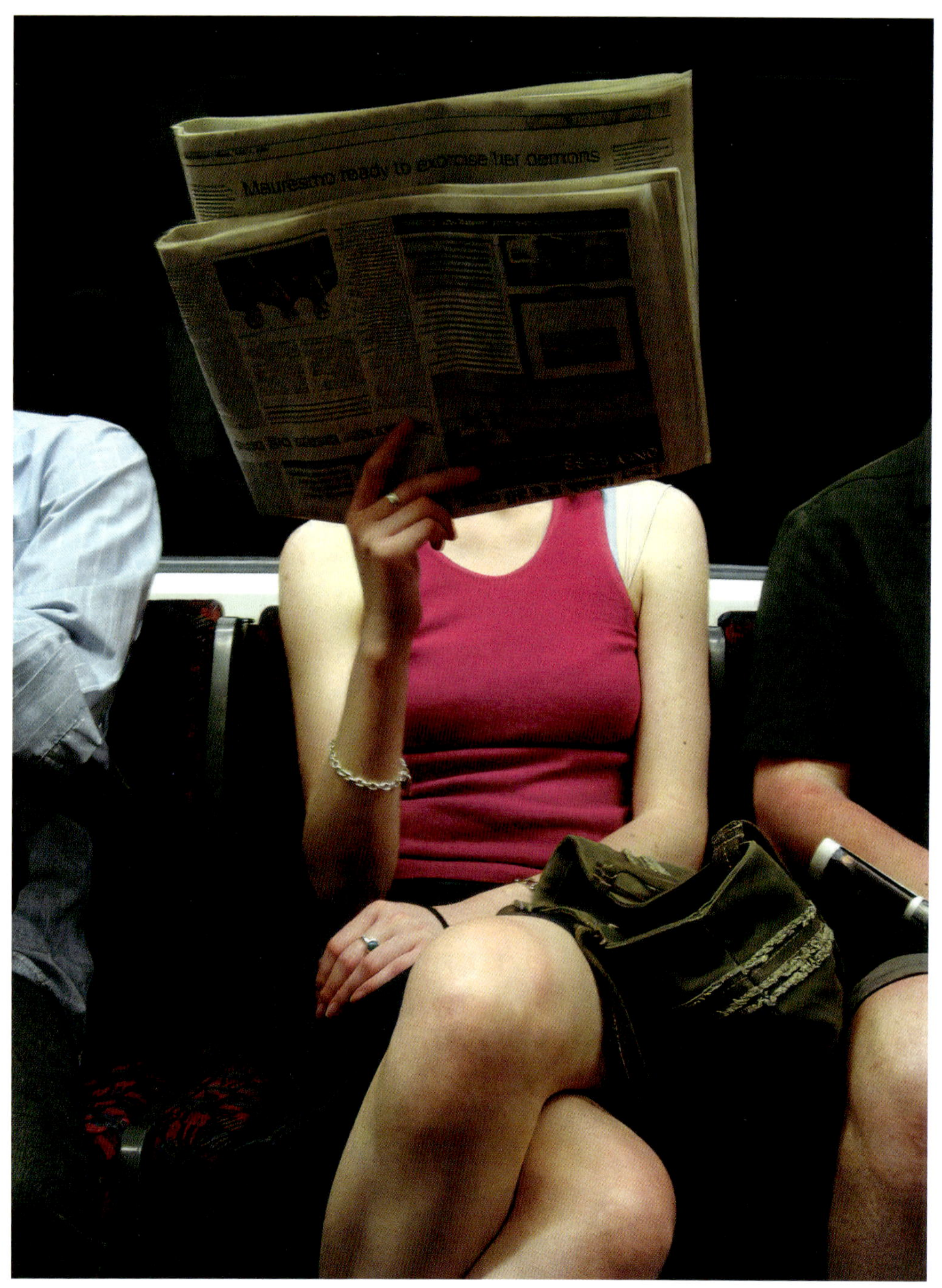

London, England, 2006

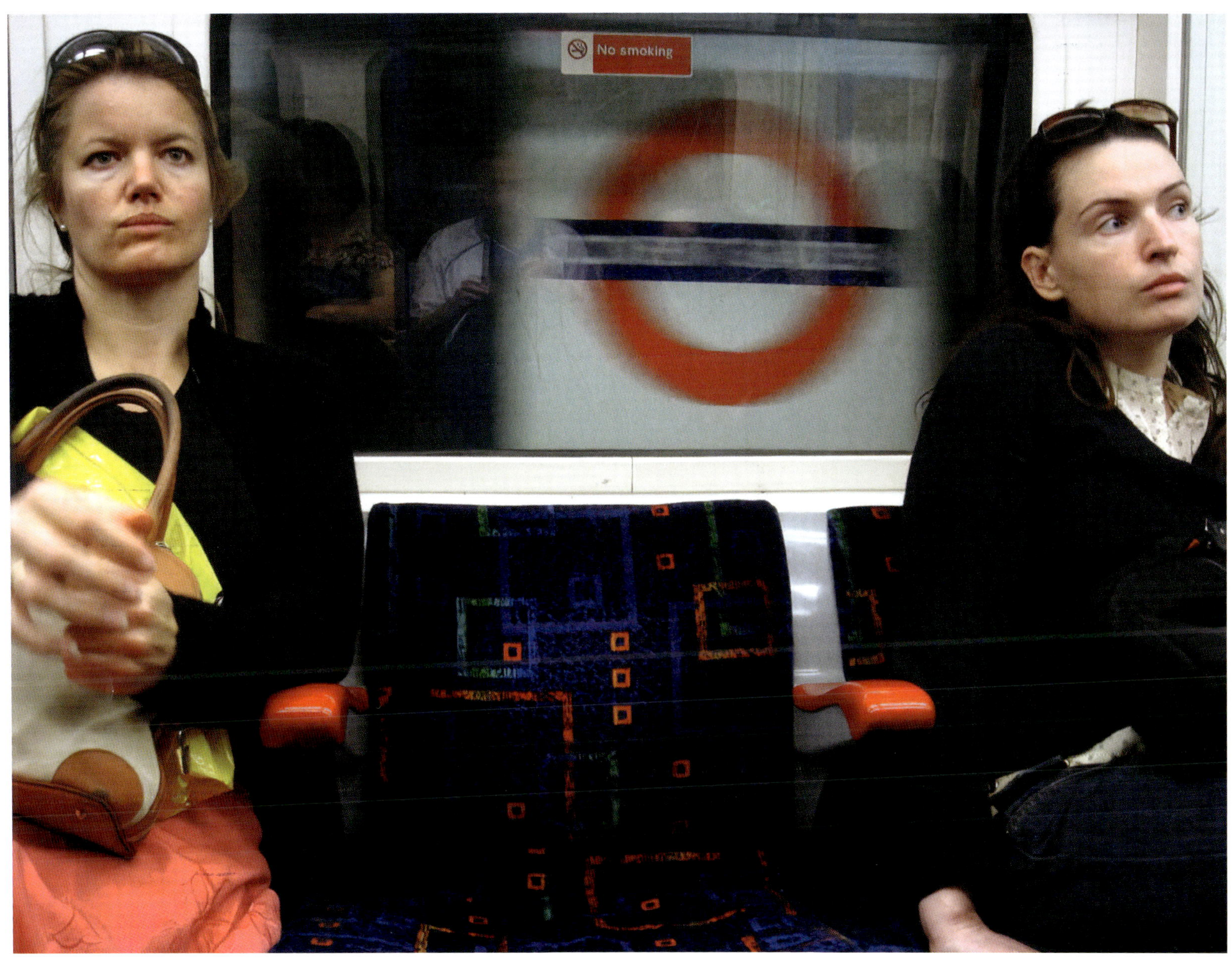

London, England, 2006

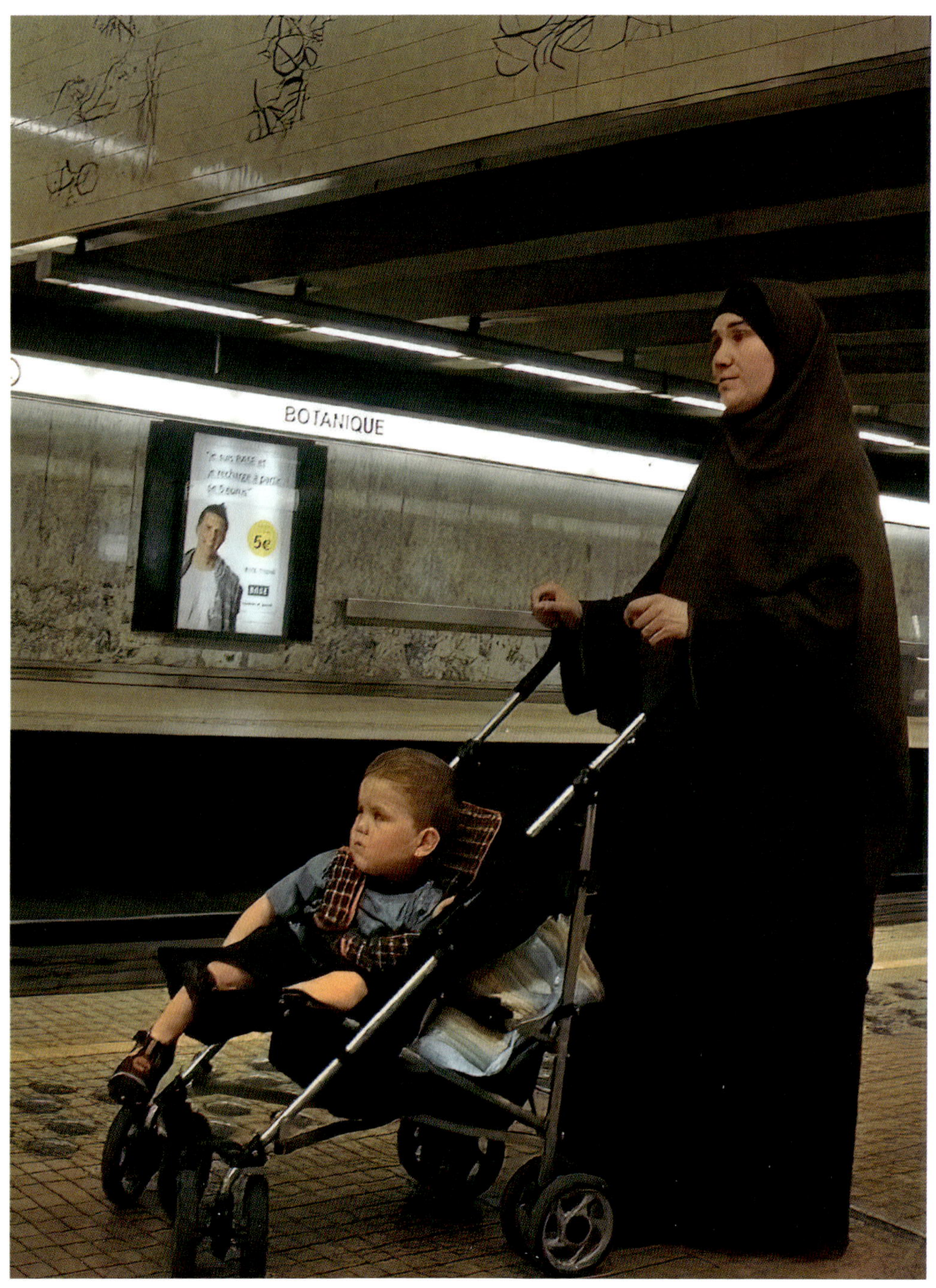

Brussels, Belgium, 2006

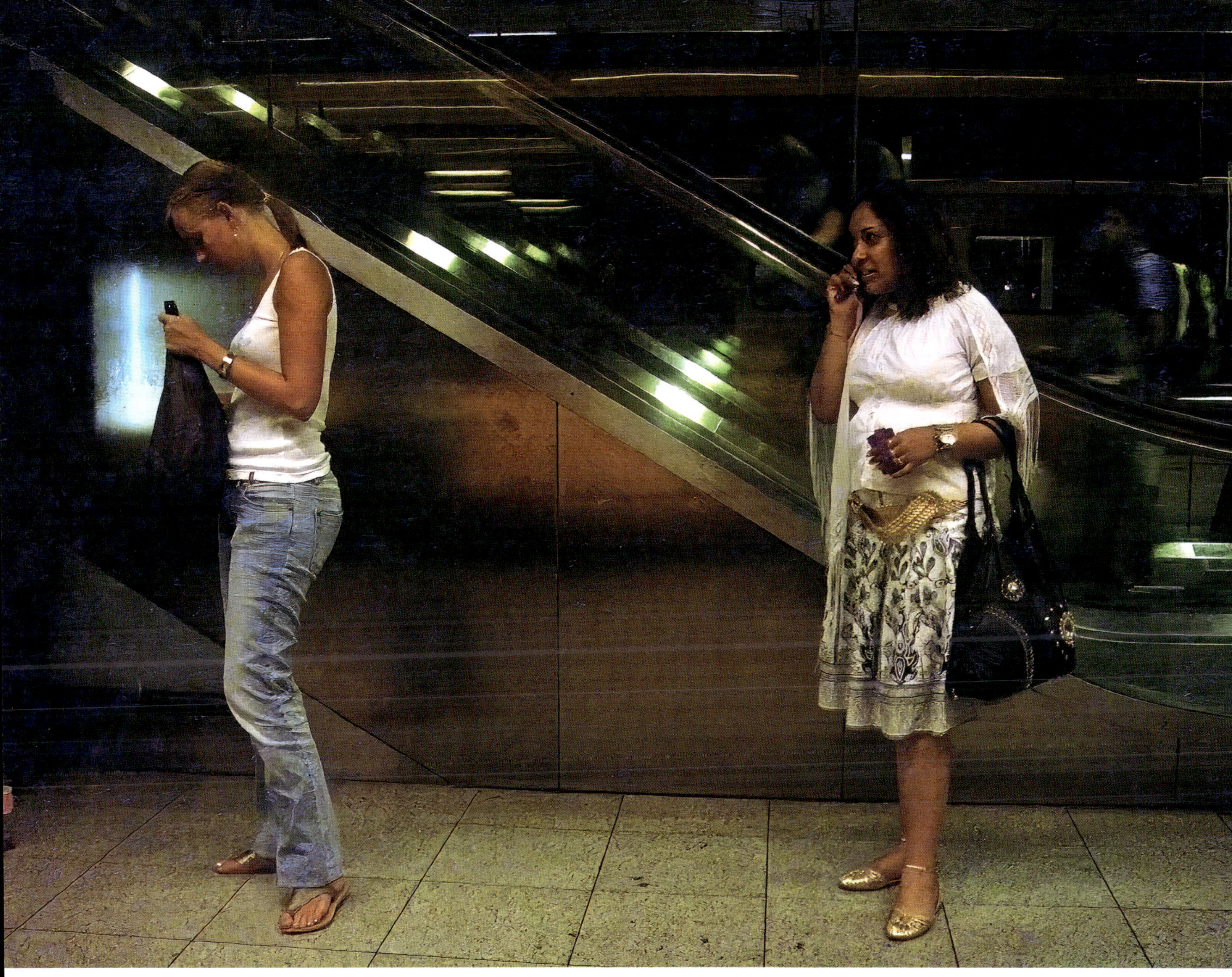

Amsterdam Subway. The Netherlands, 2006

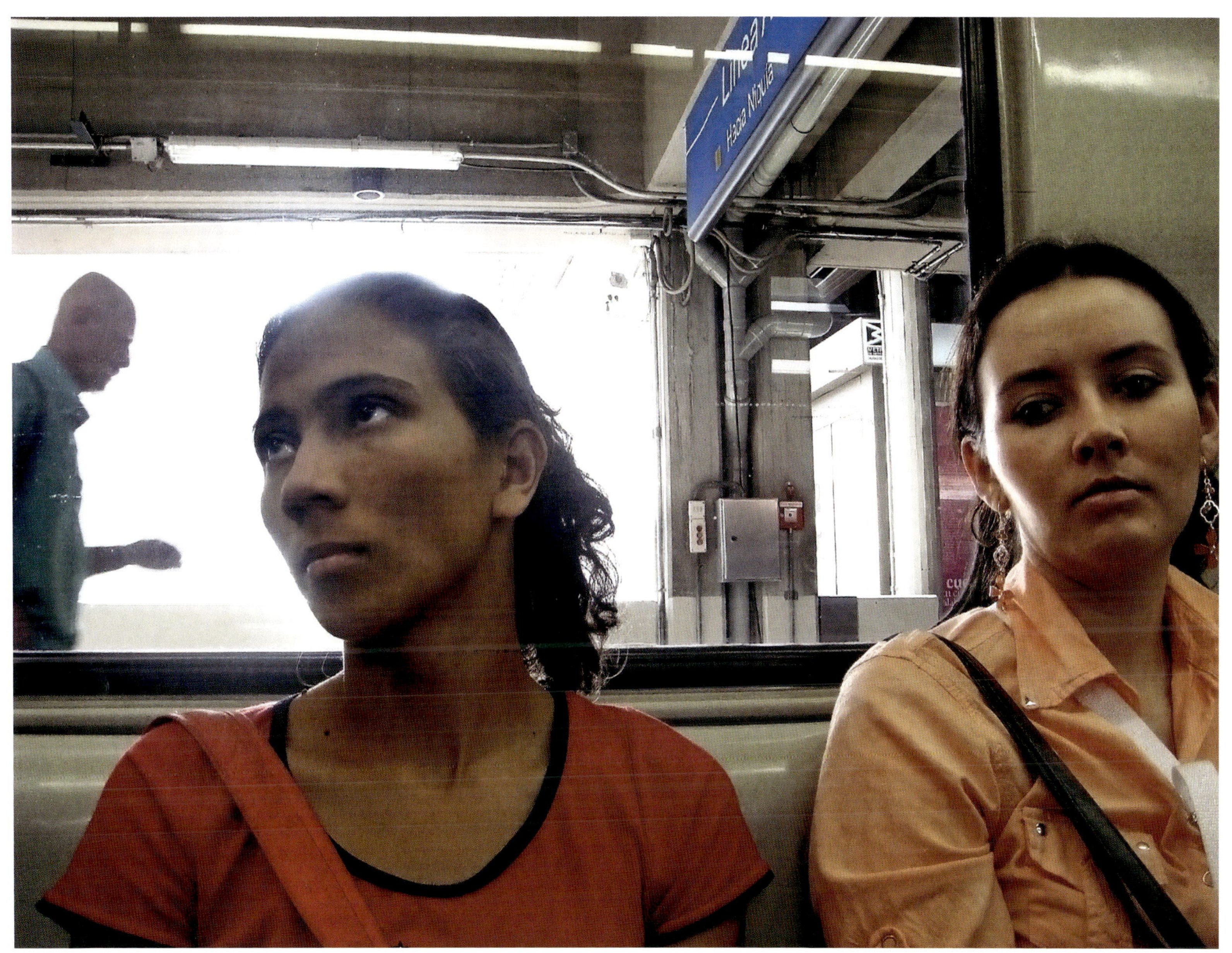

Medellín, Colombia, 2007

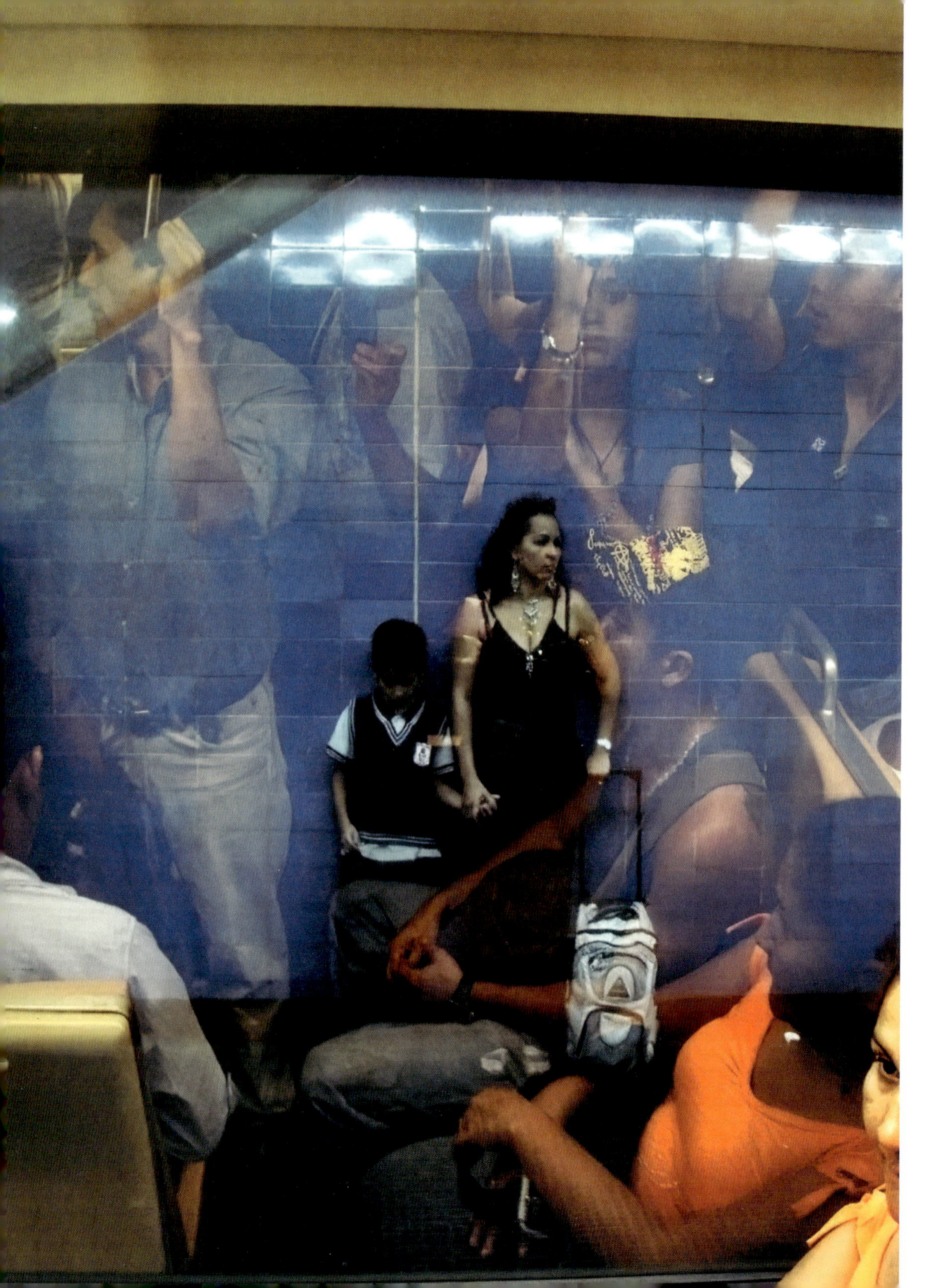

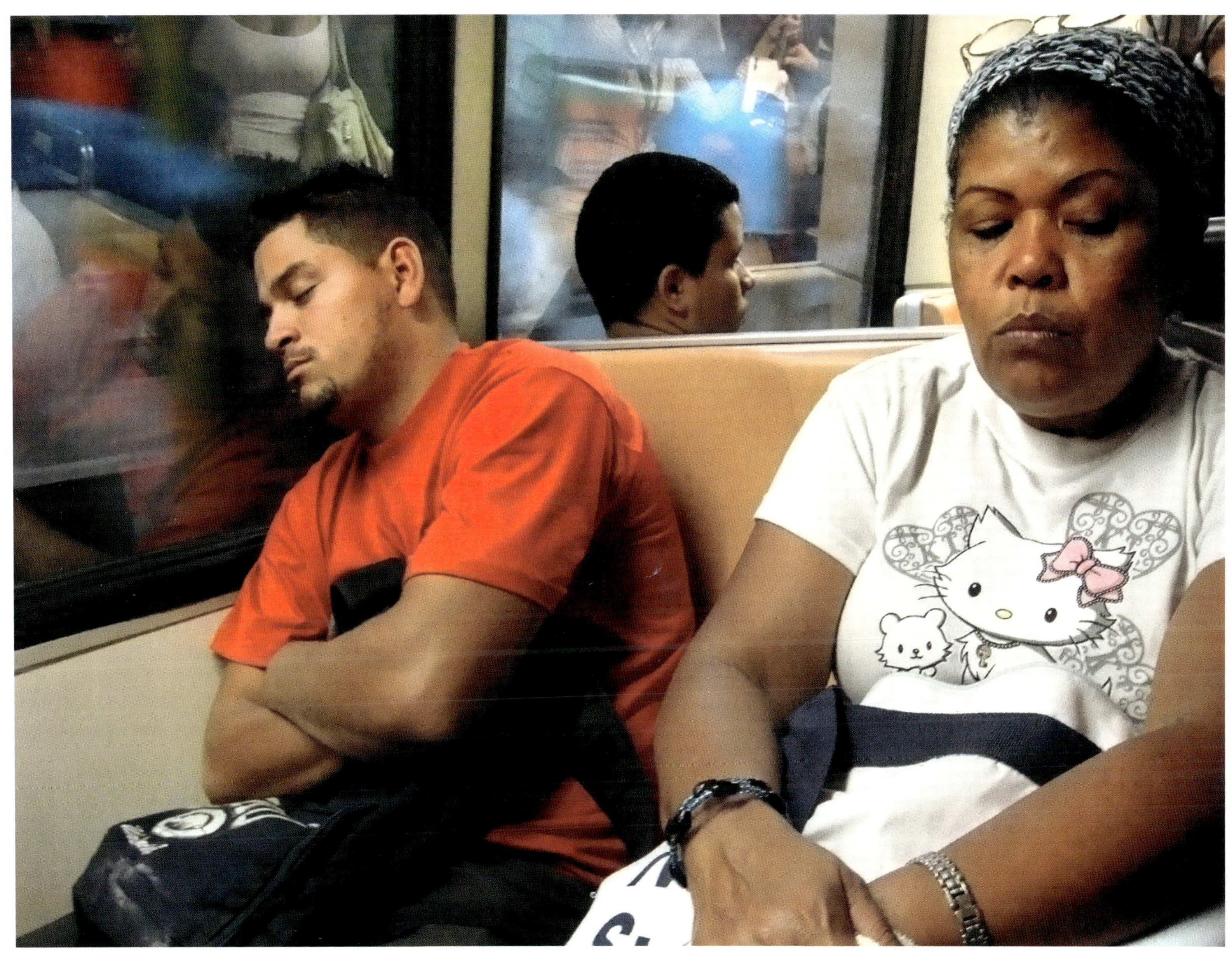

Left: Caracas, Venezuela, 2007

Caracas, Venezuela, 2007

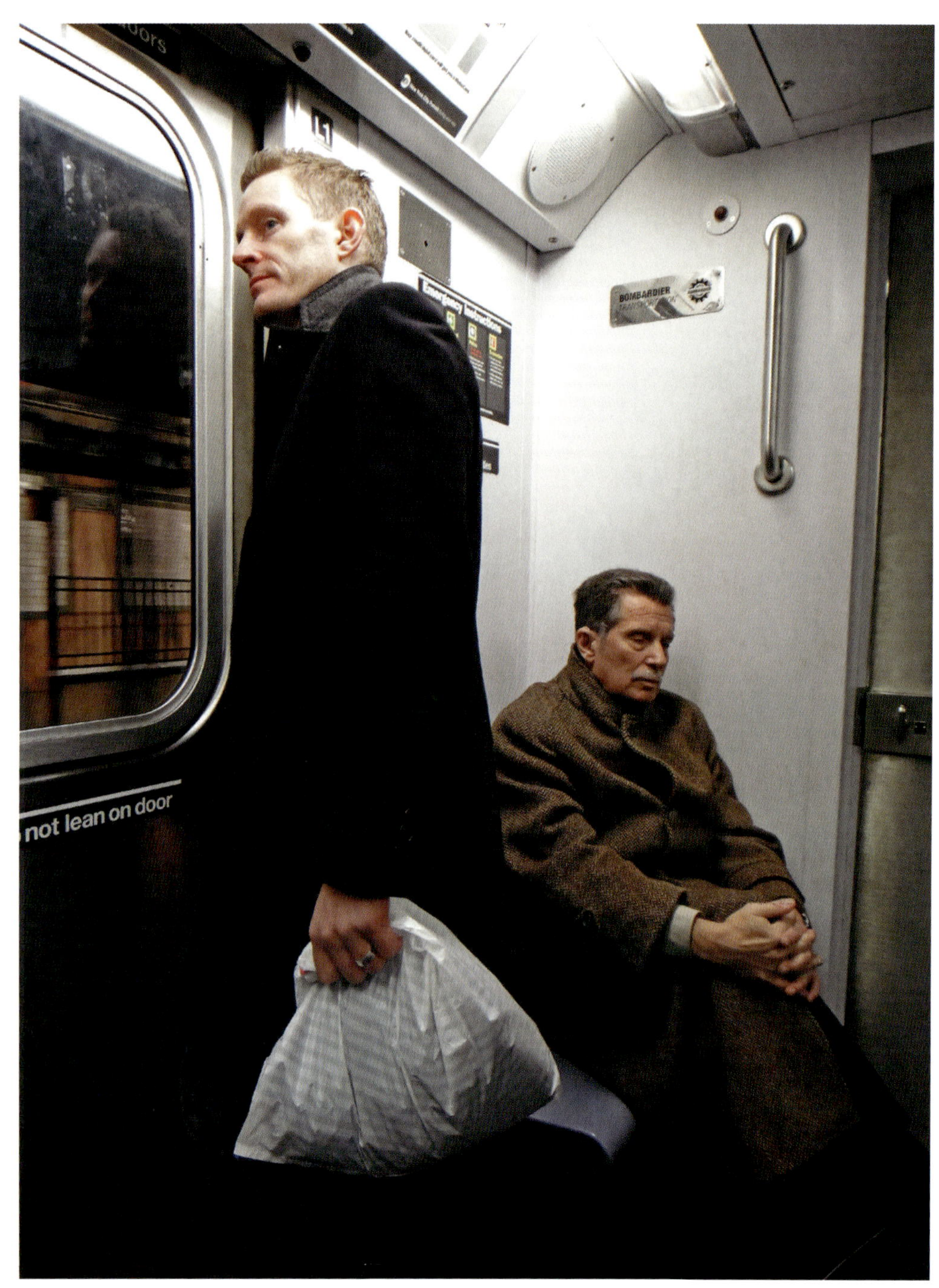

New York City, 2011

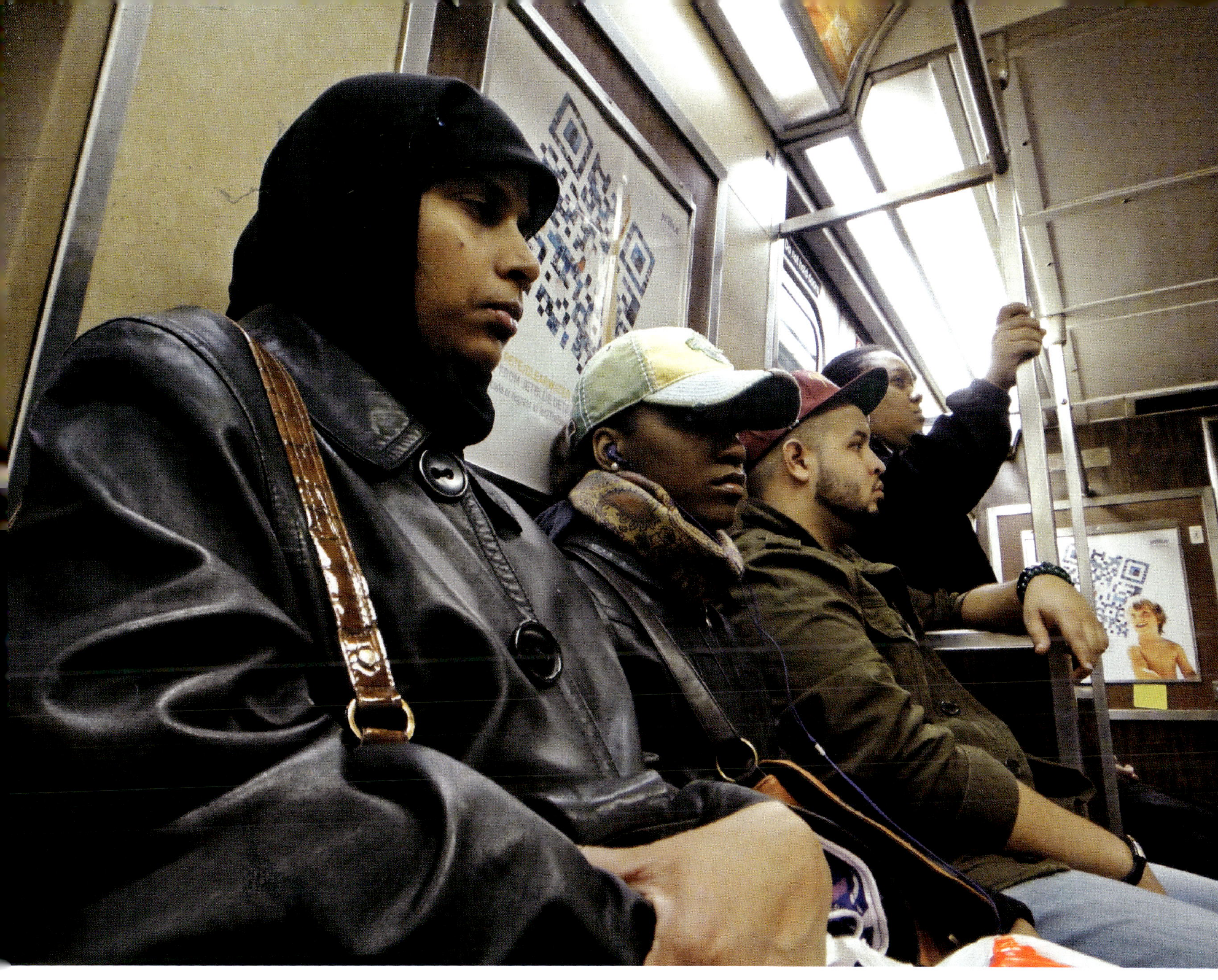

Now York City, 2011

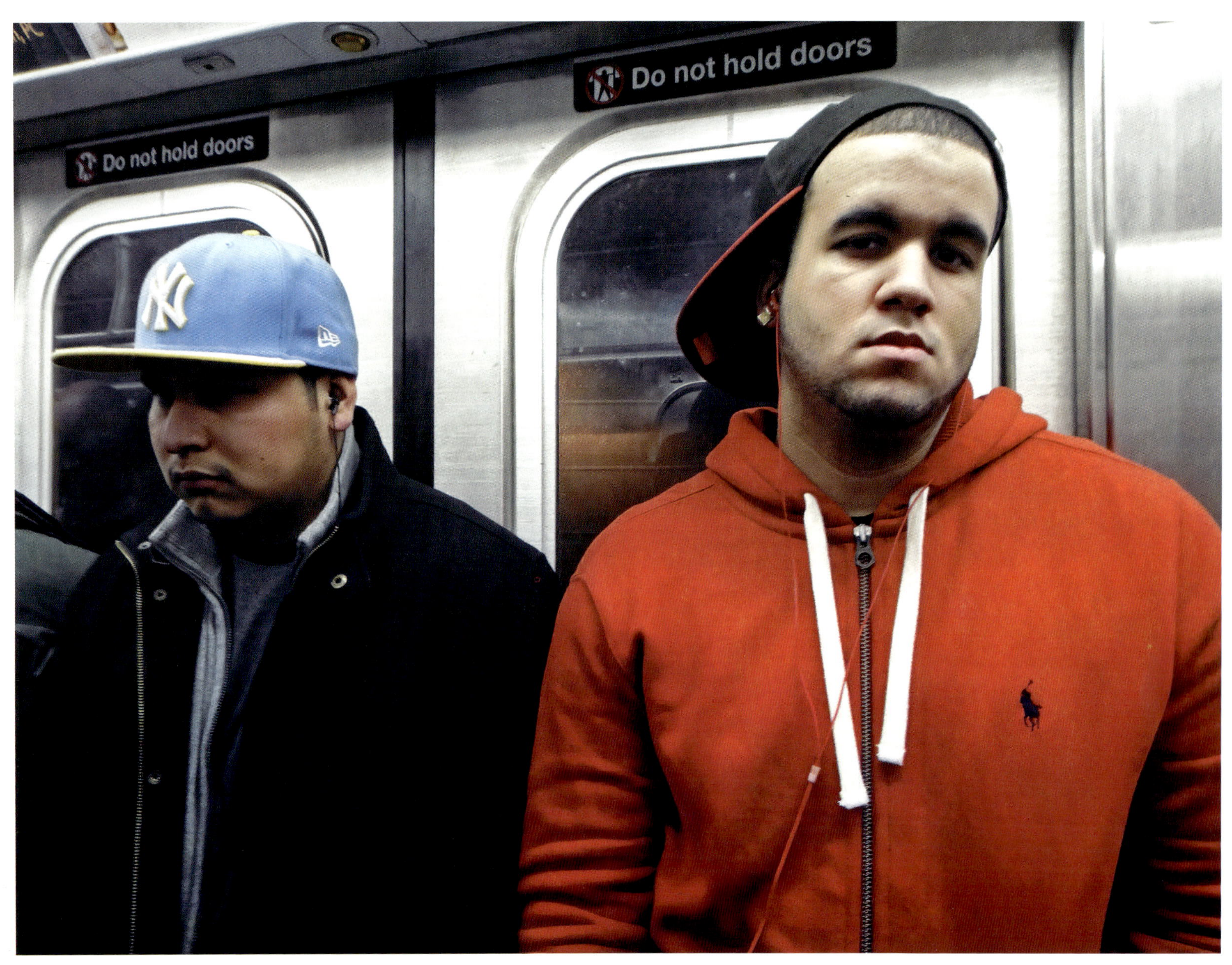

New York City, 2011

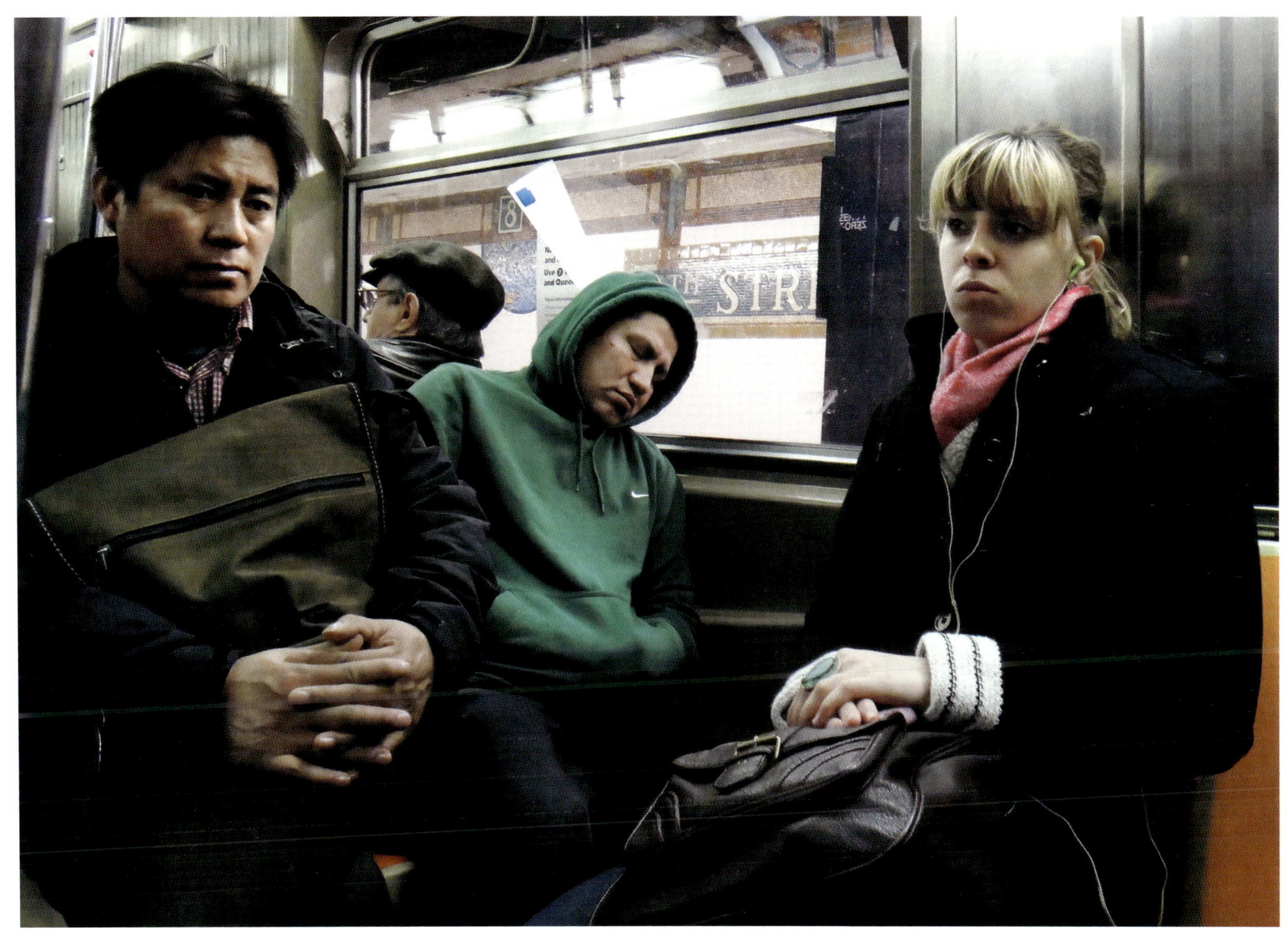

New York City, 2011

Subway Face

by Langston Hughes

That I have been looking
For you all my life
Does not matter to you.
You do not know.

You never knew.
Nor did I.
Now you take the Harlem train uptown;
I take a local down.

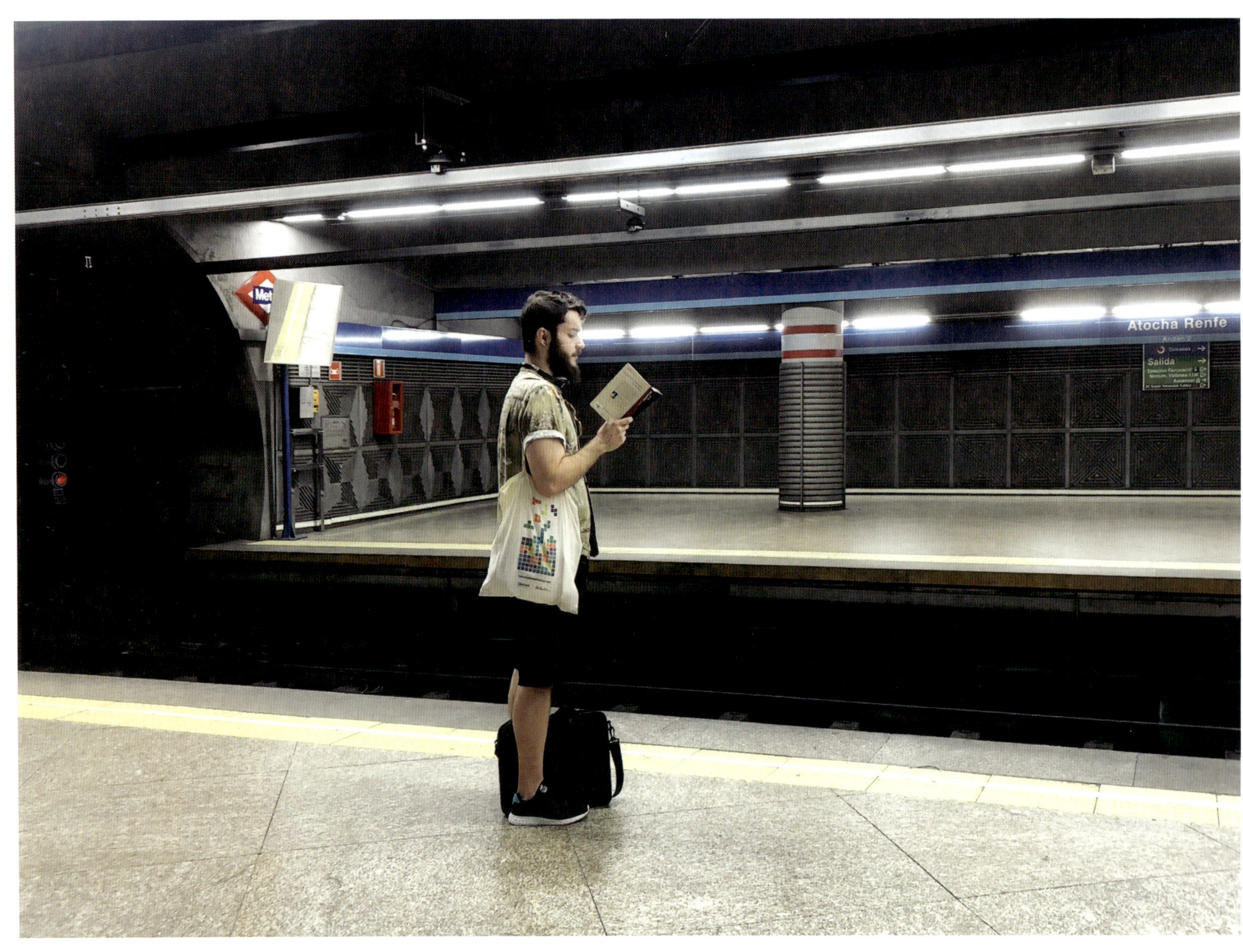

Puerta de Atocha Train Station.
Madrid, Spain, 2018

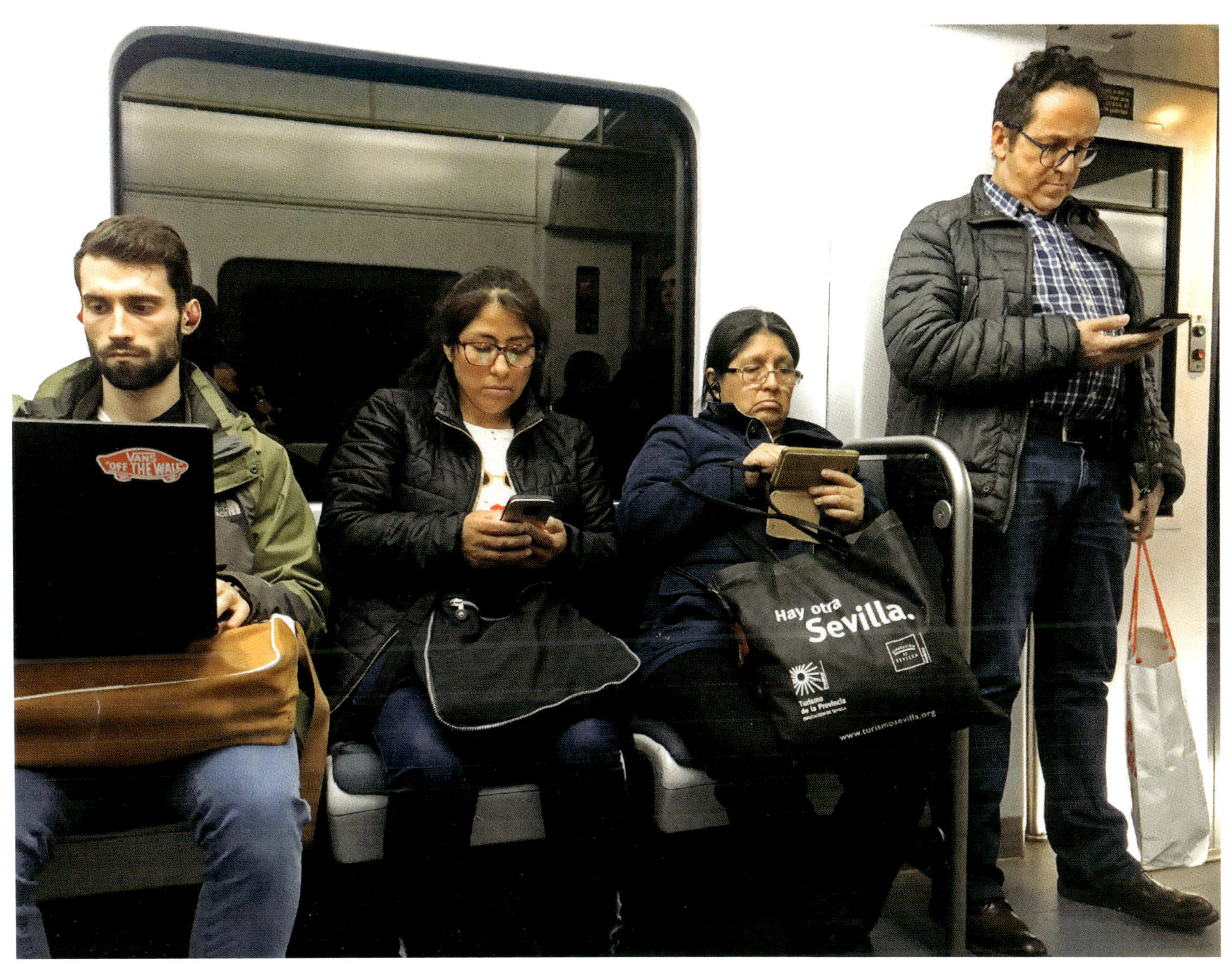

Madrid, Spain, 2018

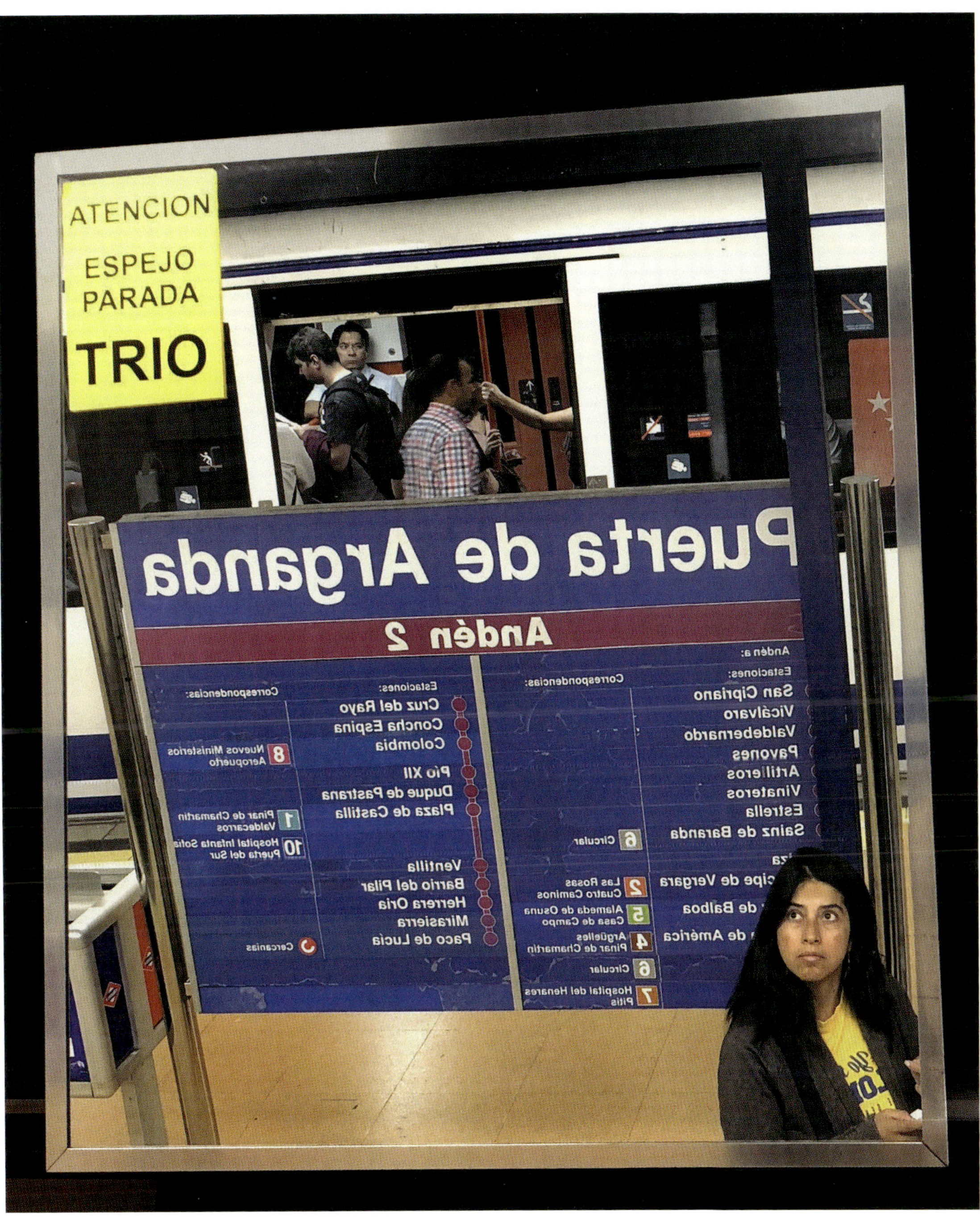

Puerta de Atocha Train Station.
Madrid, Spain, 2018

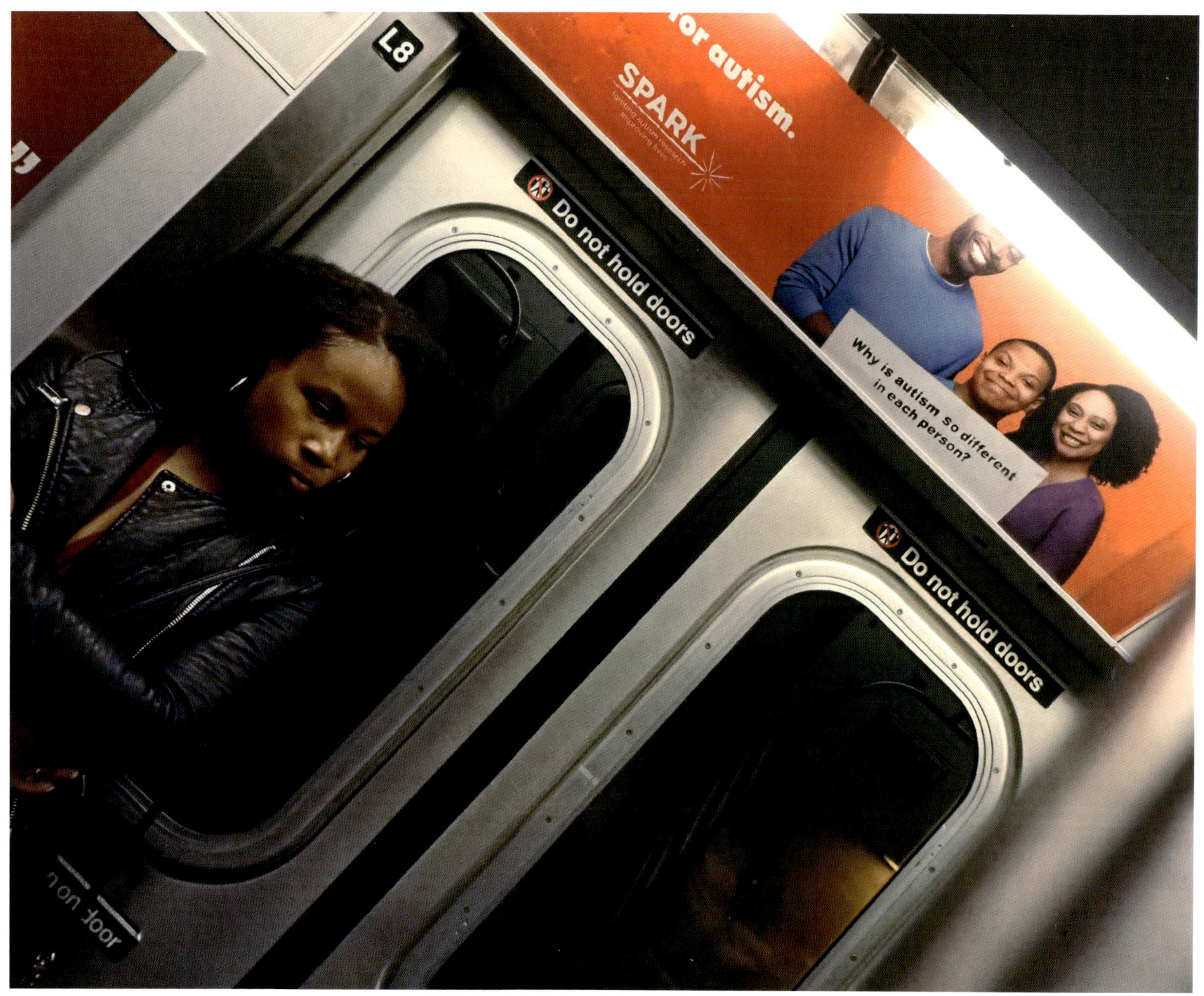

New York City, 2018

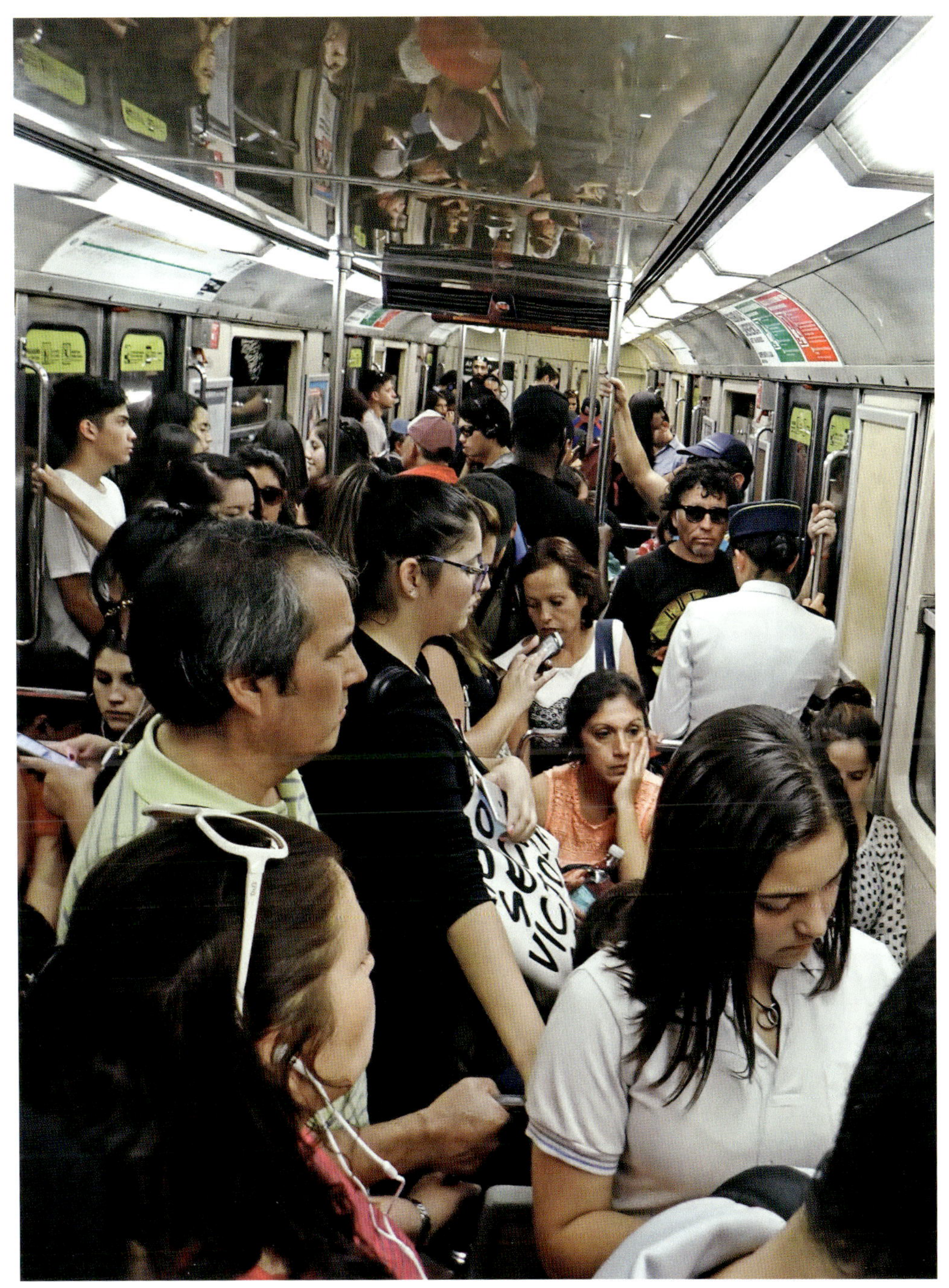

Santiago de Chile, 2018

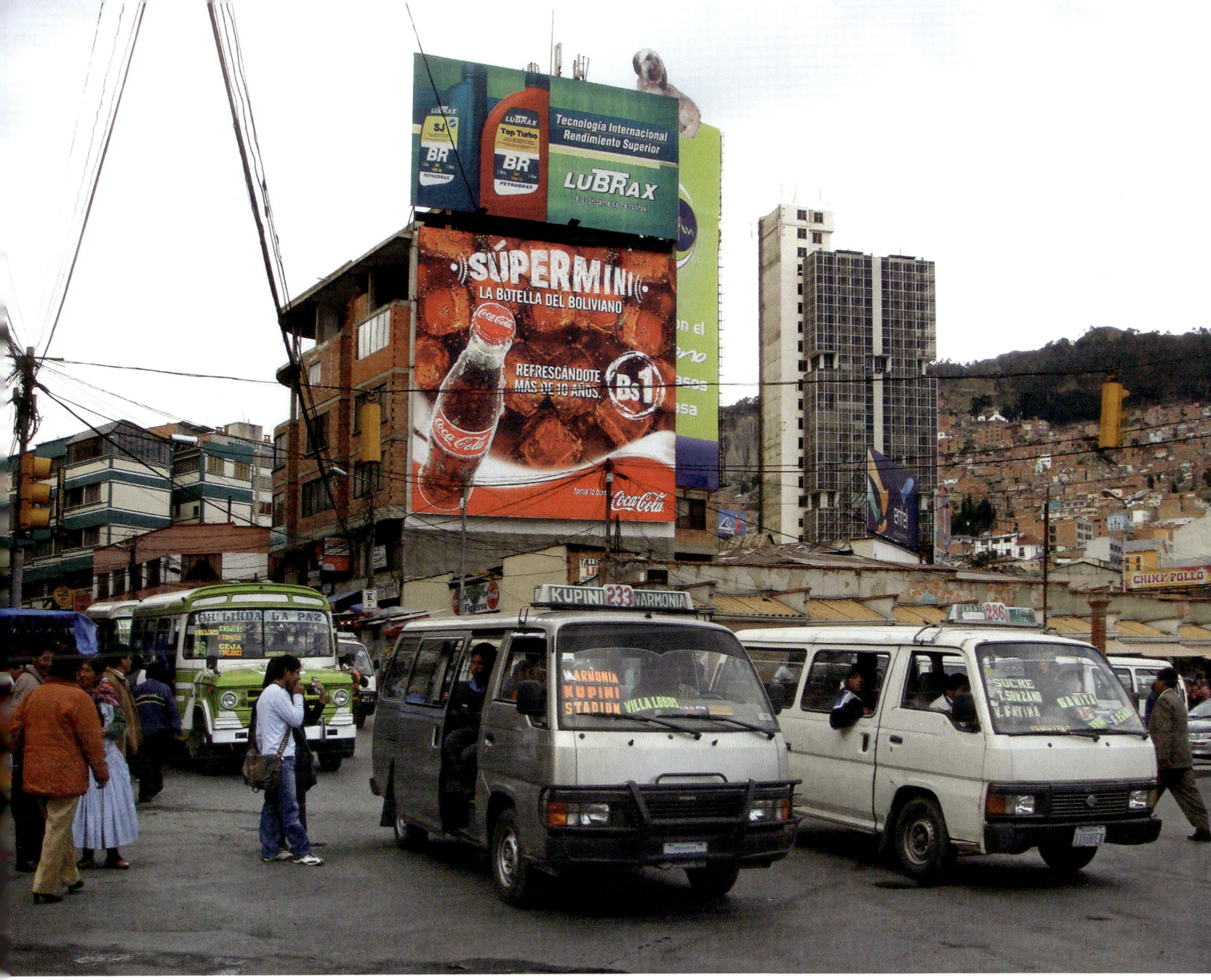

La Paz, Bolivia, 2007

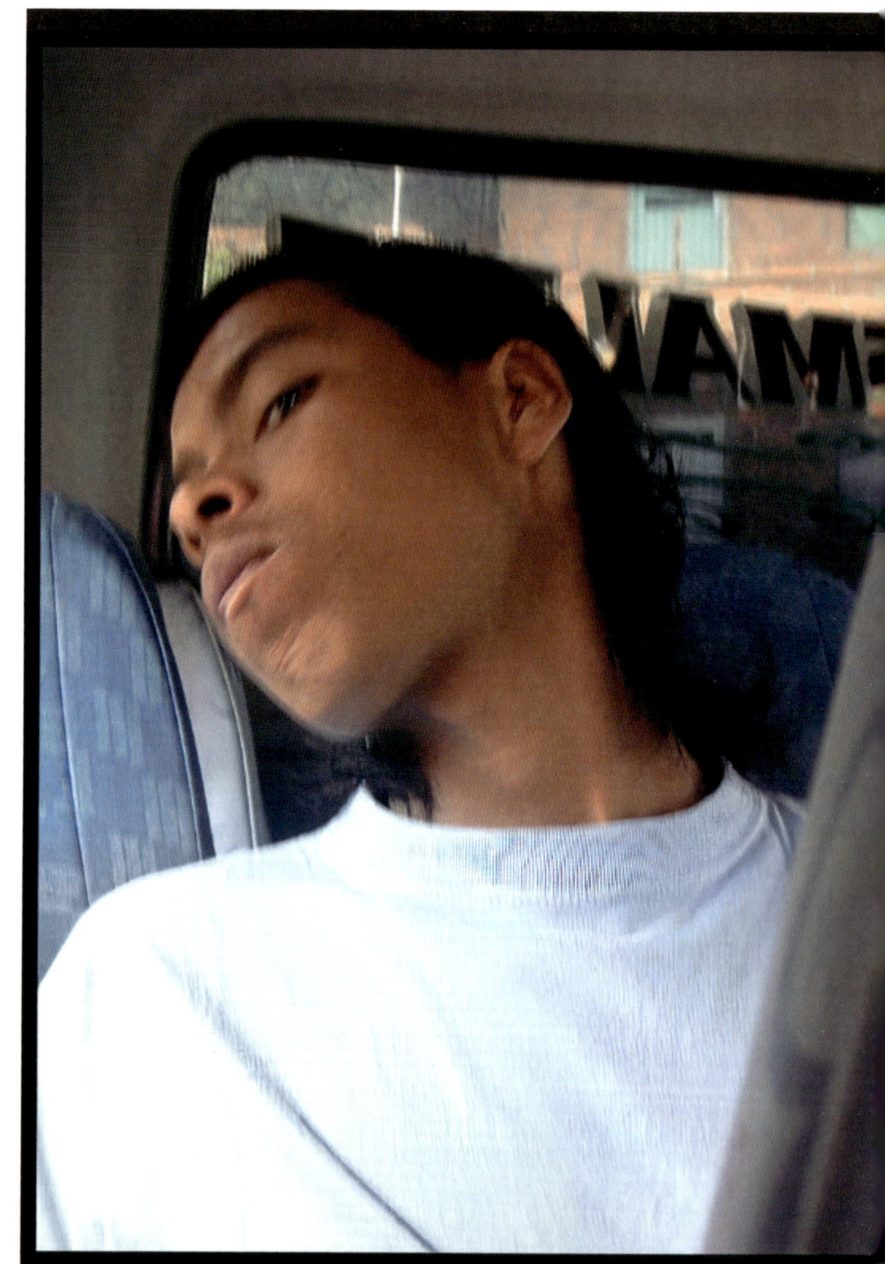

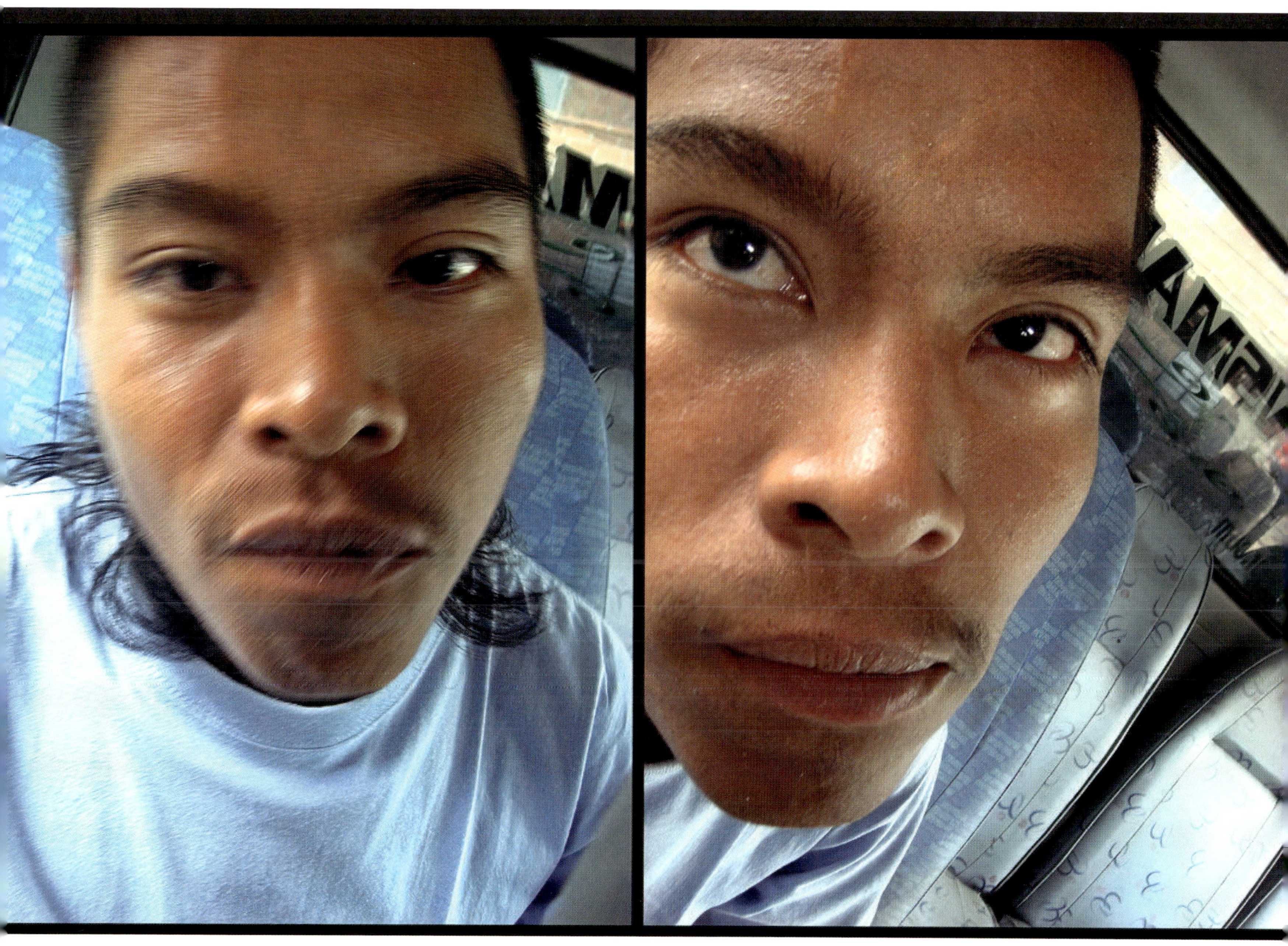

Coming down in public transport from Comuna 3 Manrique,
a marginal settlement on the hillsides above Medellín. Colombia, 2007

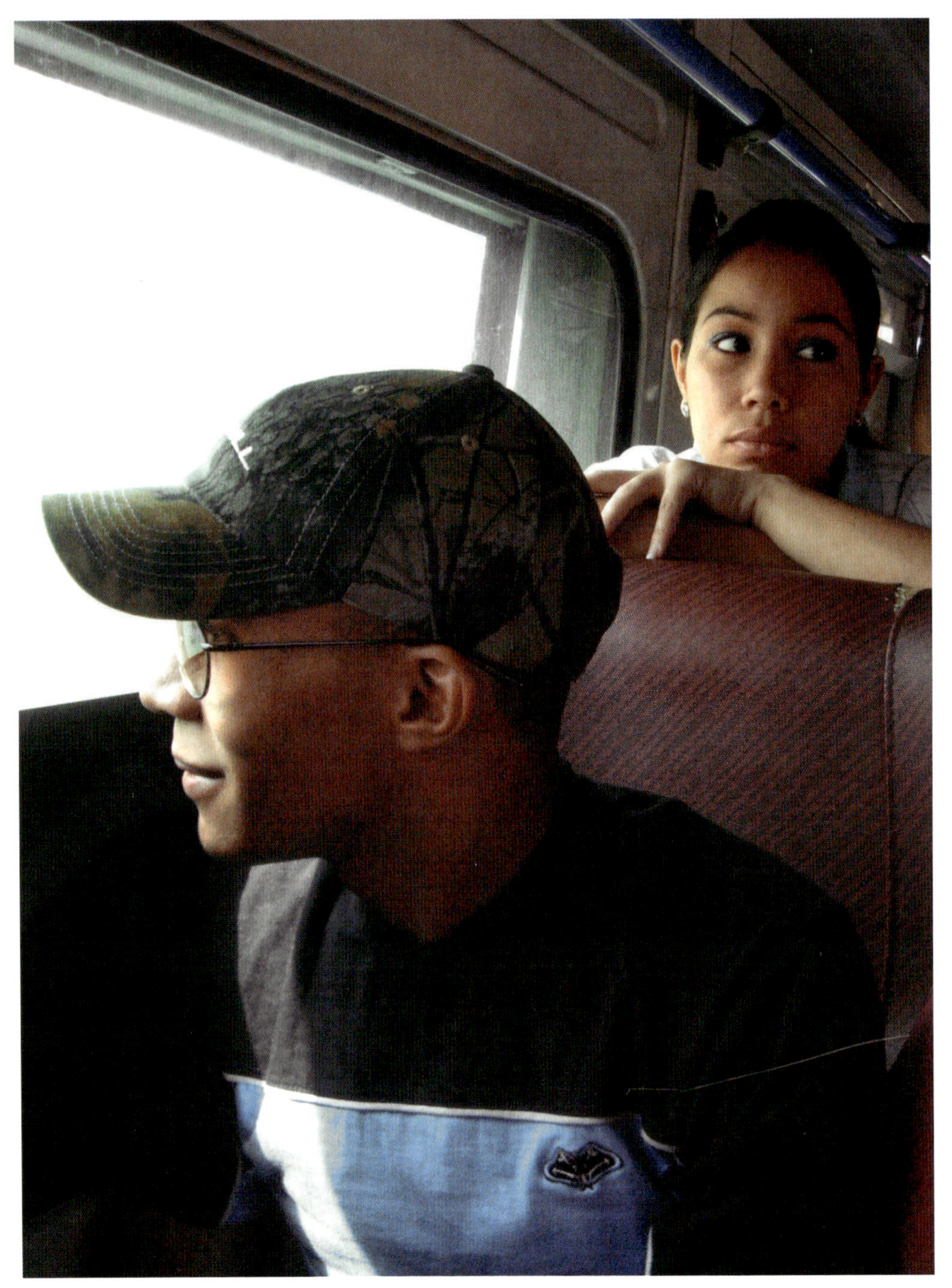

Santo Domingo, Dominican Republic, 2007

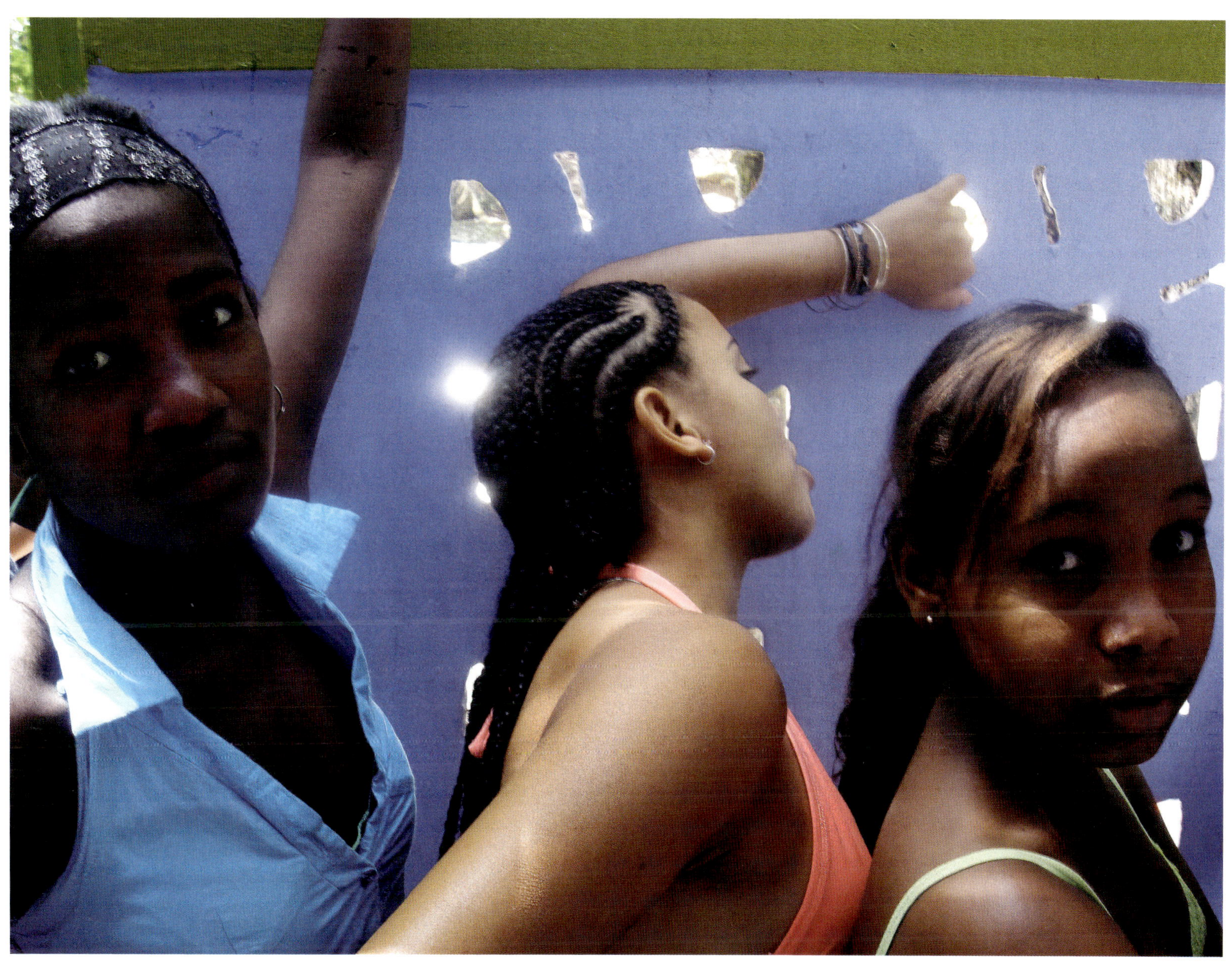

Waiting for a bus outside of Santo Domingo.
Dominican Republic, 2007

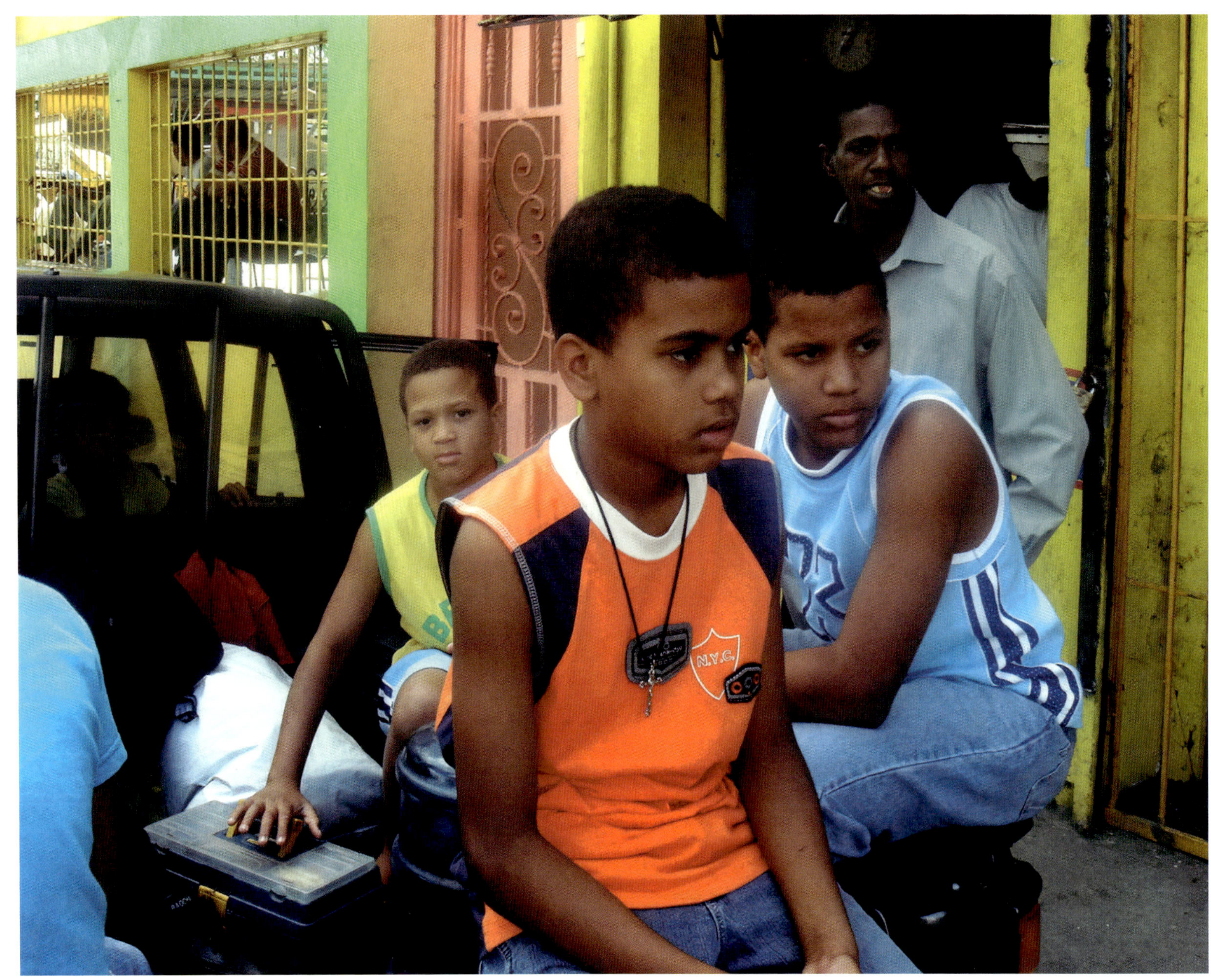

Santo Domingo, Dominican Republic, 2007

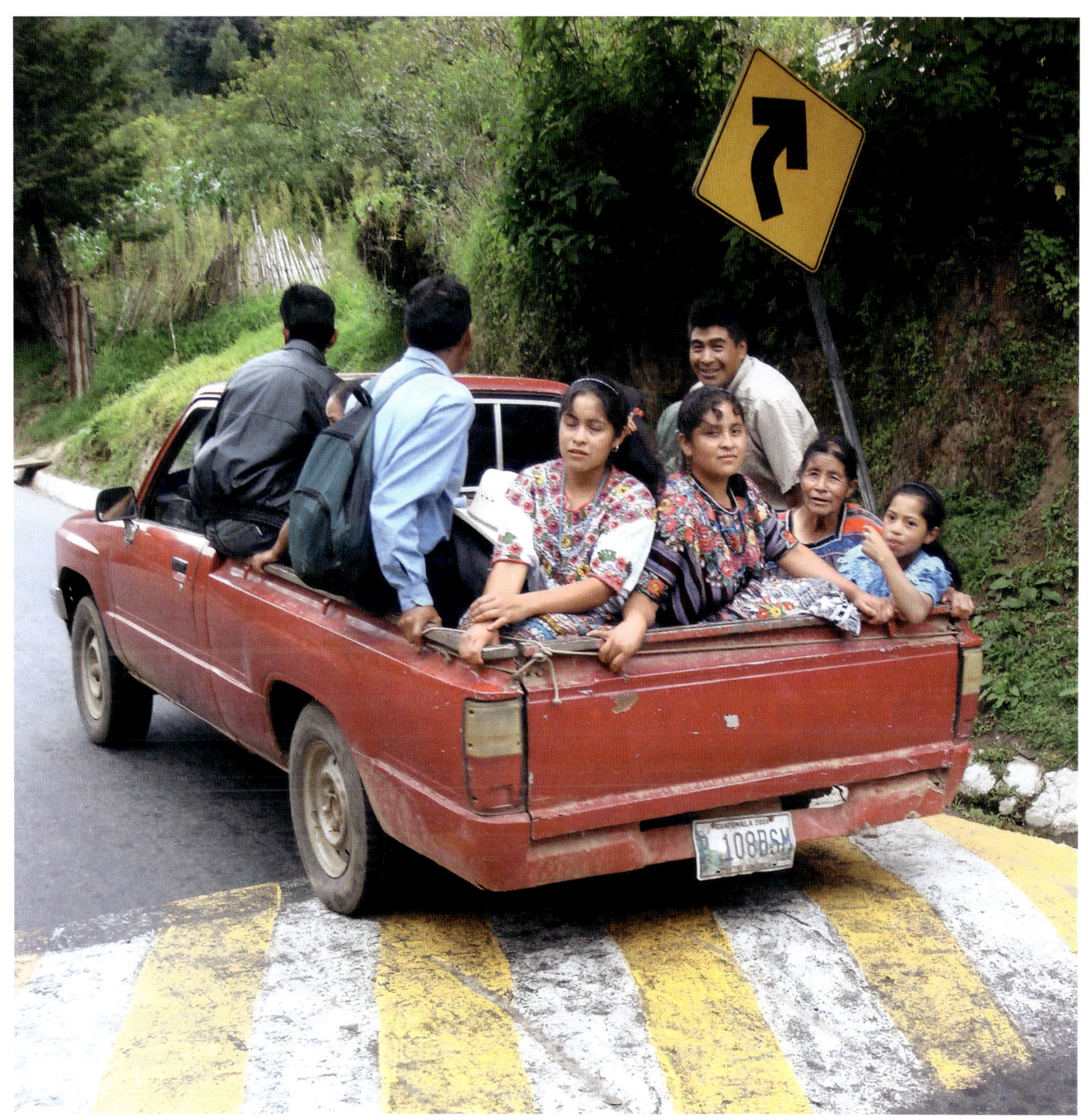

Quiché, Guatemala, 2007

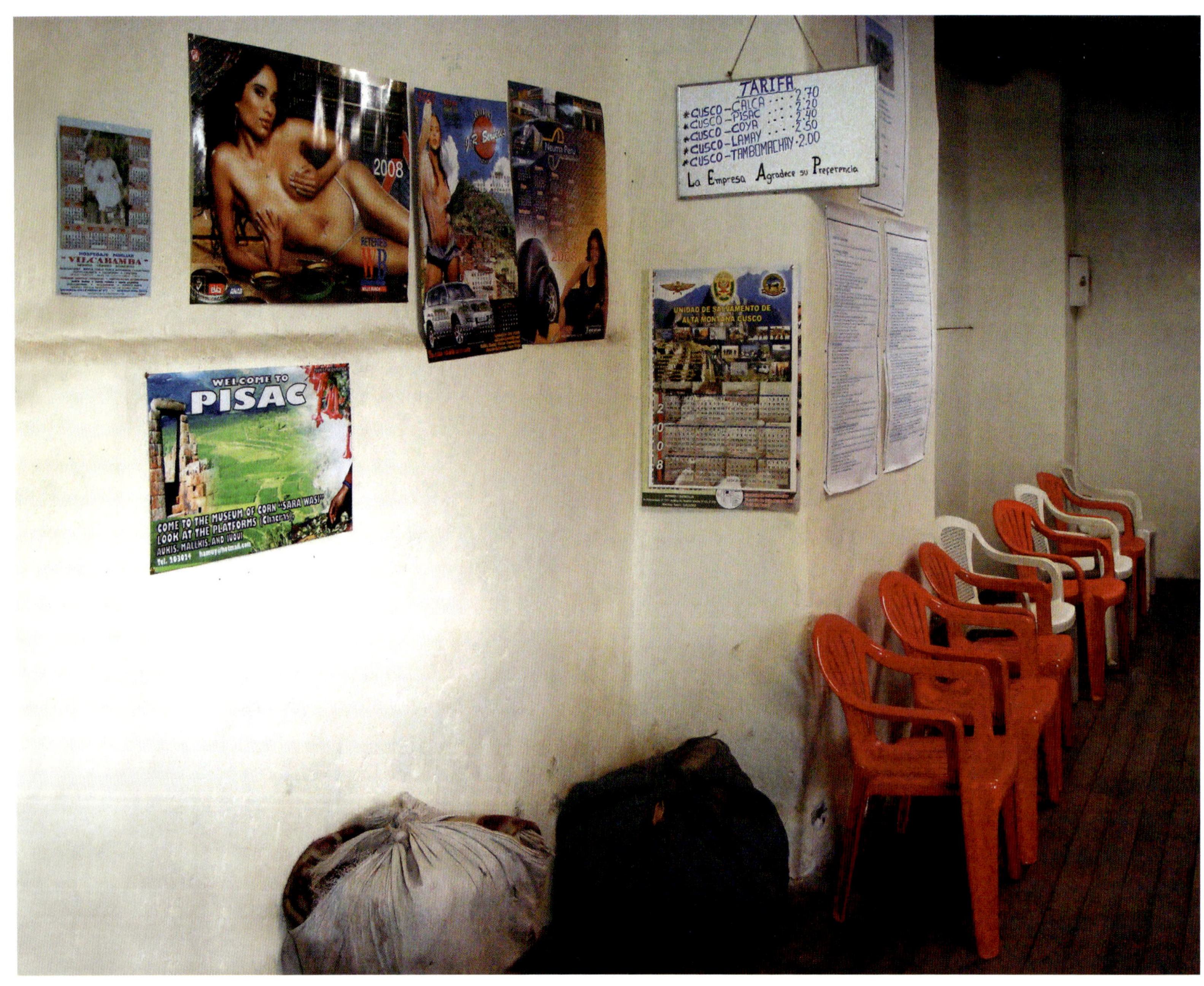

Bus station. Pisac, Peru, 2008

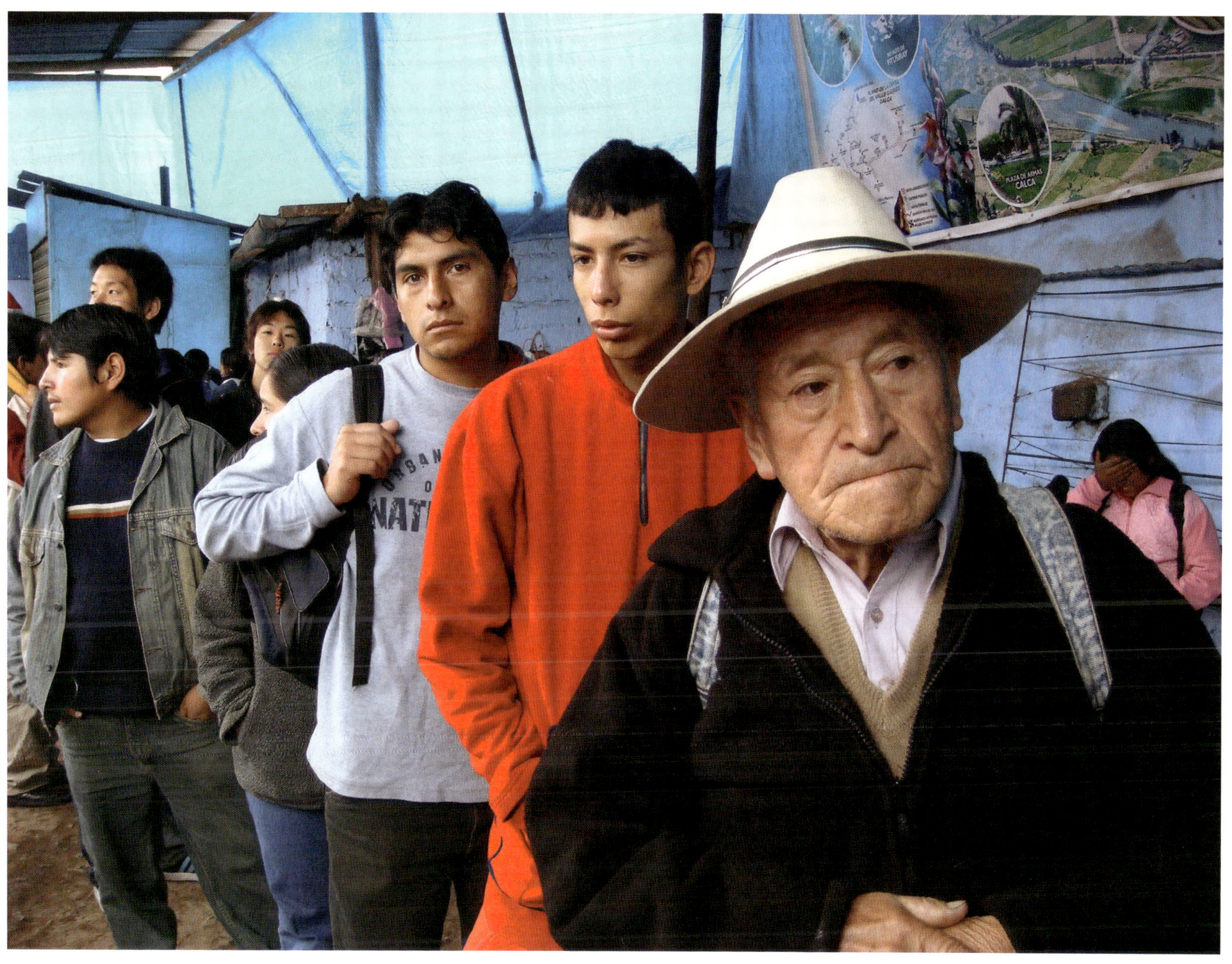

Bus station. Pisac, Peru, 2008

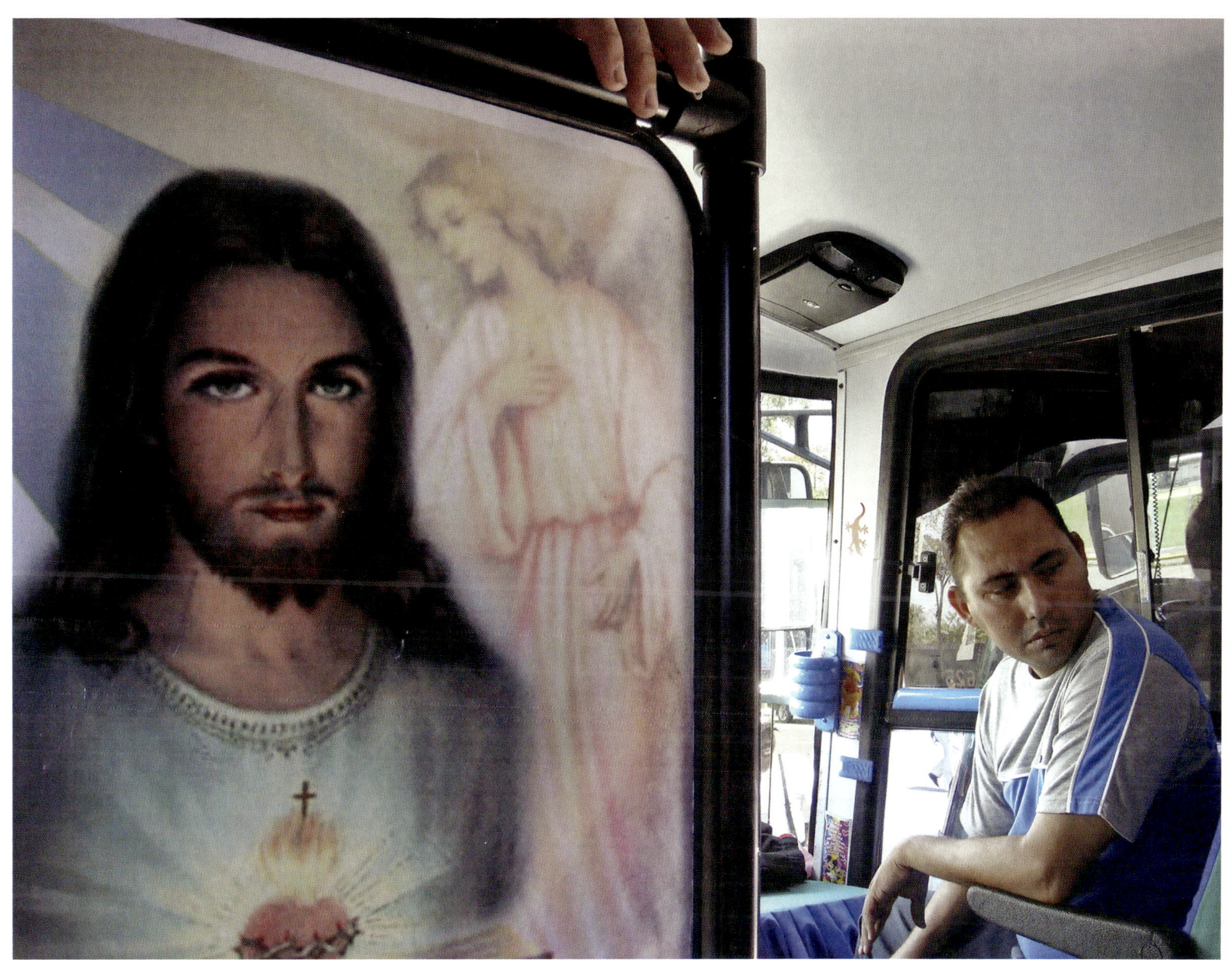

Bus from Santo Domingo in Táchira state, to
Guasdualito in the state of Apure. Venezuela, 2007

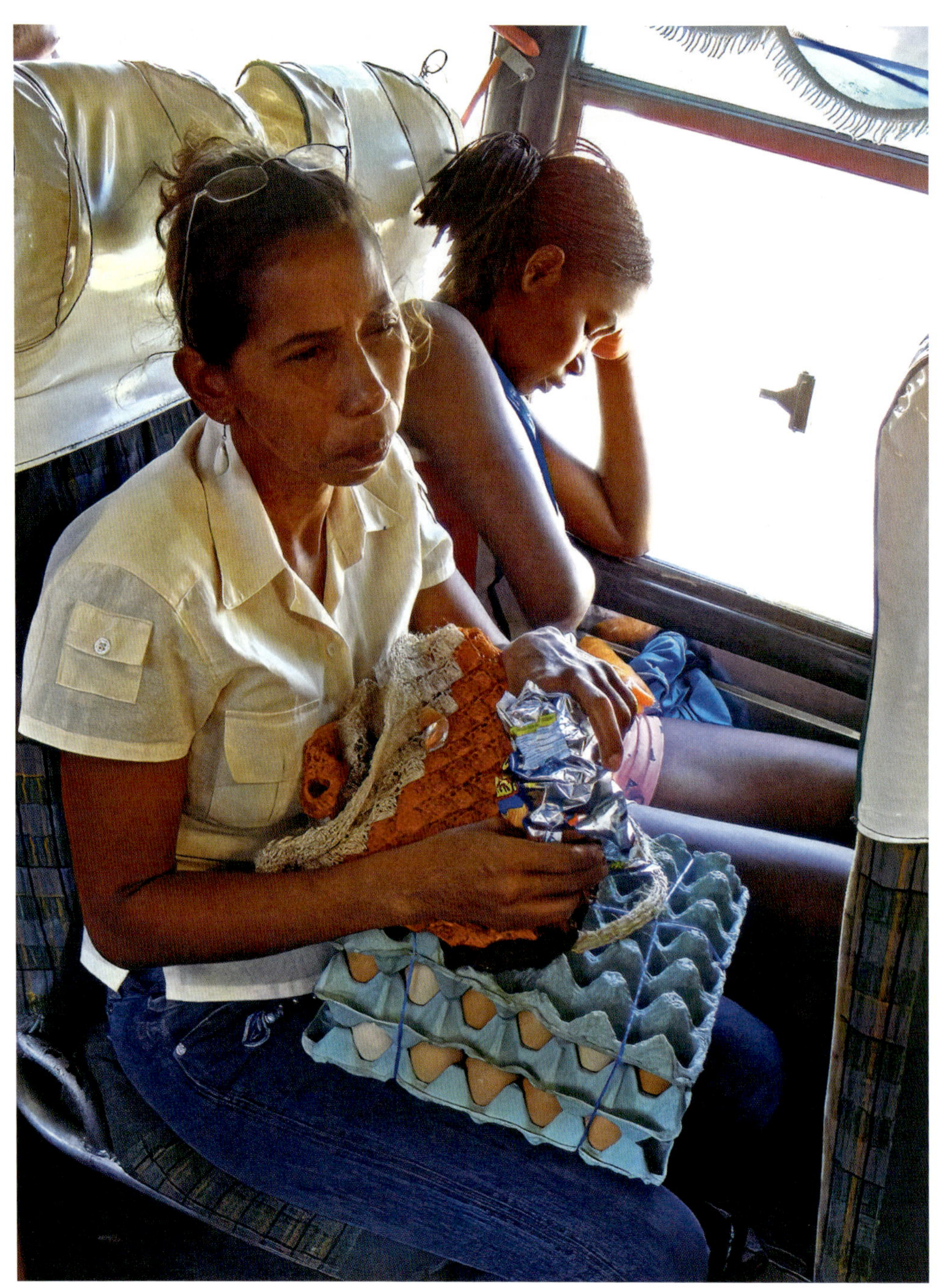

Santa Marta, Colombia, 2008

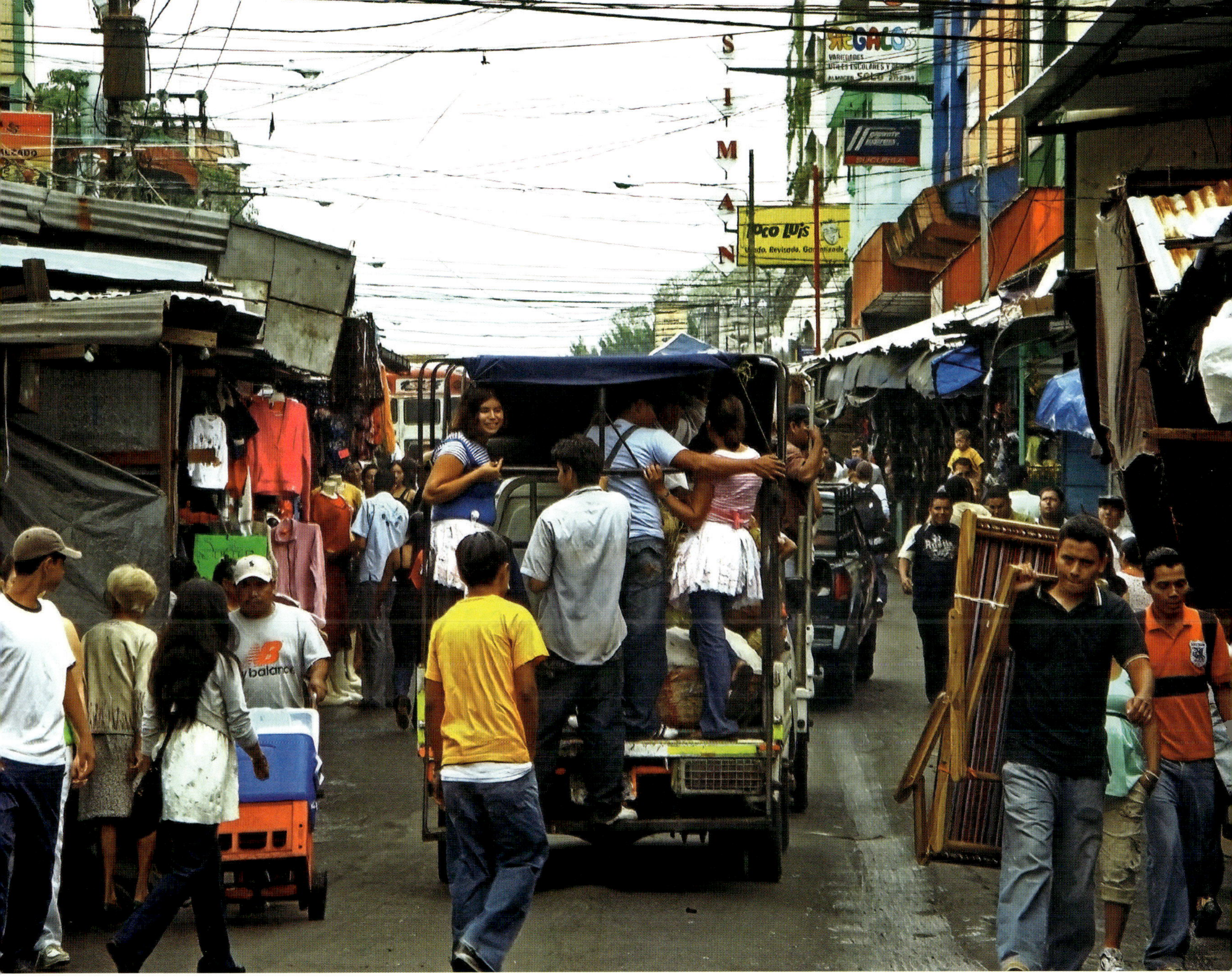

San Salvador, El Salvador, 2008

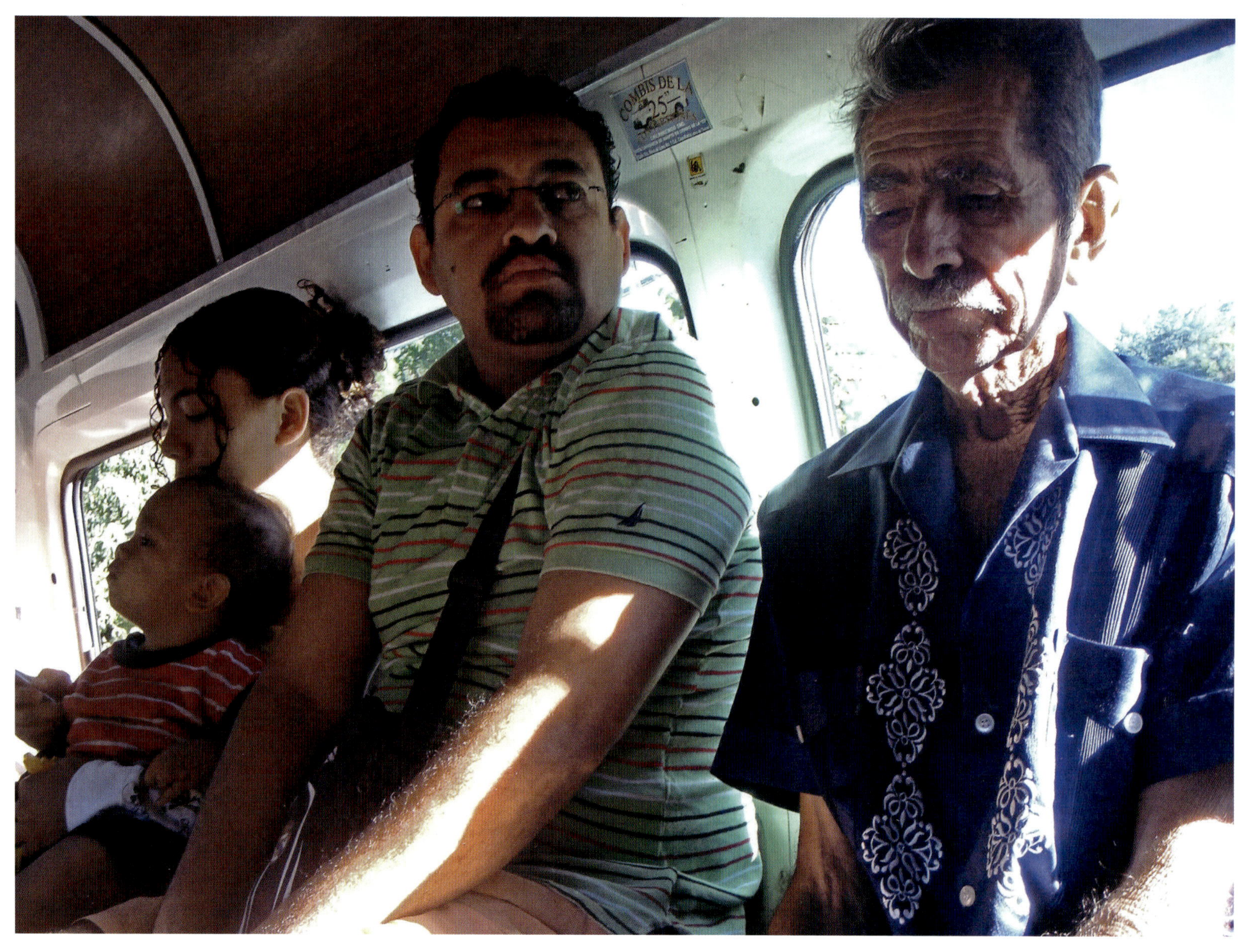

Tierra Colorada, Guerrero, Mexico, 2009

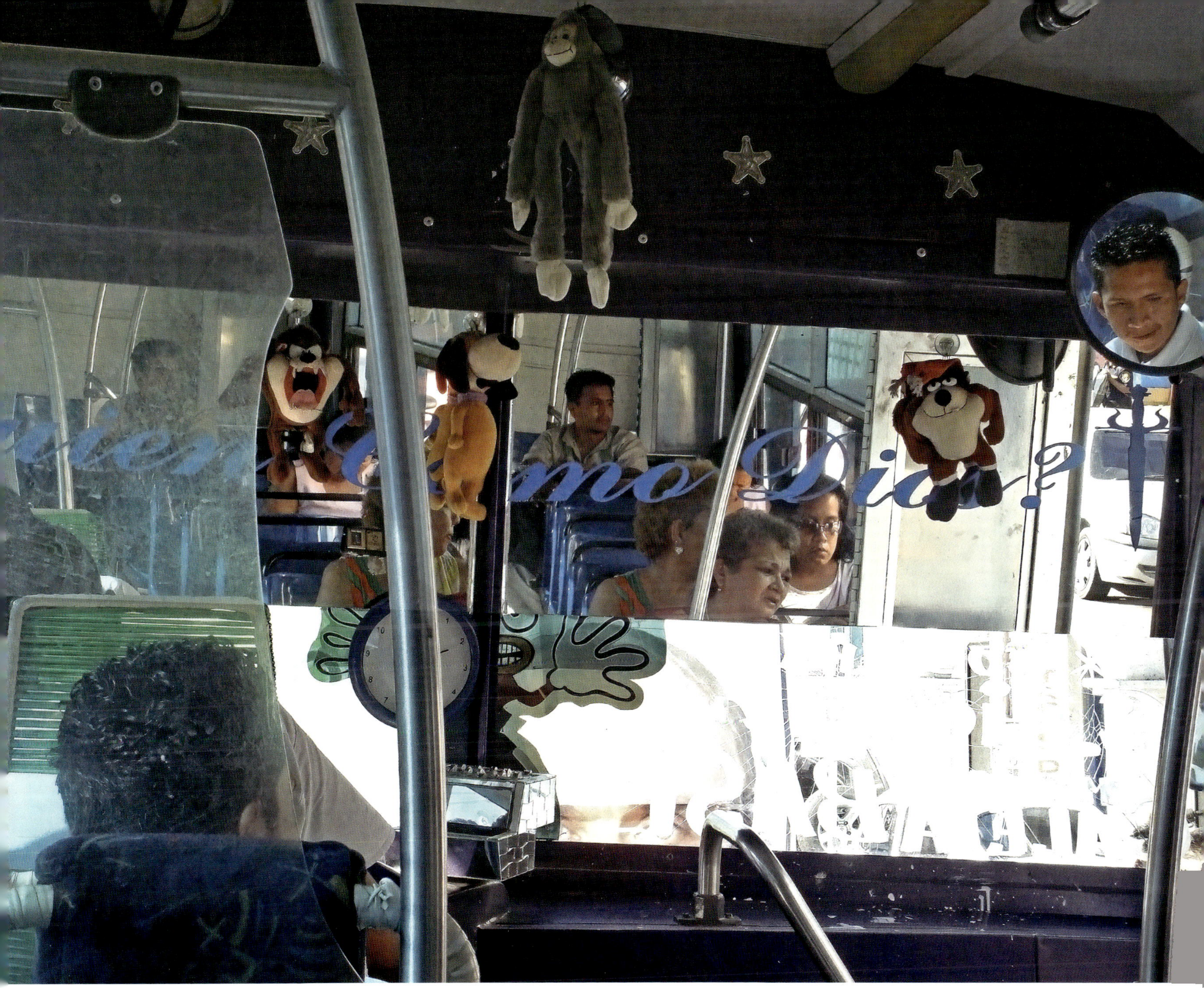

Acapulco, Mexico, 2009

Regardless of which city in the world, public transportation is one of the truest displays of humanity. The faces that can be seen—whether distracted, tired, happy, sad, excited, or thoughtful—make us reflect on the hundreds of situations that people experience while reaching their destinations.

For this reason, Jonathan Moller, by portraying with his lens the people who routinely use the buses or subways, creates an additional incentive for all governments to promote equal access to citizens—regardless of social class—to a modern, efficient, and sustainable public system of transportation.

As the population of cities grows and there is an increase on demand, we face challenges to promote mobility, the development of transport infrastructure, and the energy transition of its different actors, with the aim that not only people move but that social, economic, and environmental justice are likewise propelled forward.

This can only be achieved with communities, with local and national authorities, with all players in the transport sector, with unions, businessmen, social organizations, academia, and with all of society at large. Only in this way can we build the countries in which we all want to live.

In Colombia, we have identified unique challenges to promote mobility, the development of transportation infrastructure, and the energy transition. We have tasked ourselves with making Colombia a world power of life.

For this reason, it is essential for us to decarbonize transport in all its modes—road, rail, river, air, and sea—through the use of technologies that are increasingly efficient and less polluting.

Not with impositions, nor by excluding anyone, but instead with agreements in which everyone can participate, move forward, and fulfill their dreams...

Guillermo Francisco Reyes González
Colombian Minister of Transportation

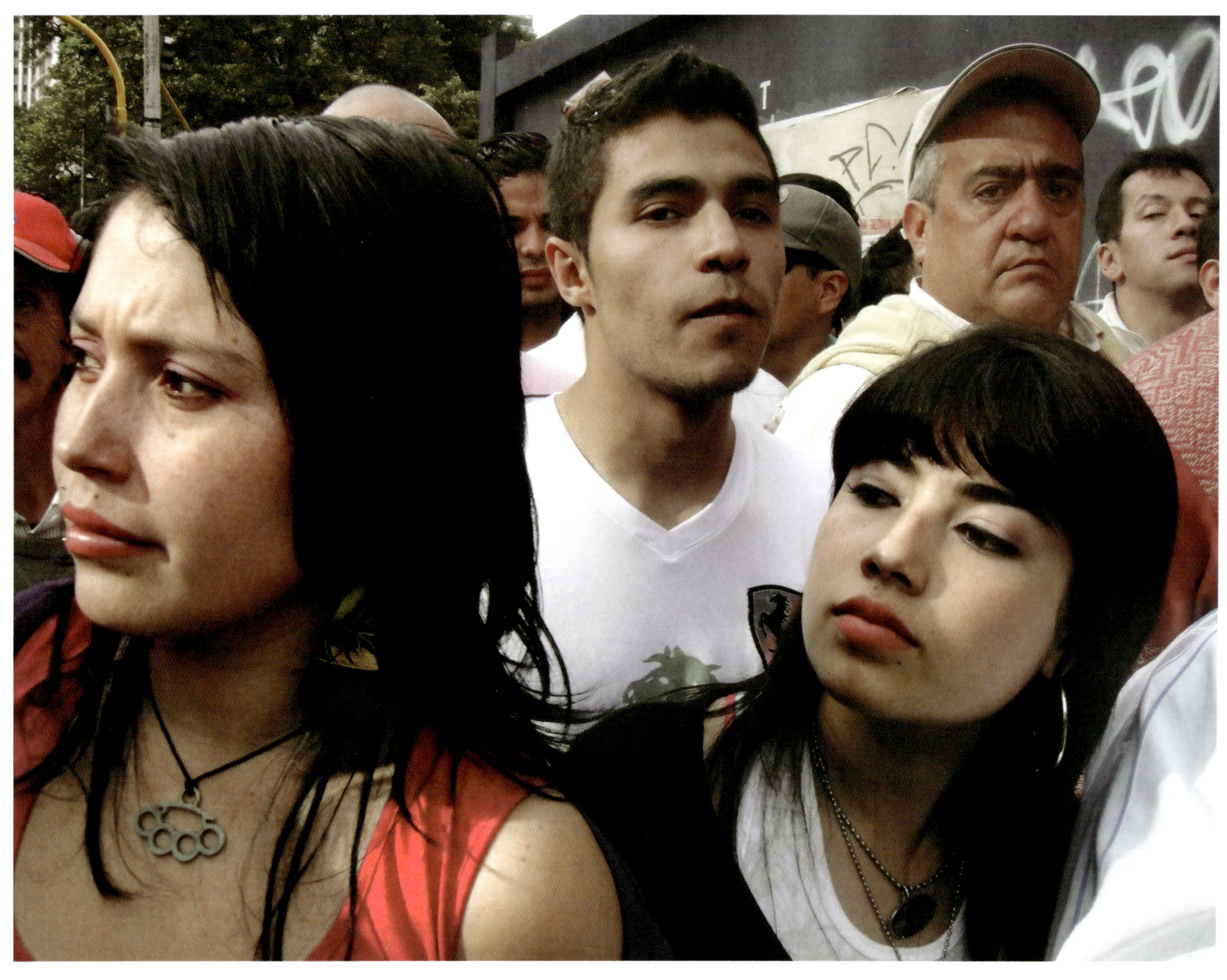

Waiting for a bus. Bogotá,
Colombia, 2009

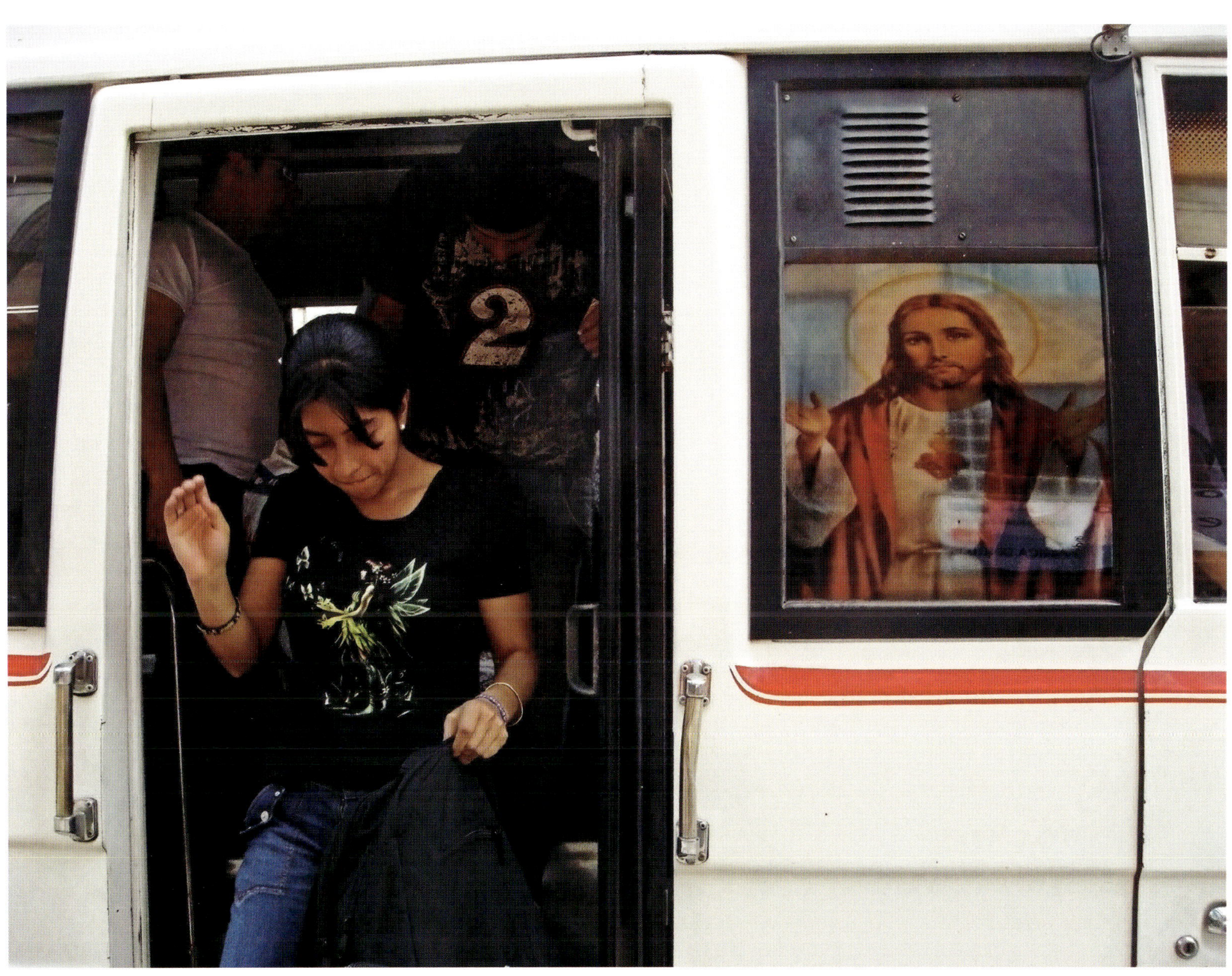

Zipaquirá, Colombia, 2009

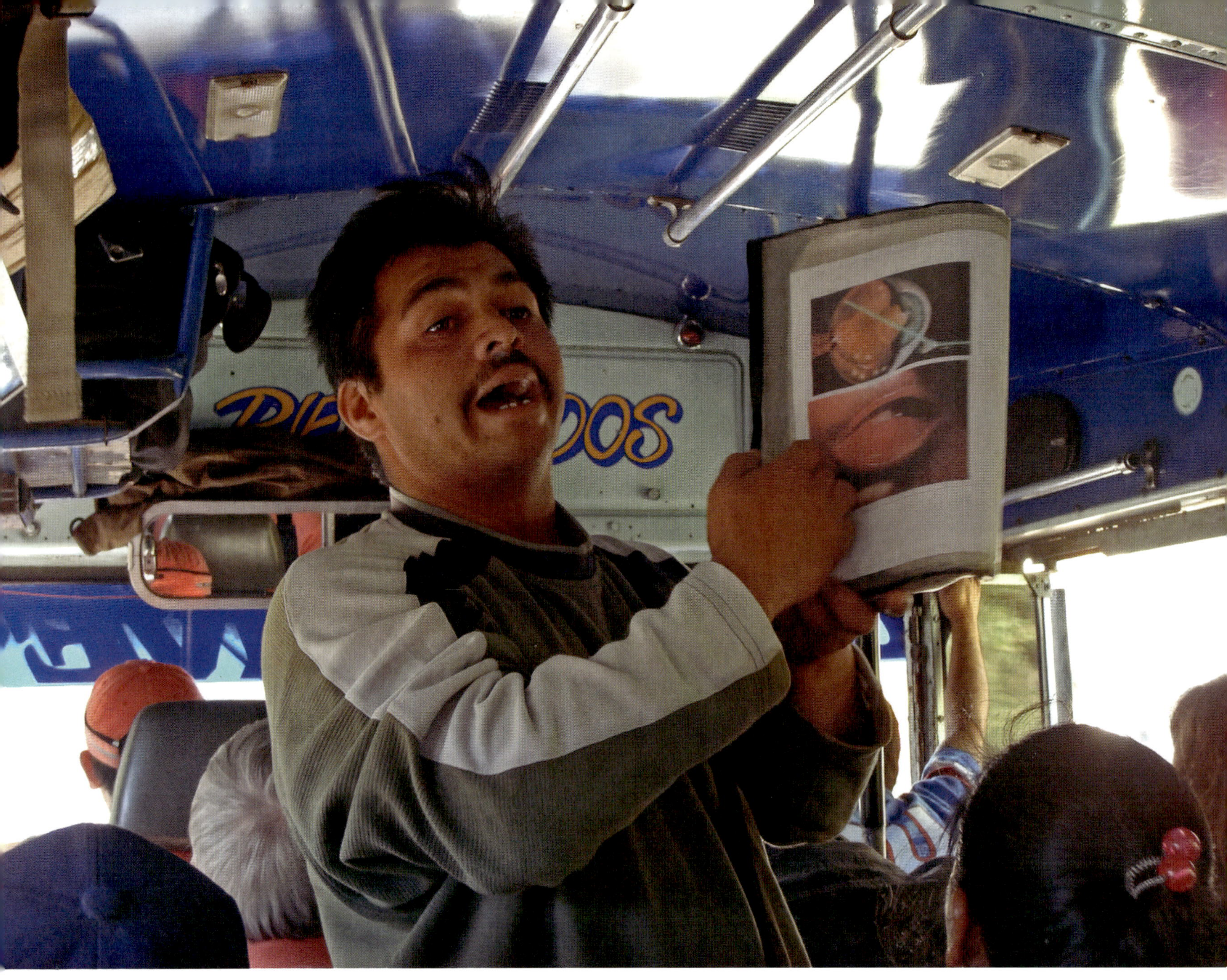

A man selling snake oil remedies on a bus
in Huehuetenango. Guatemala, 2009

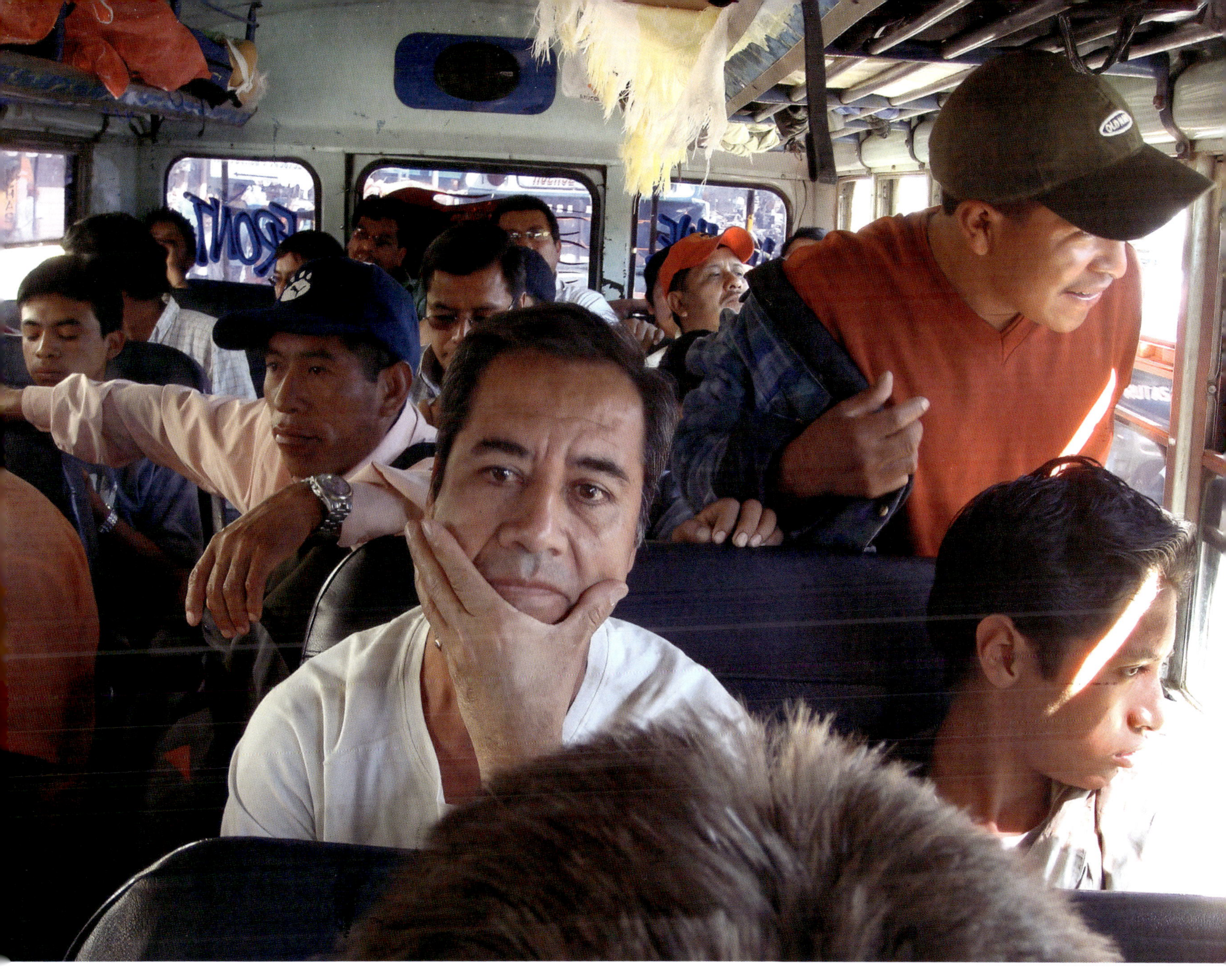

Quiché, Guatemala, 2009

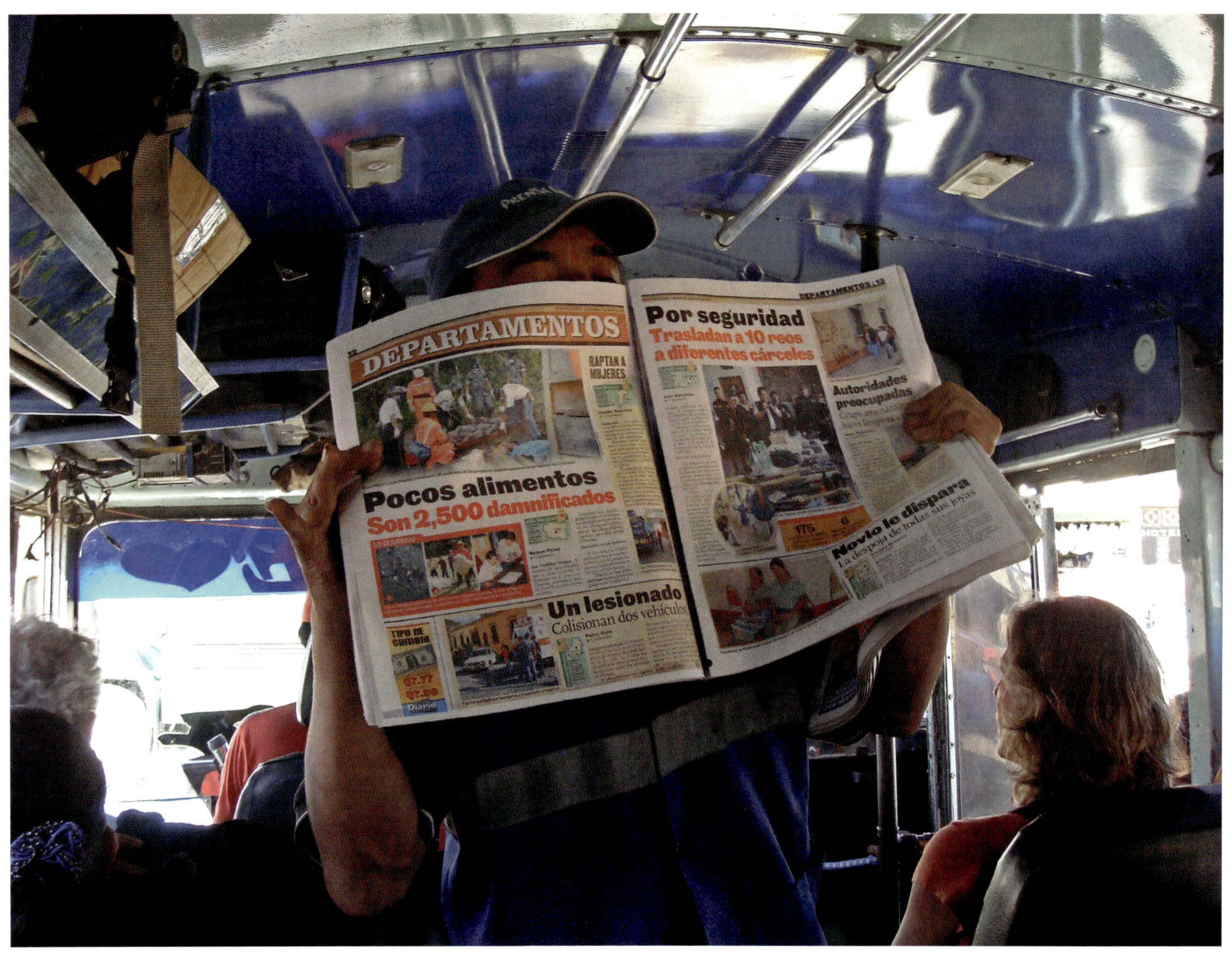

Quiché, Guatemala, 2009

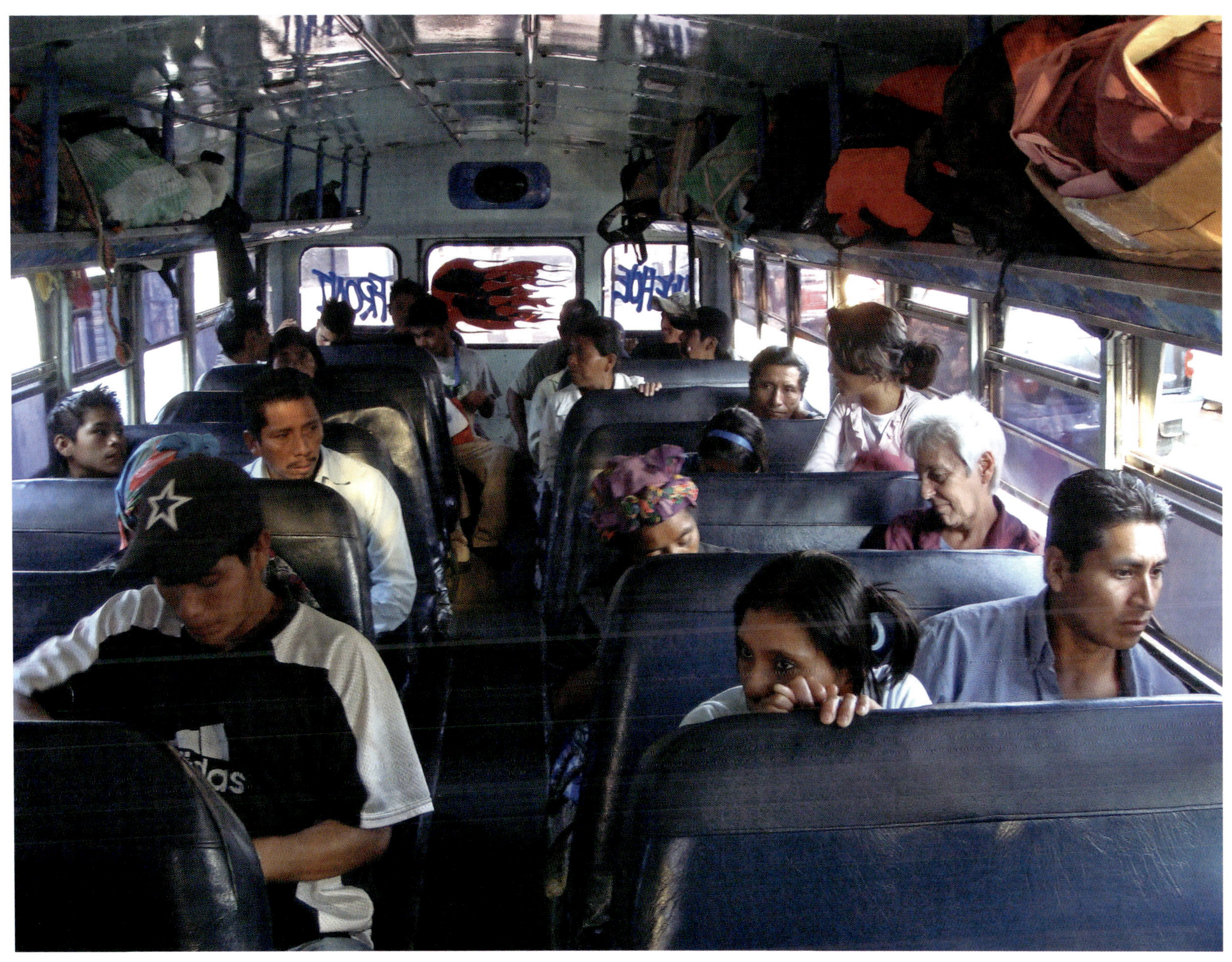

Huehuetenango, Guatemala, 2009

93

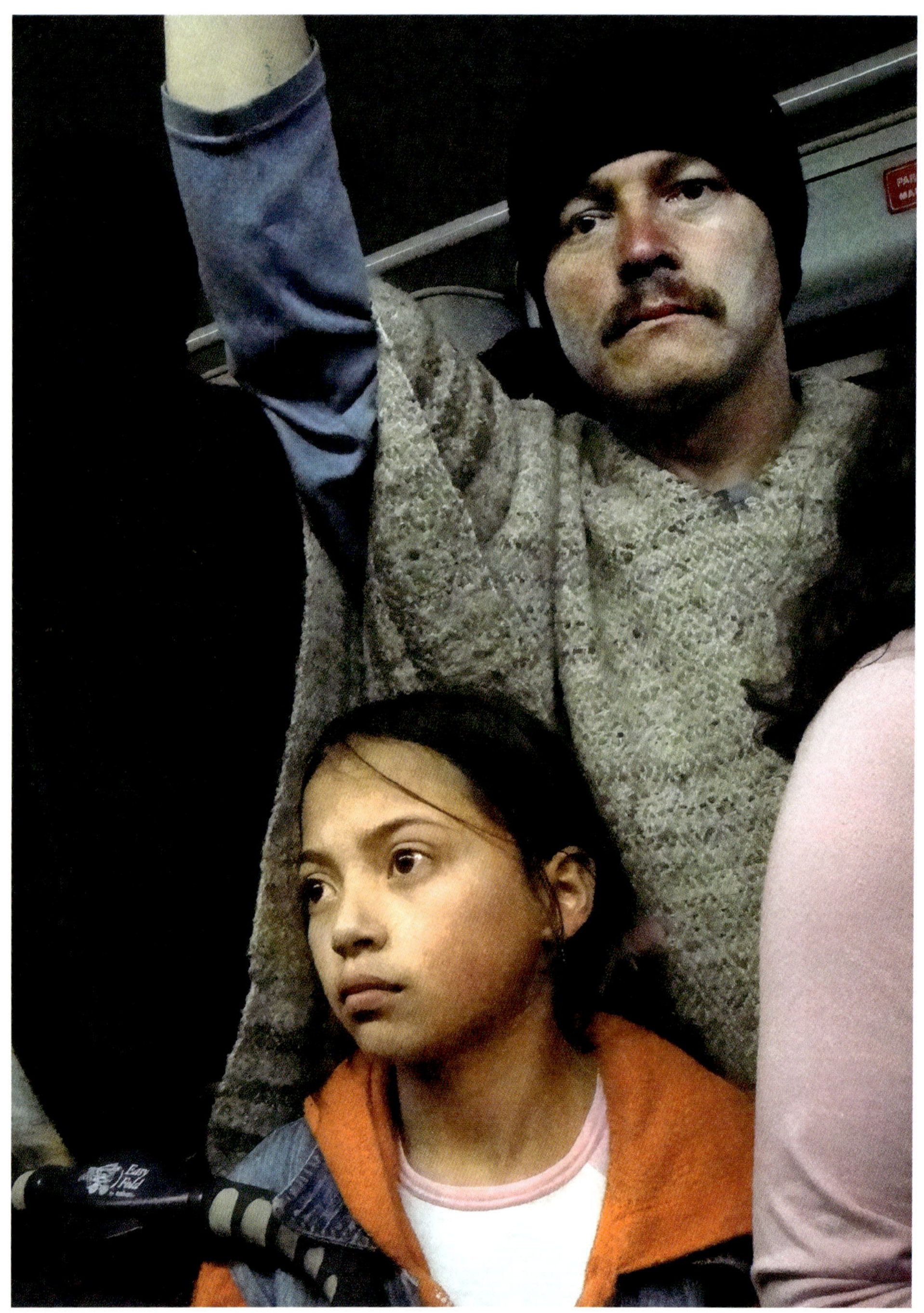

The TransMilenio rapid transit bus system.
Bogotá, Colombia, 2009

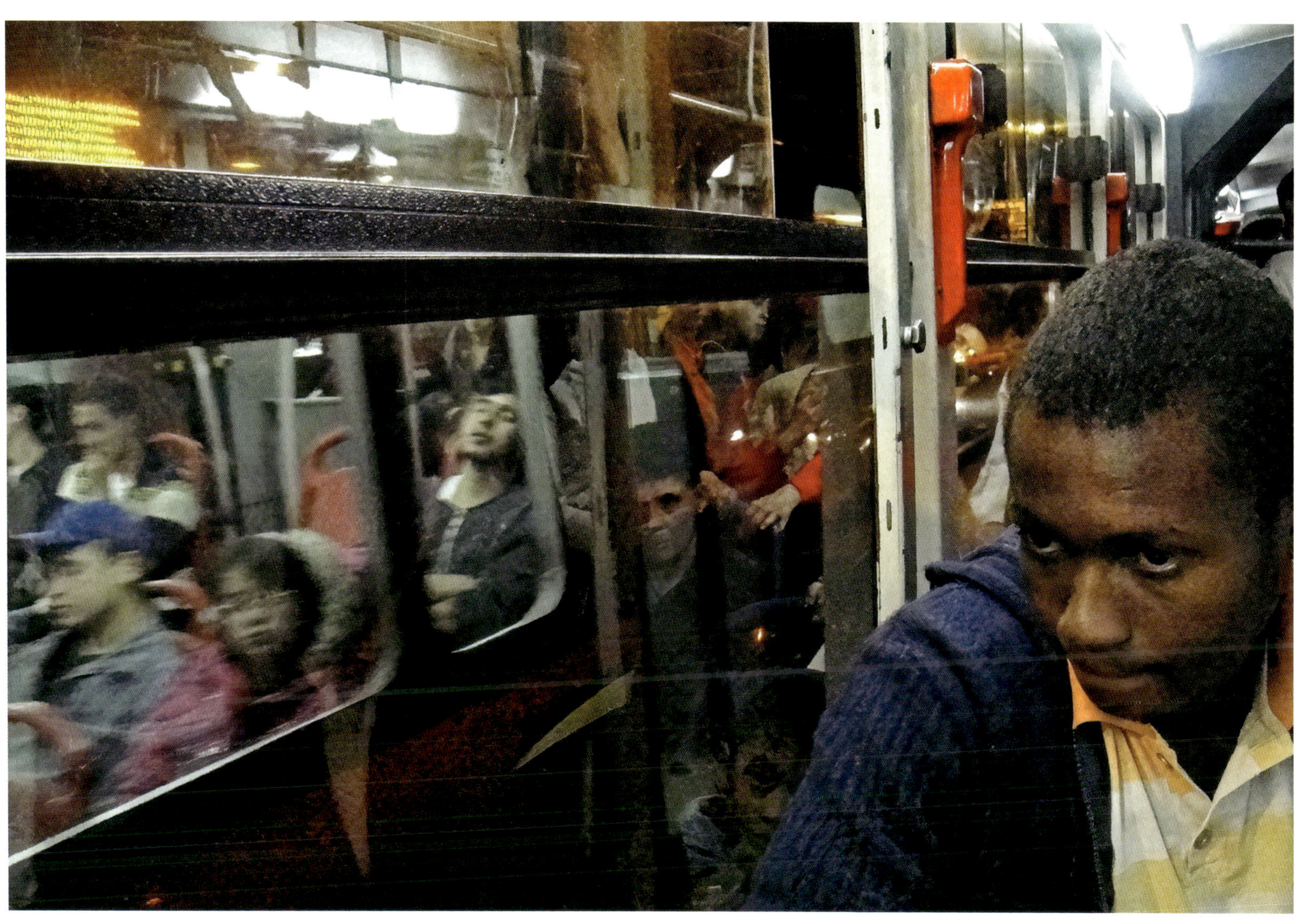

The TransMilenio rapid transit bus system.
Bogotá, Colombia, 2009

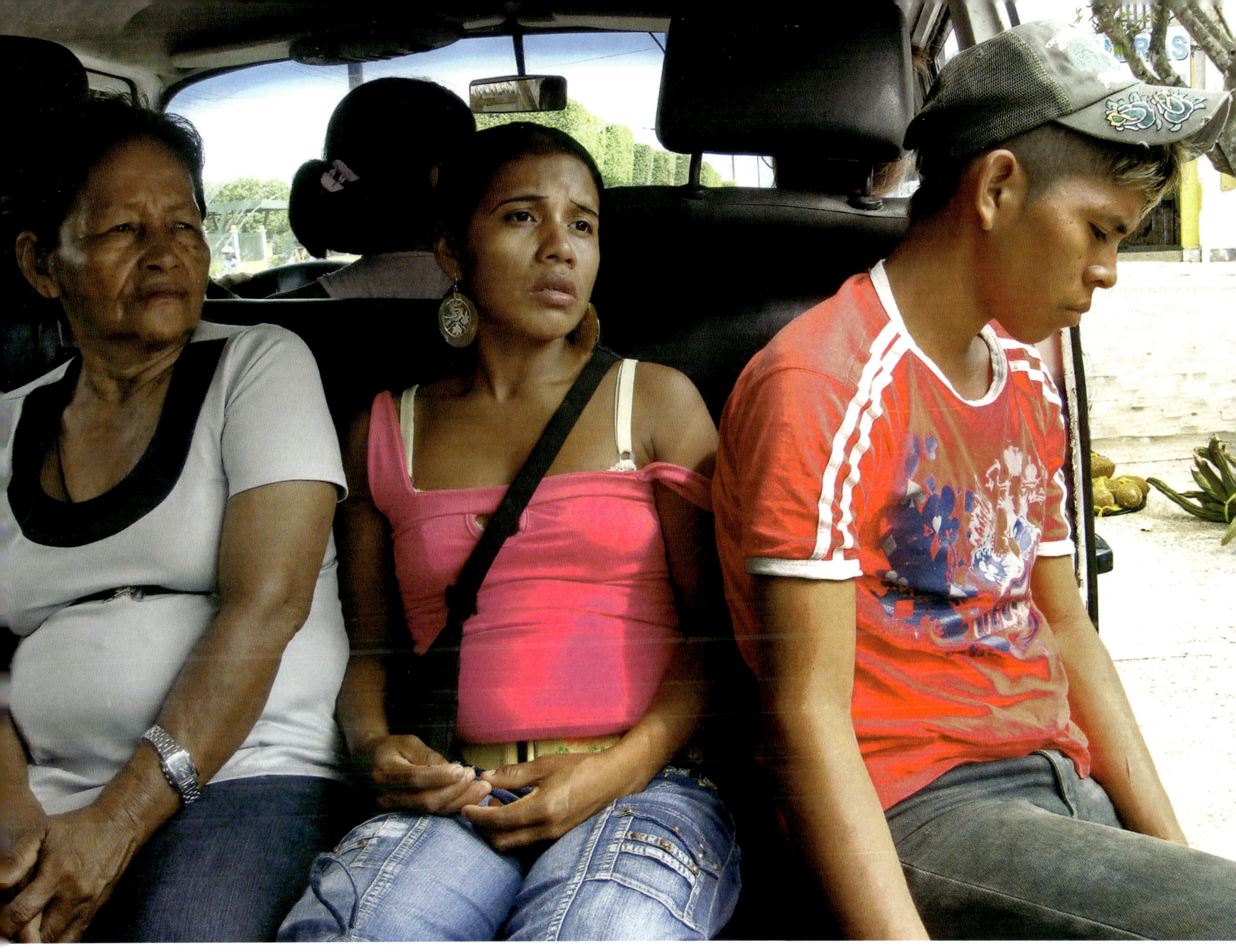

Tabatinga. Amazonas, Brazil, 2010

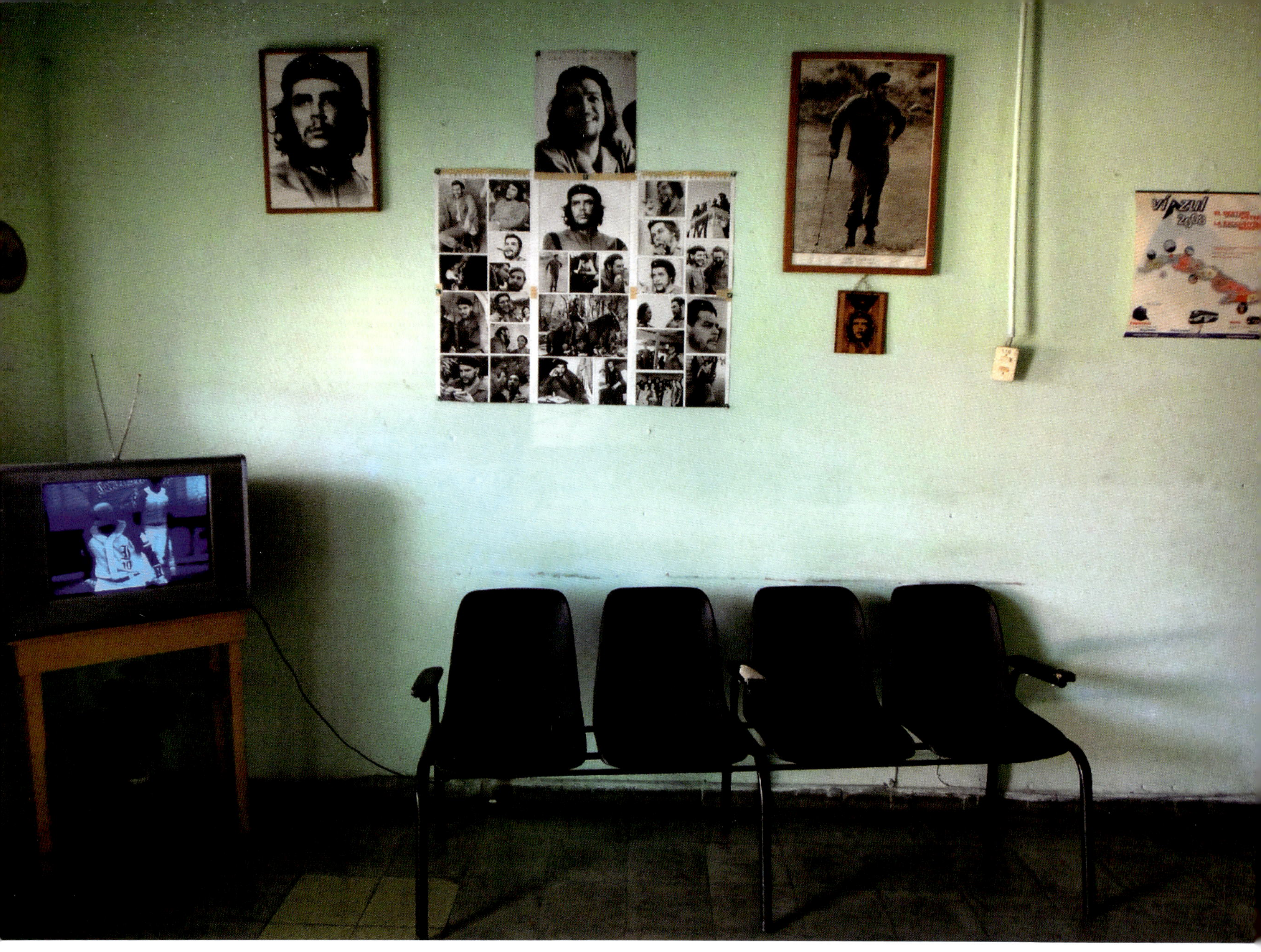

Trinidad Bus Station. Cuba, 2010

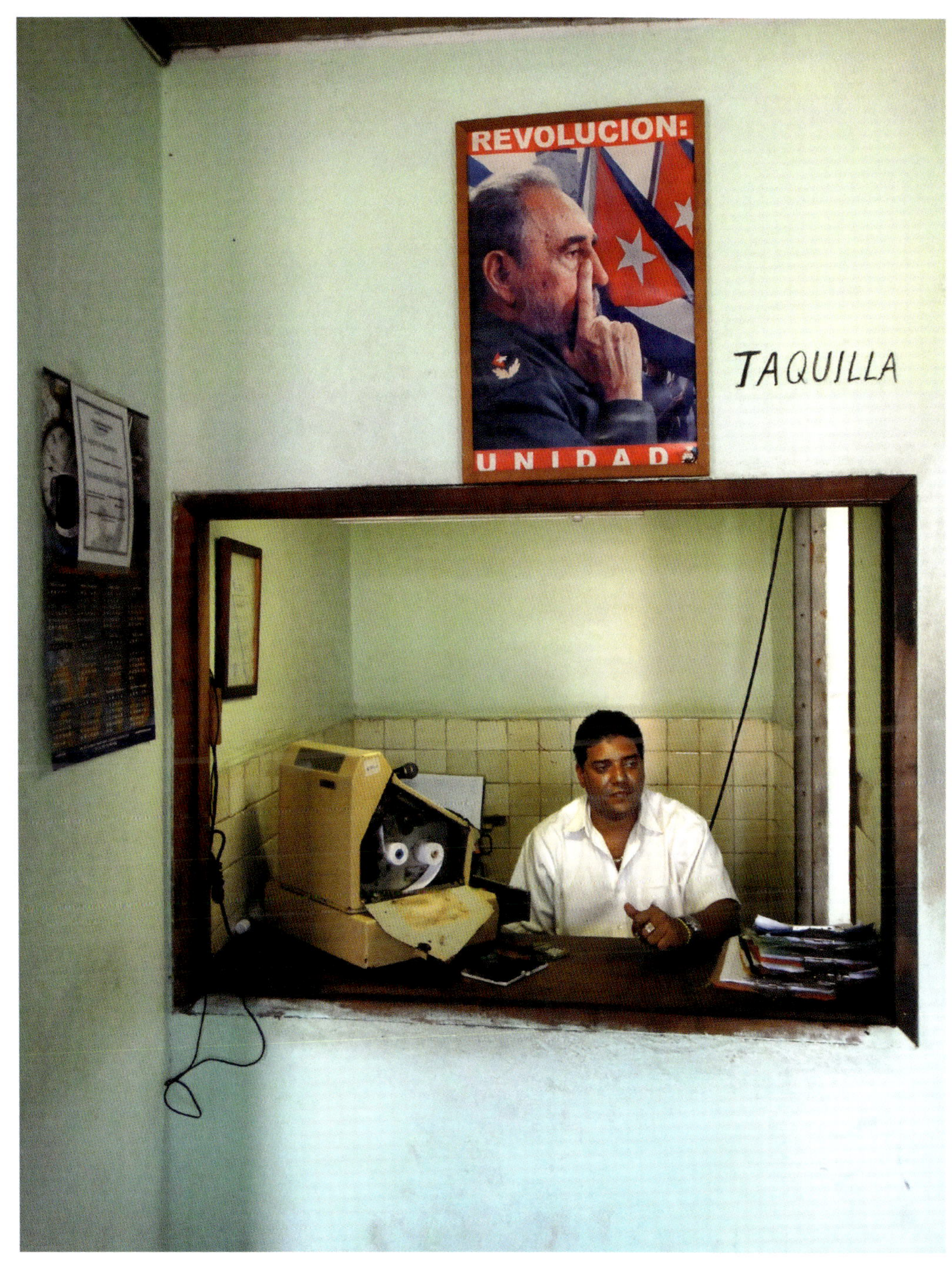

Trinidad Bus Station. Cuba, 2010

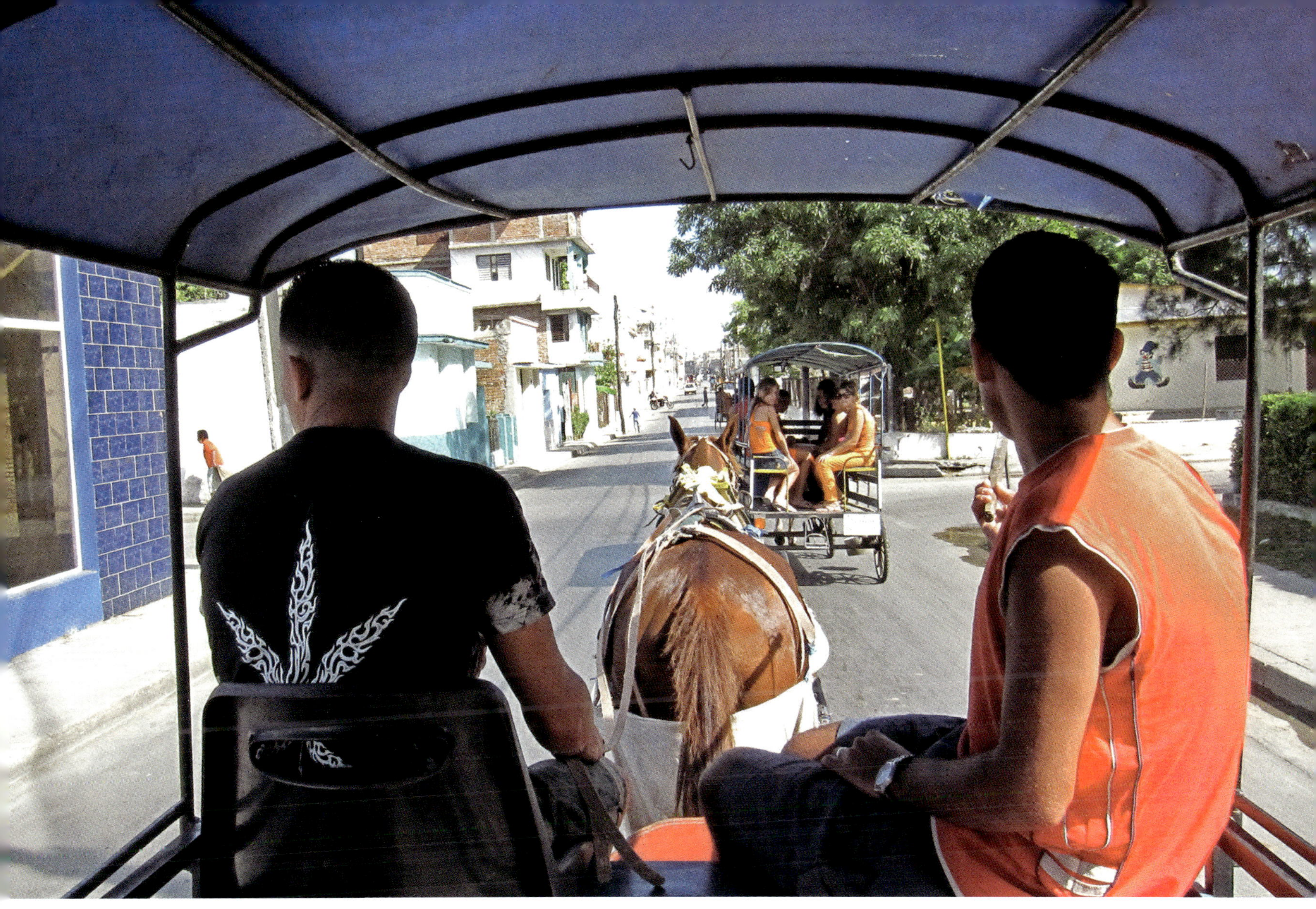

Local transportation in the city of
Santa Clara. Cuba, 2010

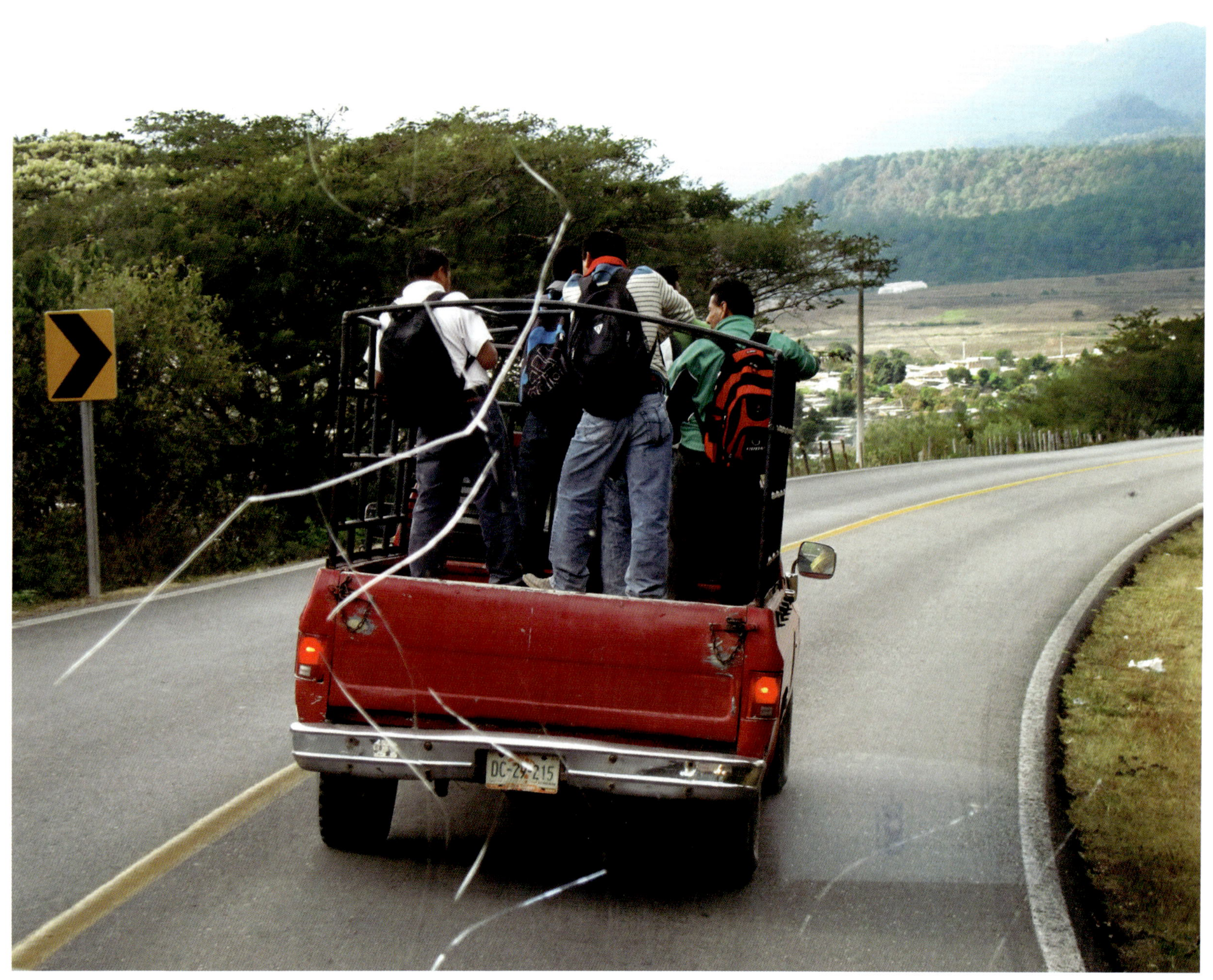

Chimaltenango, Guatemala, 2013

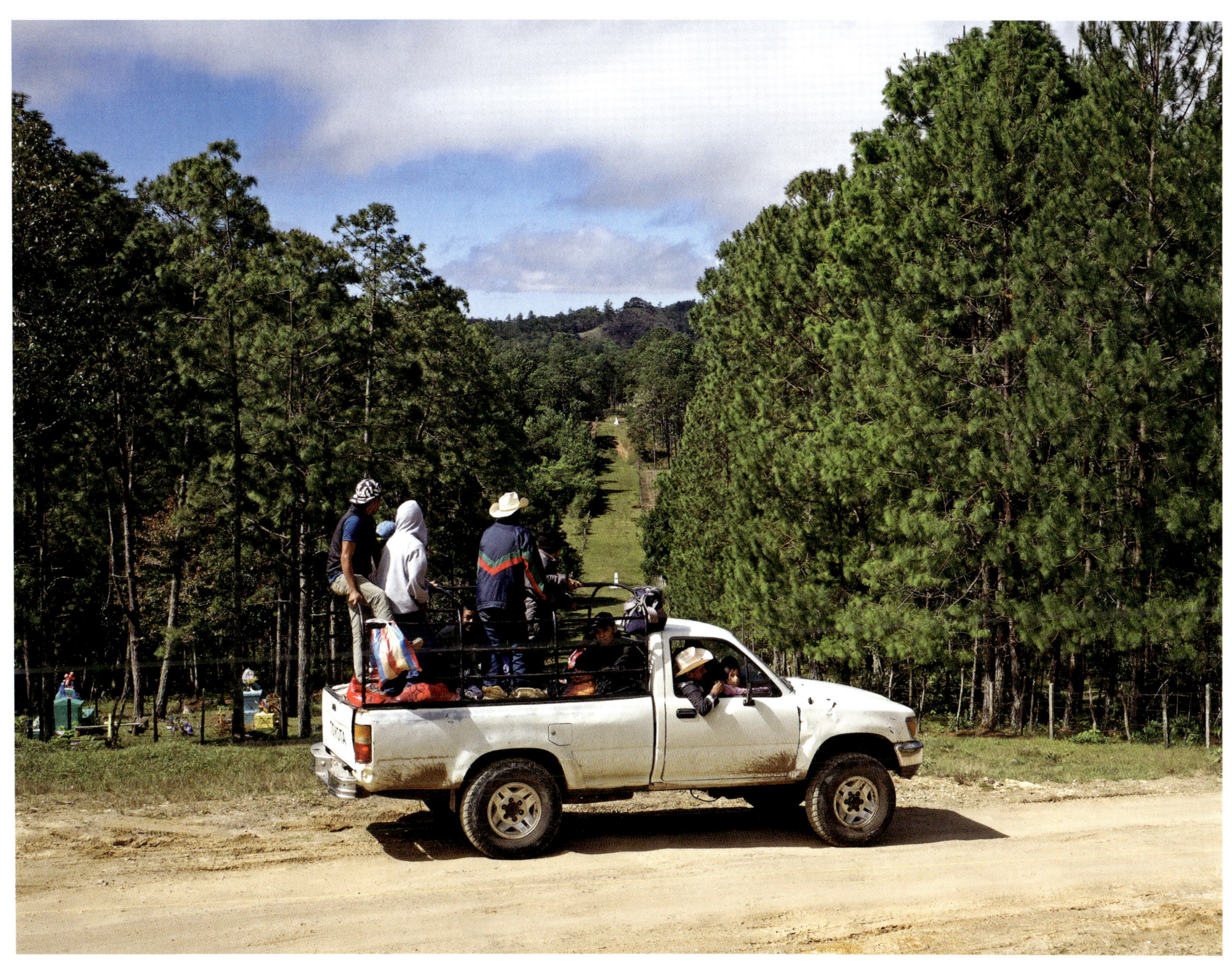

People crossing a rural, open border from Guatemala into Mexico. Part of the international border between Huehuetenango, Guatemala and Chiapas, Mexico, 2017

The National Bus Terminal.
Havana, Cuba, 2013

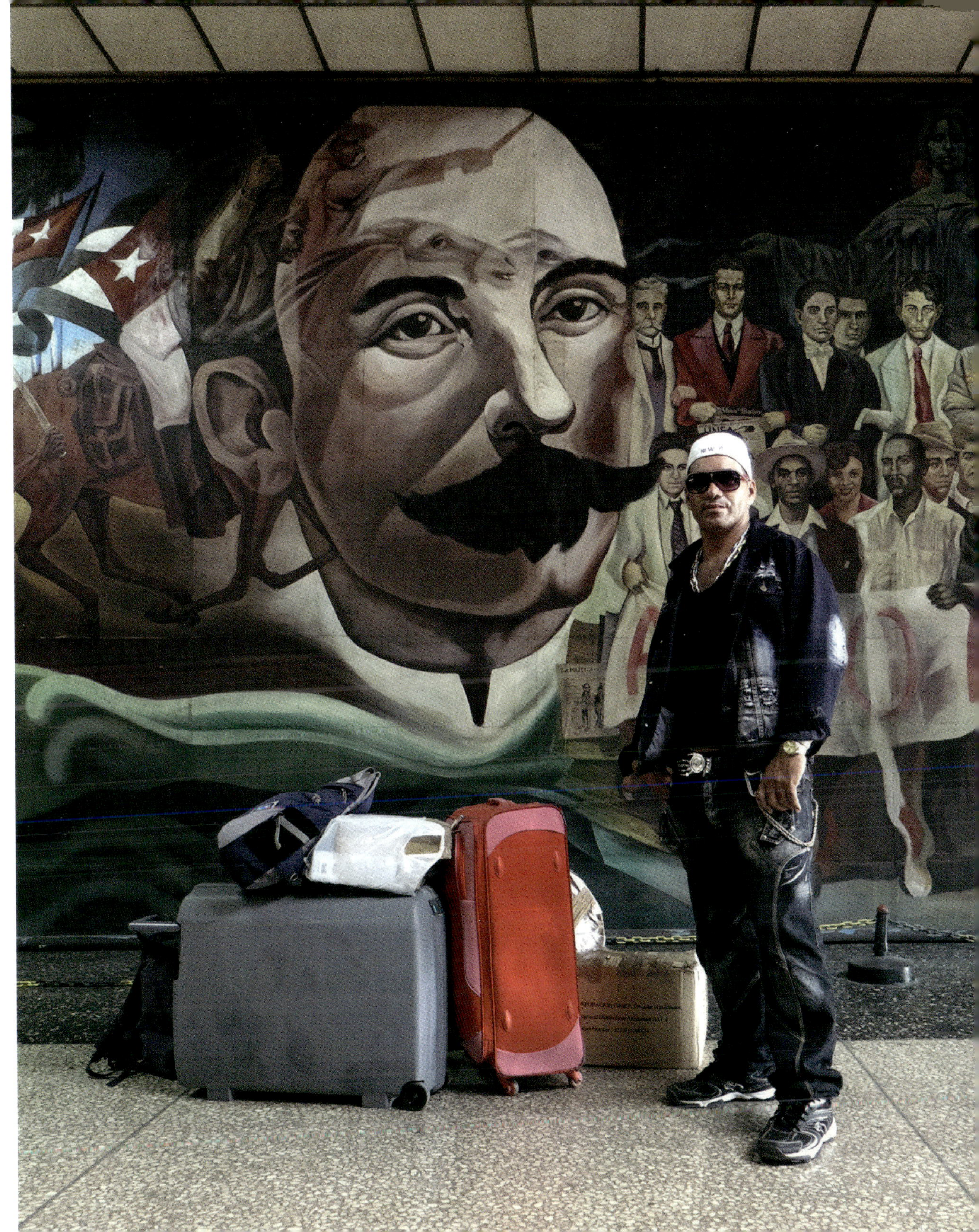

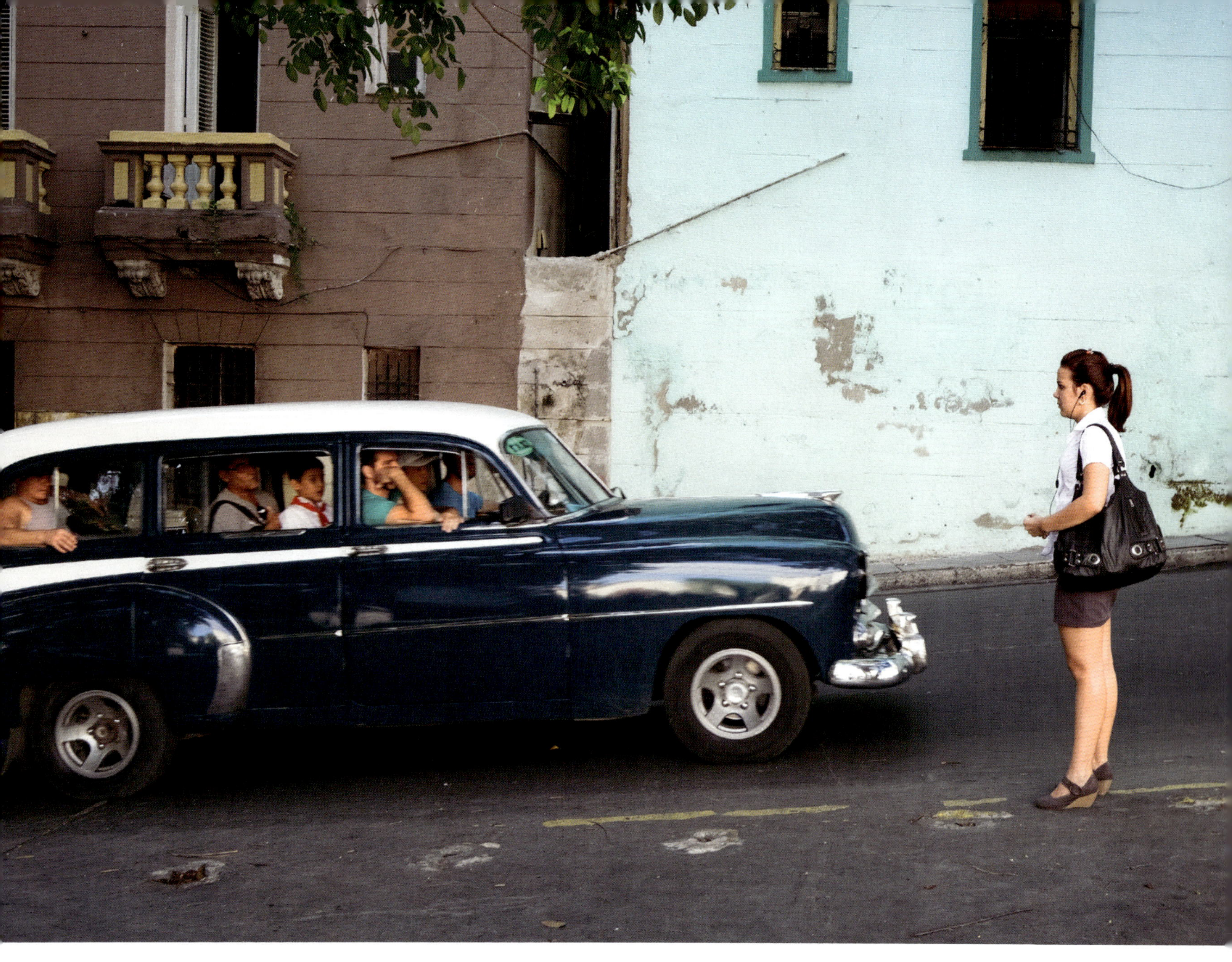

A woman waits for an *almendrón*, a collective taxi.
Havana, Cuba, 2015

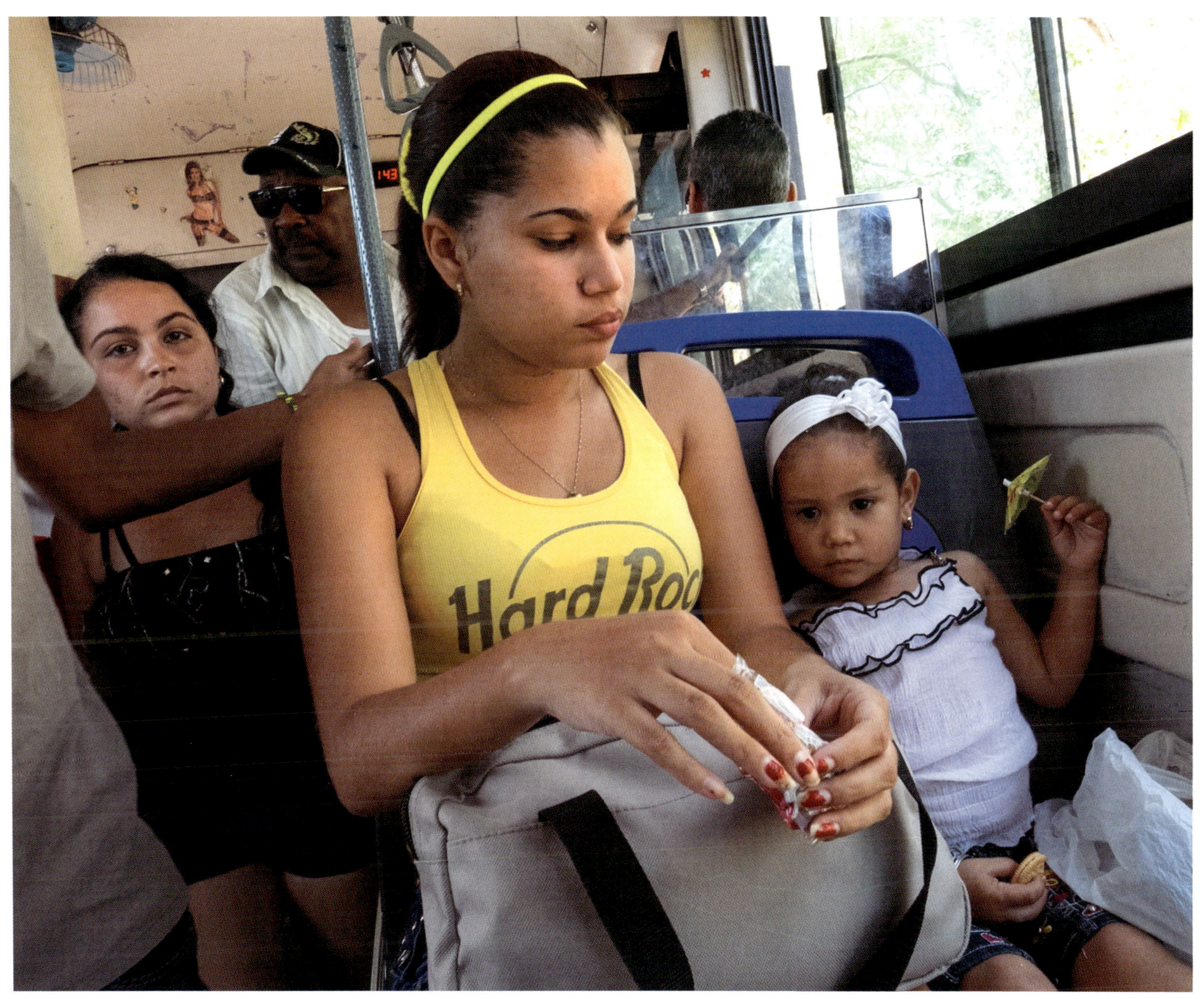

Bus P-15, from Alamar to Guanabacoa.
Havana, Cuba, 2015

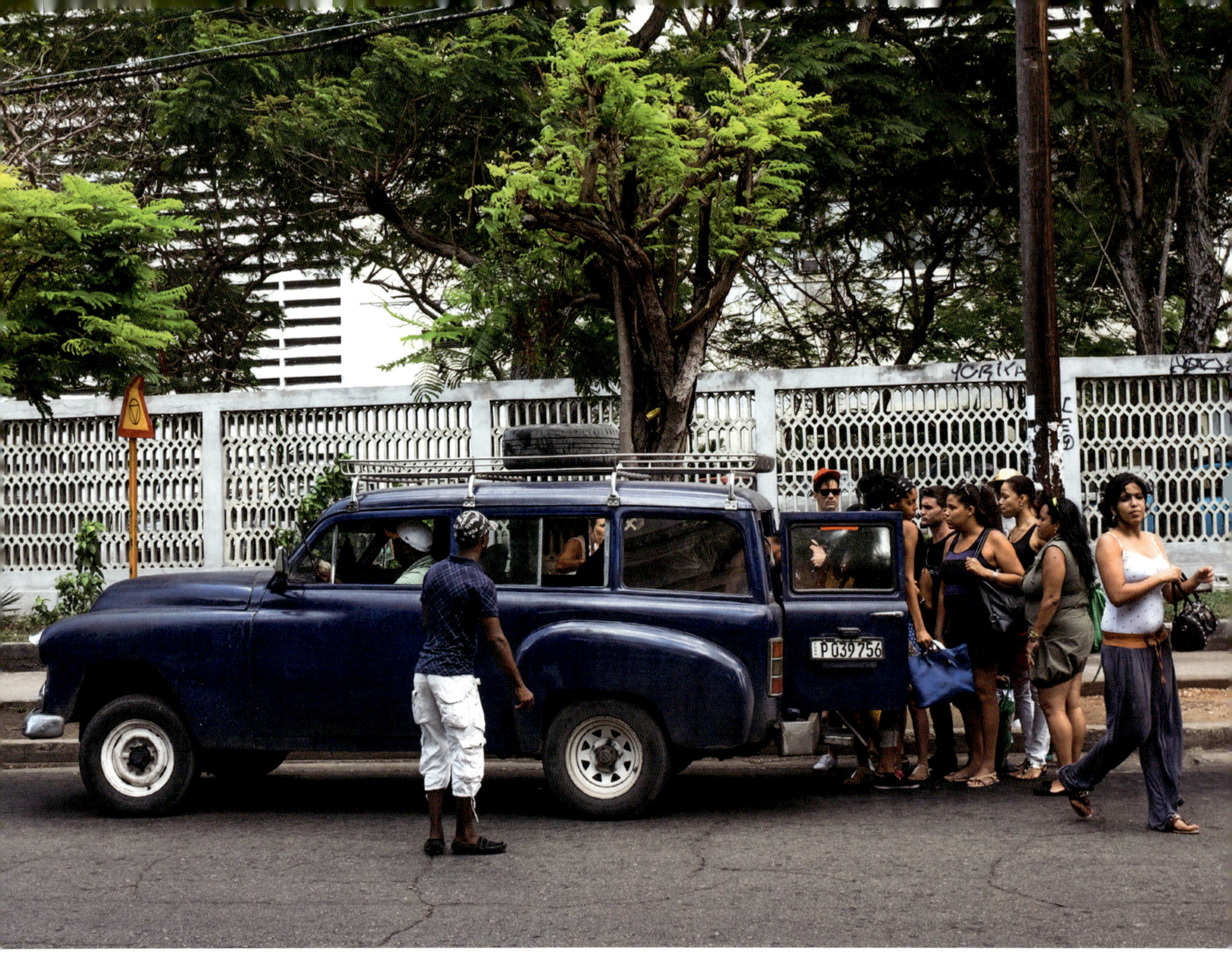

Many of the *máquinas* or *almendrones*, old American cars from the 1950s, are operated as collective taxis
which always follow the same routes through the city. Havana, Cuba, 2015

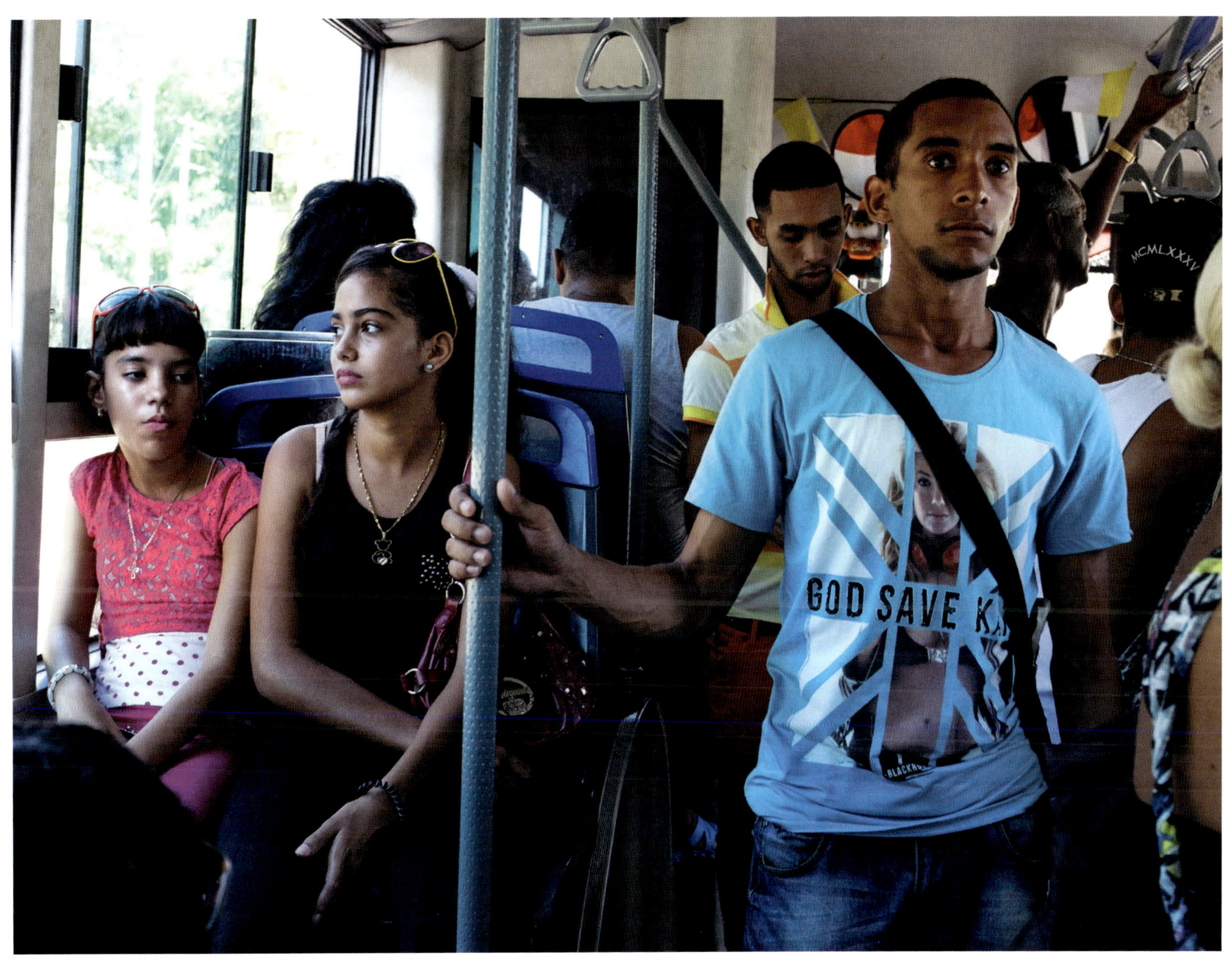

Bus P-16, from Boyeros to Plaza de la Revolución.
Havana, Cuba, 2015

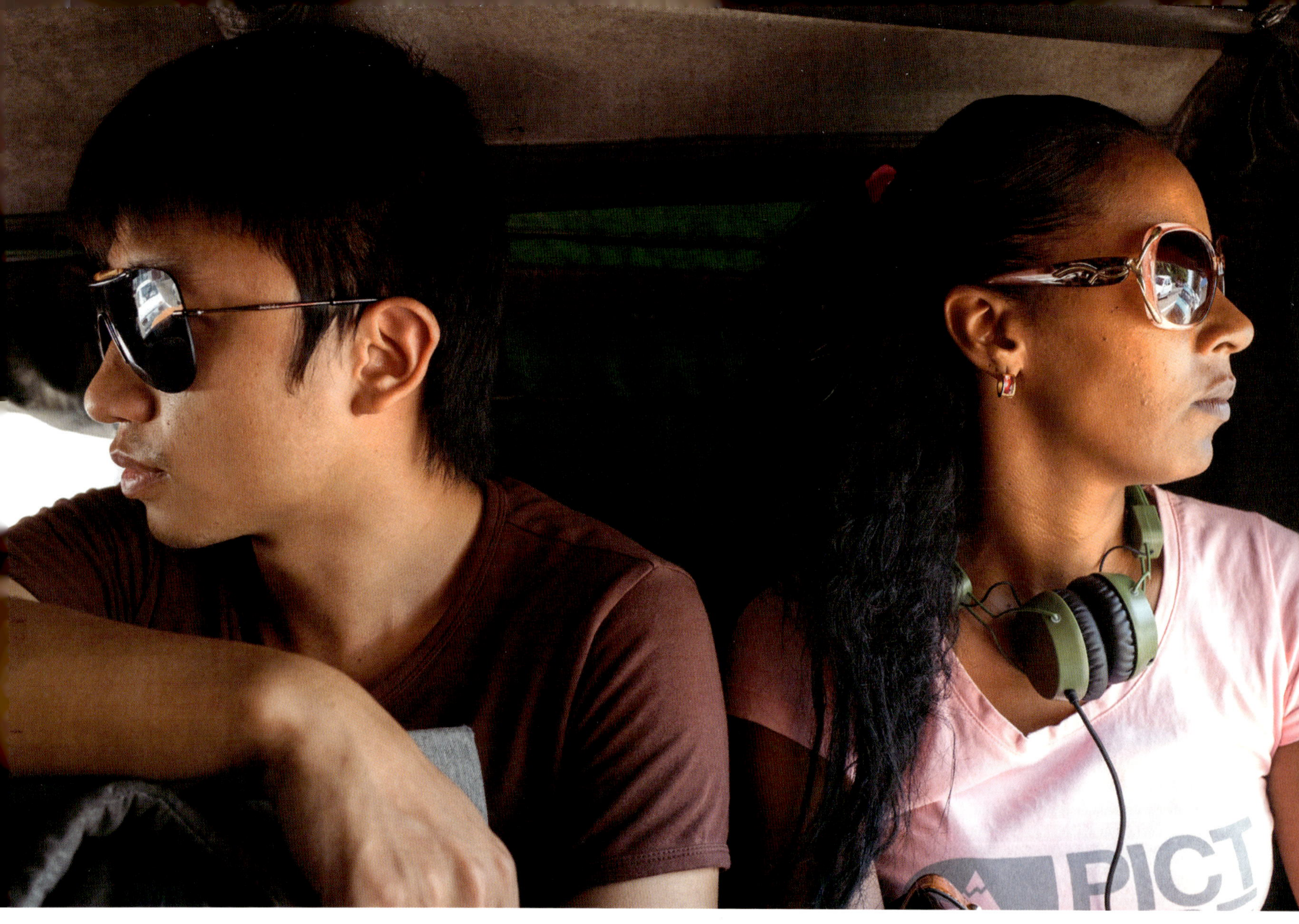

Inside of one of the collective taxis known
as an *almendrón* or a *máquina*. Havana, Cuba, 2015

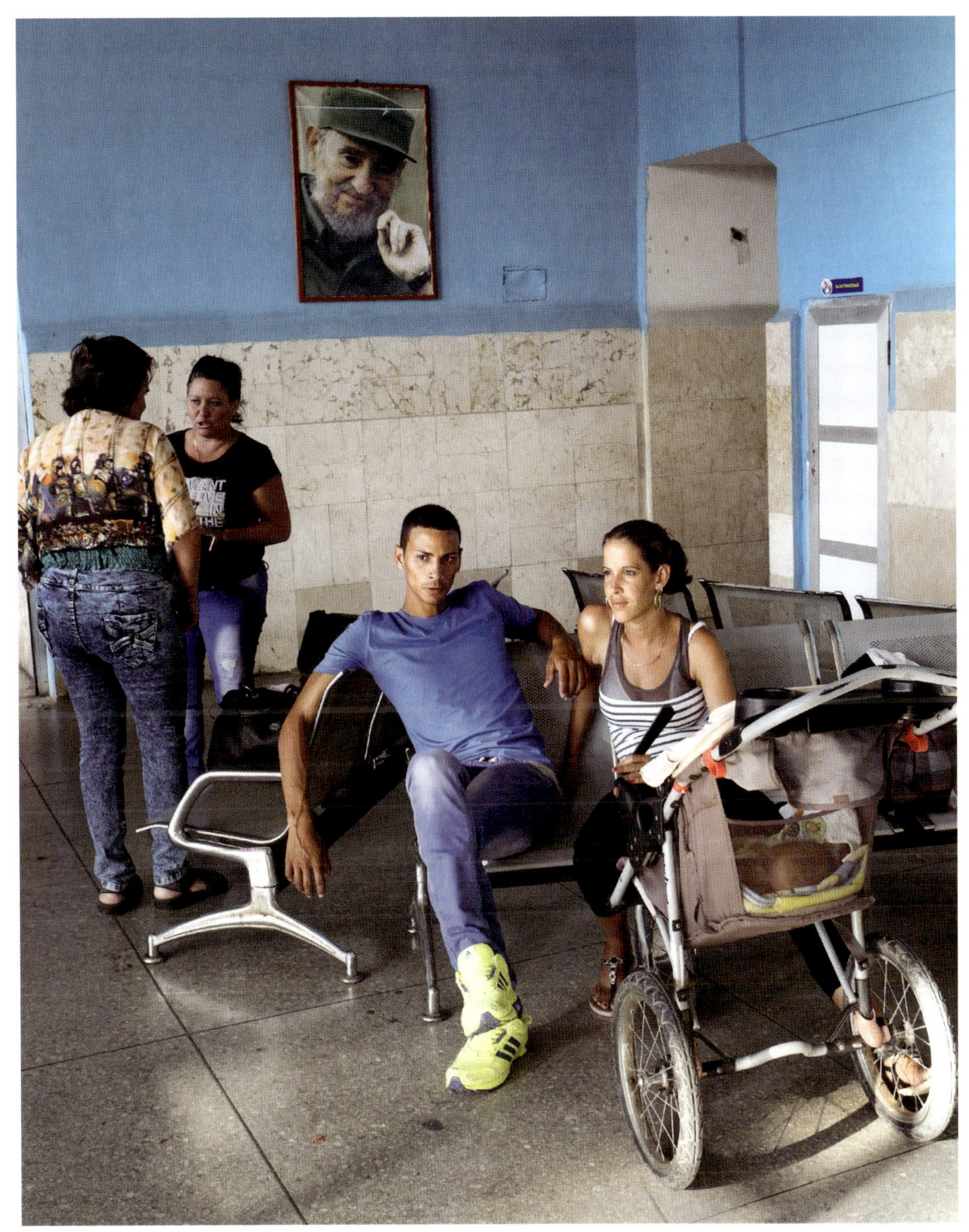

Santa Clara Bus Station. Cuba, 2016

Journey to the Center of the Photo

It's not enough to spot a subject, focus a camera lens on it, and capture an image to achieve a good photograph. Indeed, there are many elements that make up a "good" photograph. This reality is recurringly visited throughout photography's evolution—from the daguerreotype, to Lumiere's chromed plates, to the superb lenses that science has now created. Human intelligence has always defined what technological artifice can achieve. Cuban poet Eliseo Diego believed an image captured at a precise moment to be a ticket to posterity—a posterity whose meaning is established in art.

Like poetry, a good snapshot suggests various relationships and alludes to worlds that the imagination then explores. Cartier-Bresson, French photographer, believed that the mind, the eye, and the heart formed a single axis in photography. Jonathan "Jonás" Moller's work is nourished by this evolution and by the tradition of photojournalism; he is capable of capturing movement that both safeguards and subverts the still image. Faces, bodies, and objects come together and conspire, perhaps, to take us inside the photographer's experience who has been a unique and intelligent witness. Both are in motion—travelers immersed in their transits and the artist who travels along with them—allowing the viewer, to experience adventure and to scrutinize the future of those journeys, maybe more so than their pasts. For Eliseo Diego, bearing witness is the worthiest legacy of the poet. It is a witnessing that seeks, investigates, and moves instead of avoiding what lies beyond what the lens captures.

Traveling with Jonathan Moller's photography goes far beyond reporting on a location or highlighting a curiosity; rather his images direct our gaze towards their center—the center which Jules Verne, nineteenth-century French adventure writer, reminds us revolves around the imagination. Take for example, the beautiful images of Cuba that move us and bear witness to a people's resilient tenacity that results from impositions placed upon us by the most warlike power on the planet, and more importantly, a people's vitality that nevertheless radiates through. Cuban poet José Lezama Lima says that poverty is capable of radiating beauty. By traversing both on the same axis, life is illuminated, calling us to follow the path towards a better world—a true inclusion in all the diversity of human behavior. Hence, we appreciate the artist's vision—it delves into vital essence rather than colonizing surface—and it leaves us with faith that traveling in resistance also leads us towards posterity. A posterity that dignifies the humble, and like our hero, José Martí, never loses faith in human improvement.

Alpidio Alonso-Grau
Minister of Culture of the Republic of Cuba

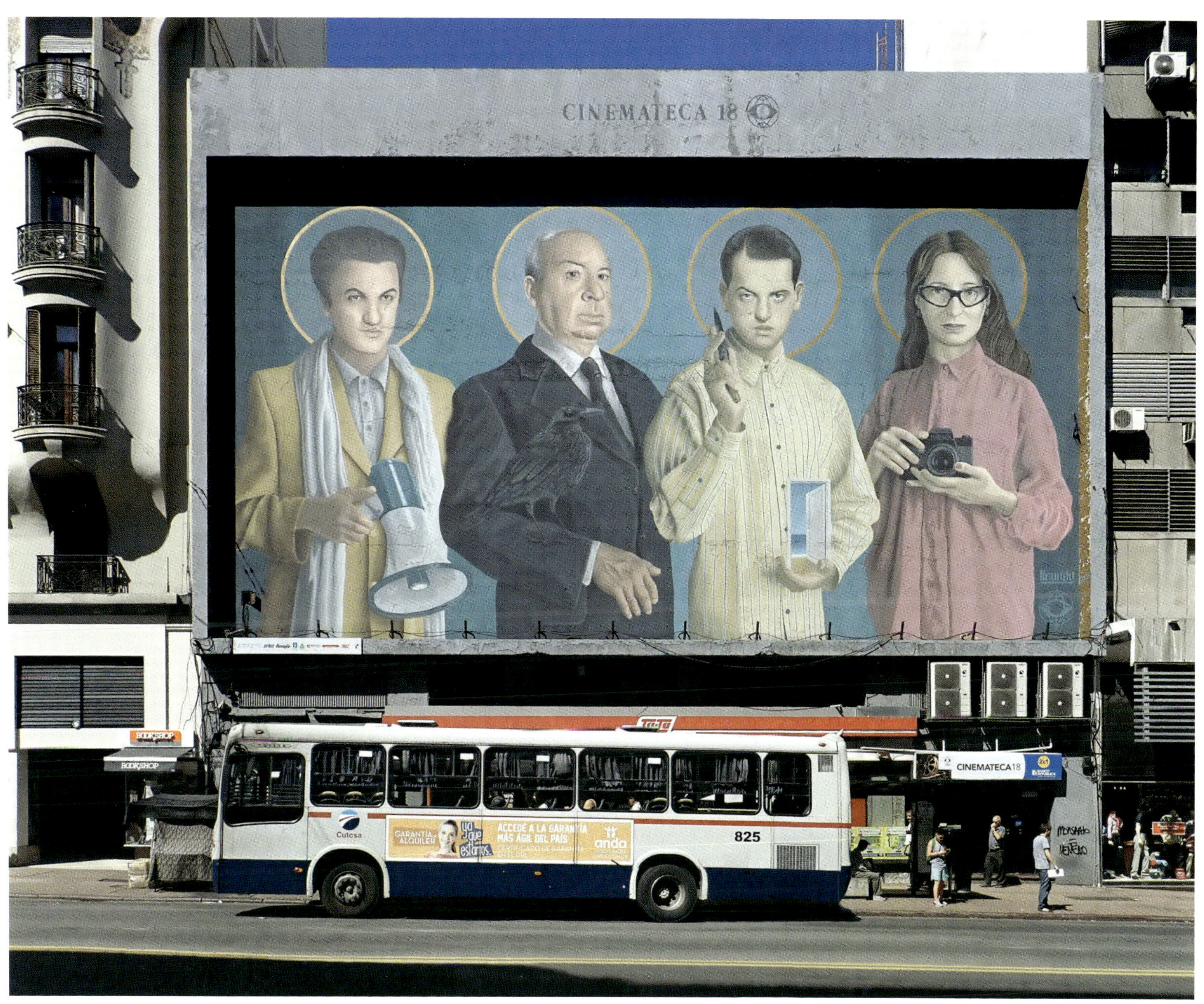

Montevideo, Uruguay, 2018

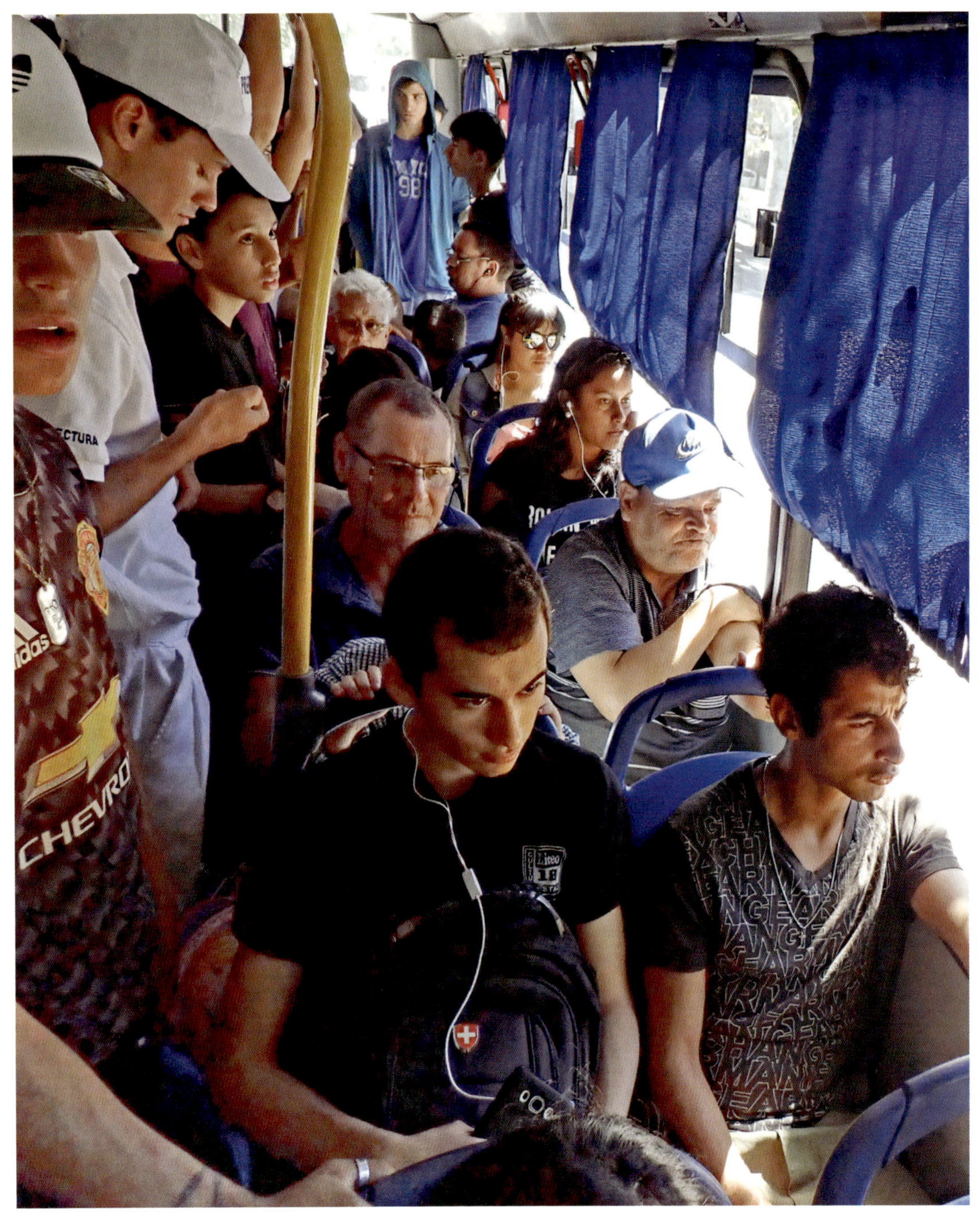

Montevideo, Uruguay, 2018

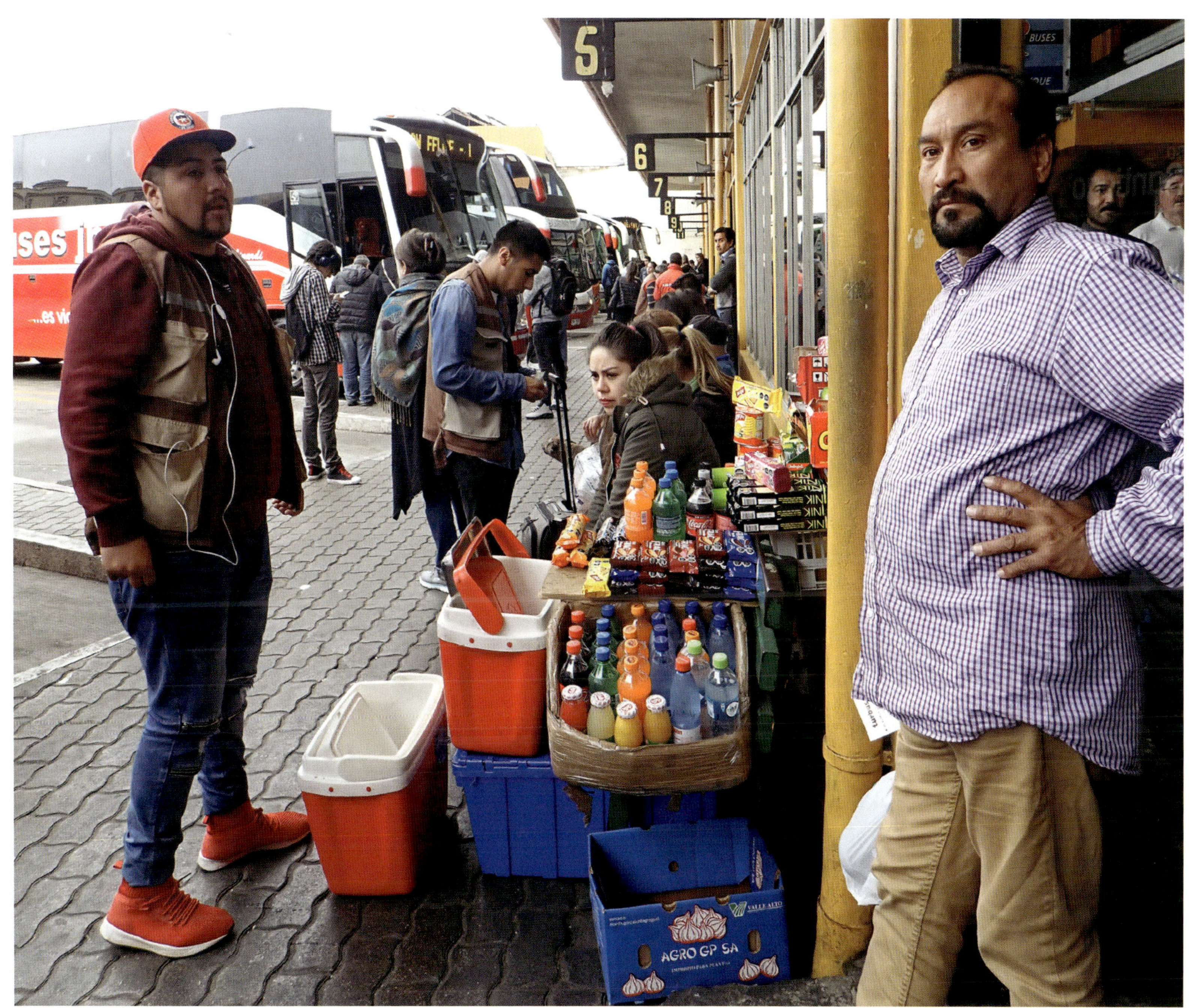

Valparaíso Bus Terminal. Chile, 2018

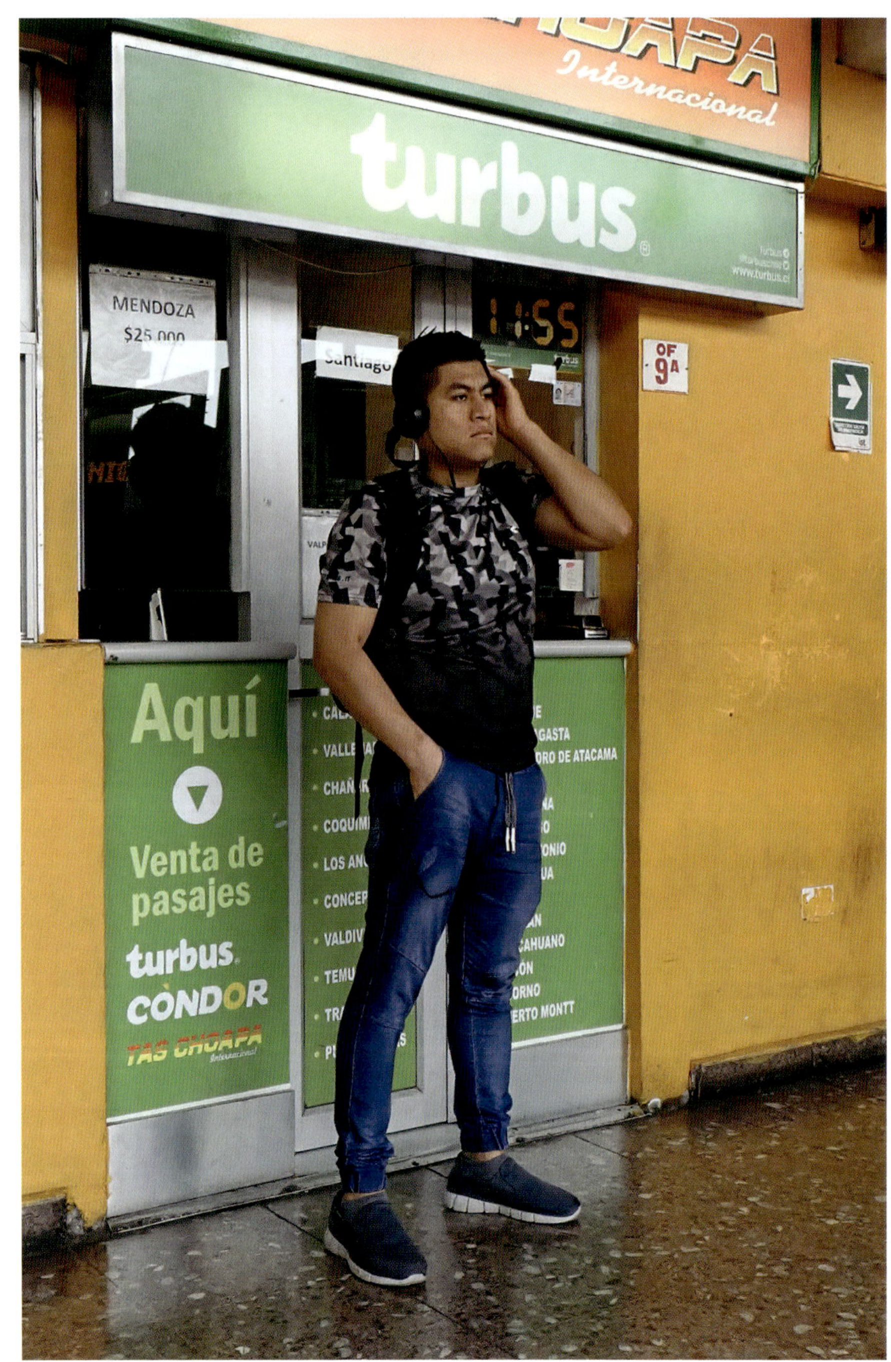

Valparaíso Bus Terminal. Chile, 2018

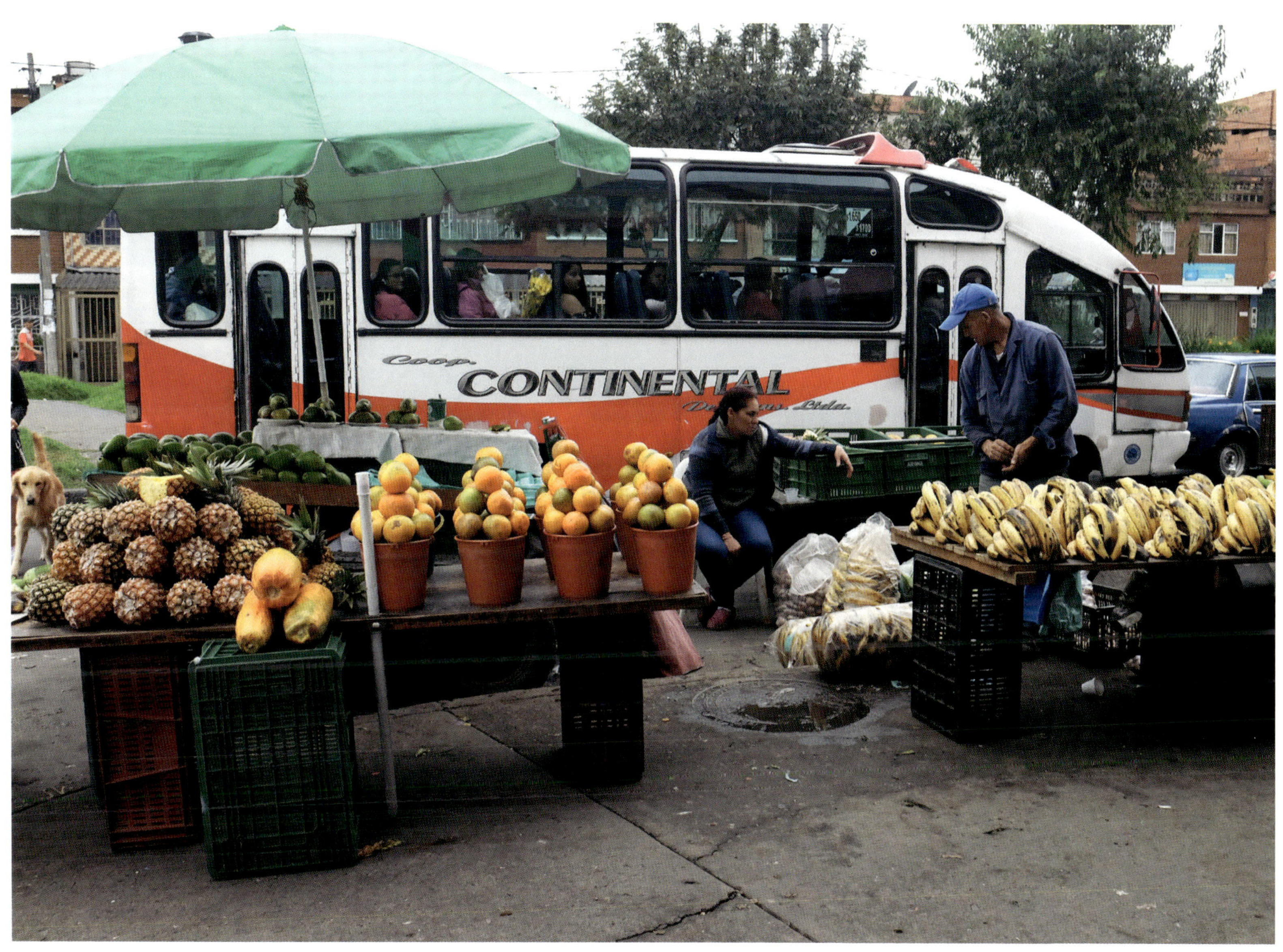

Bogotá, Colombia, 2018

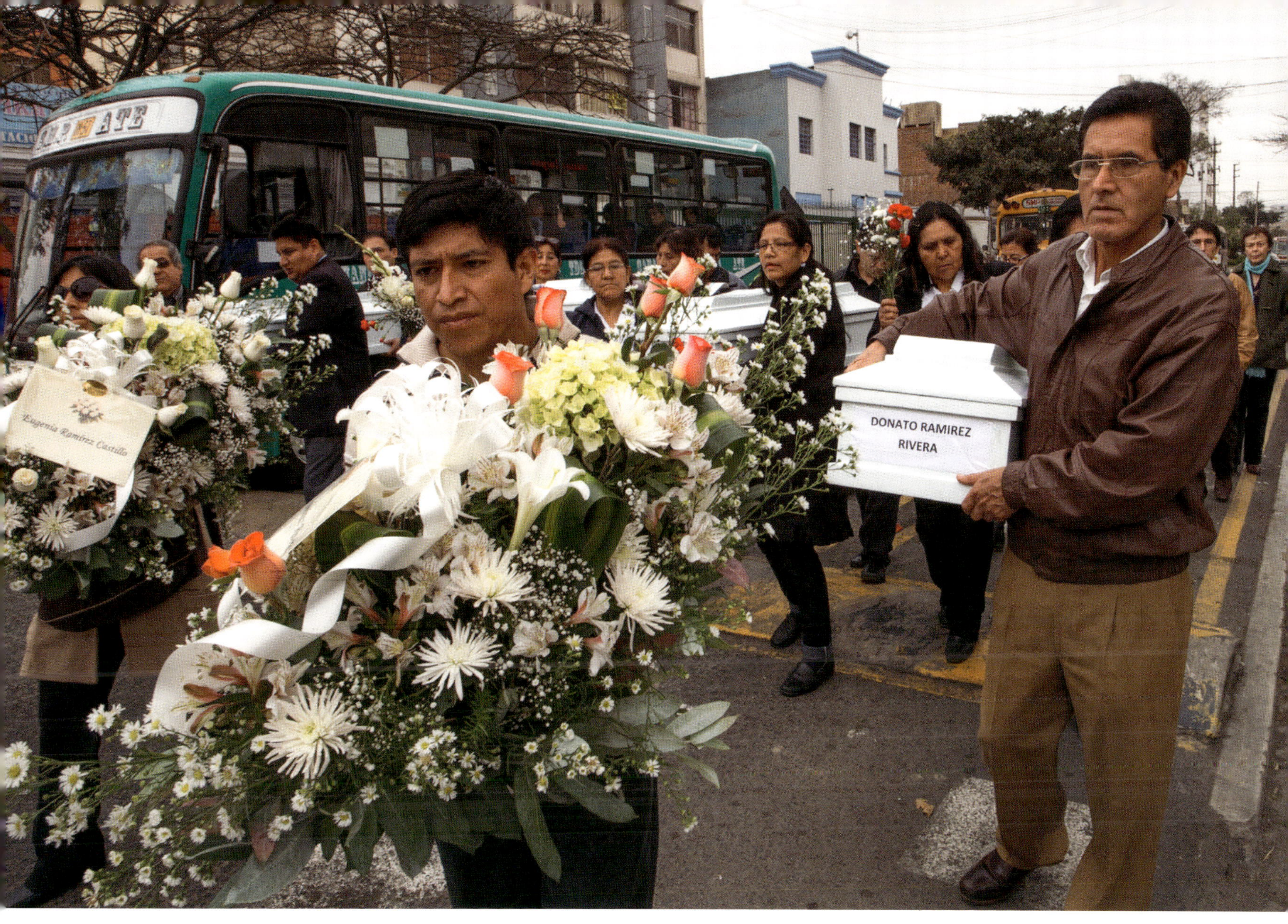

As a bus passes by, a group of people carry coffins containing the remains of people
killed by the military in the Ayacucho region in the Andes in 1986. Lima, Peru, 2013

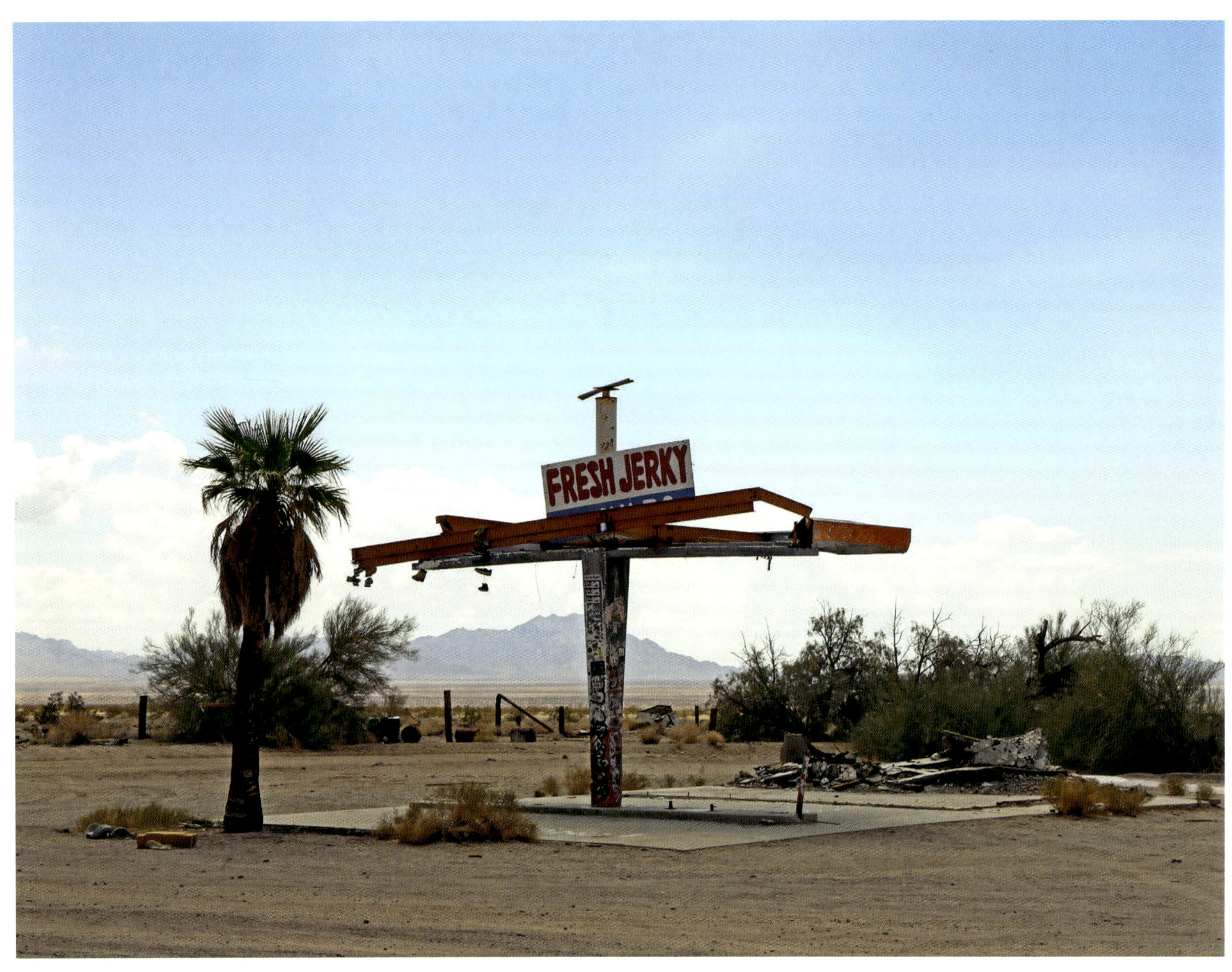

Los Angeles to Denver road trip. Mojave Desert
in southern California, 2014

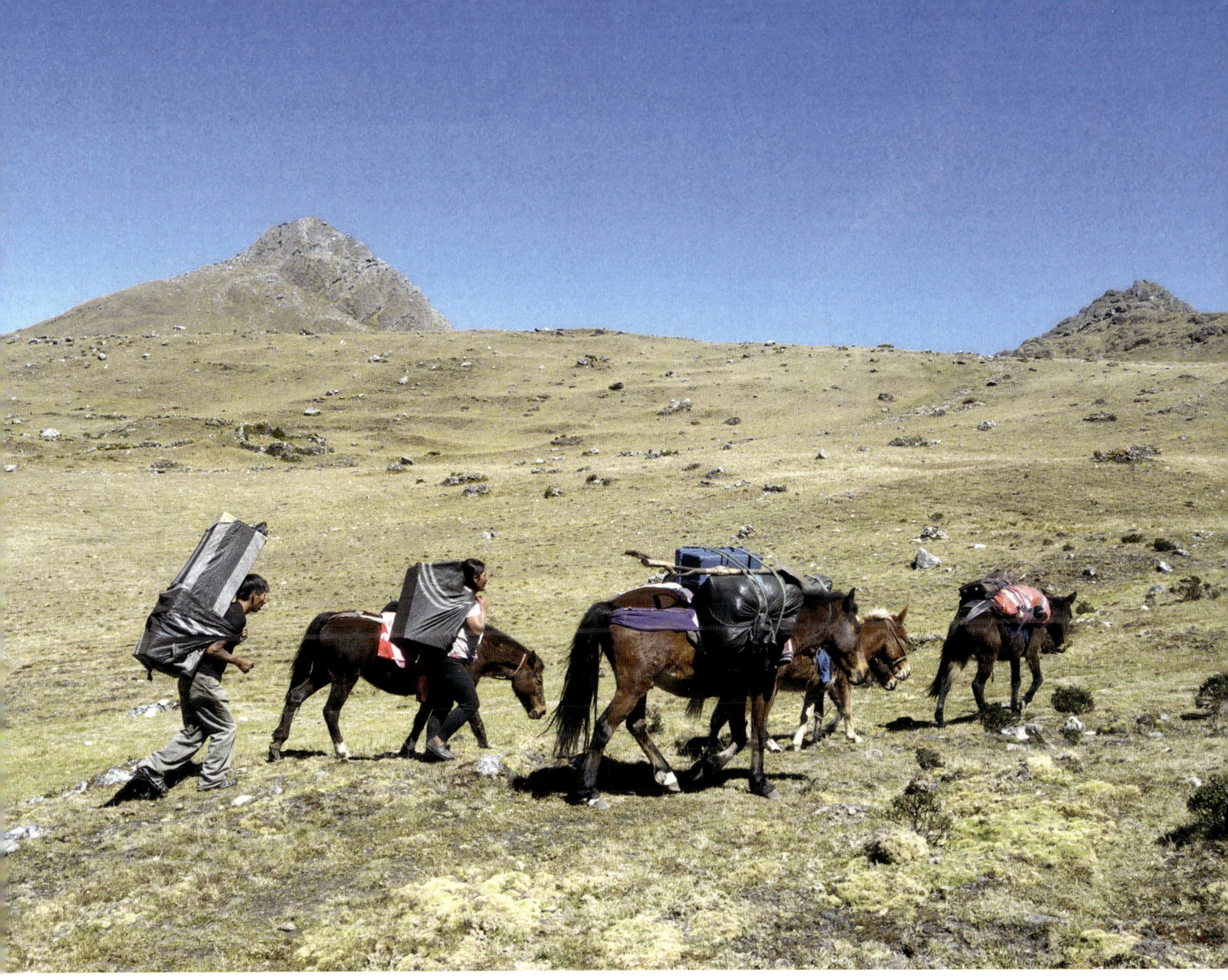

On a six-hour hike from Pucamarca out to the nearest road in Ushmay; people are carrying the skeletal remains of their relatives, some of the six men who were killed by Shining Path guerrillas in 1984, and the horses are carrying supplies used while camping out in the abandoned village of Pucamara for three nights during the exhumations. Ayacucho Region, Peru, 2012

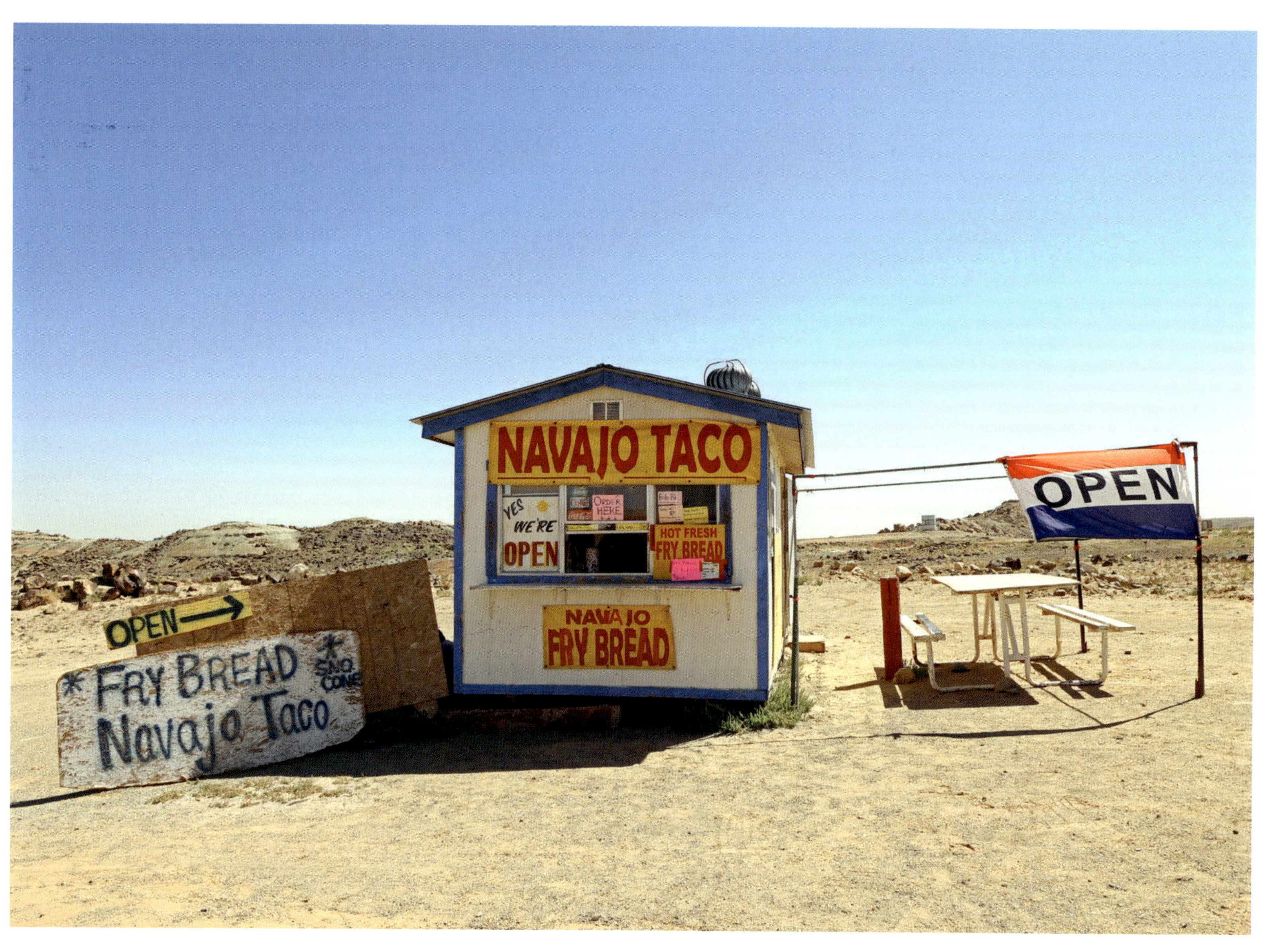

Los Angeles to Denver road trip.
New Mexico, 2014

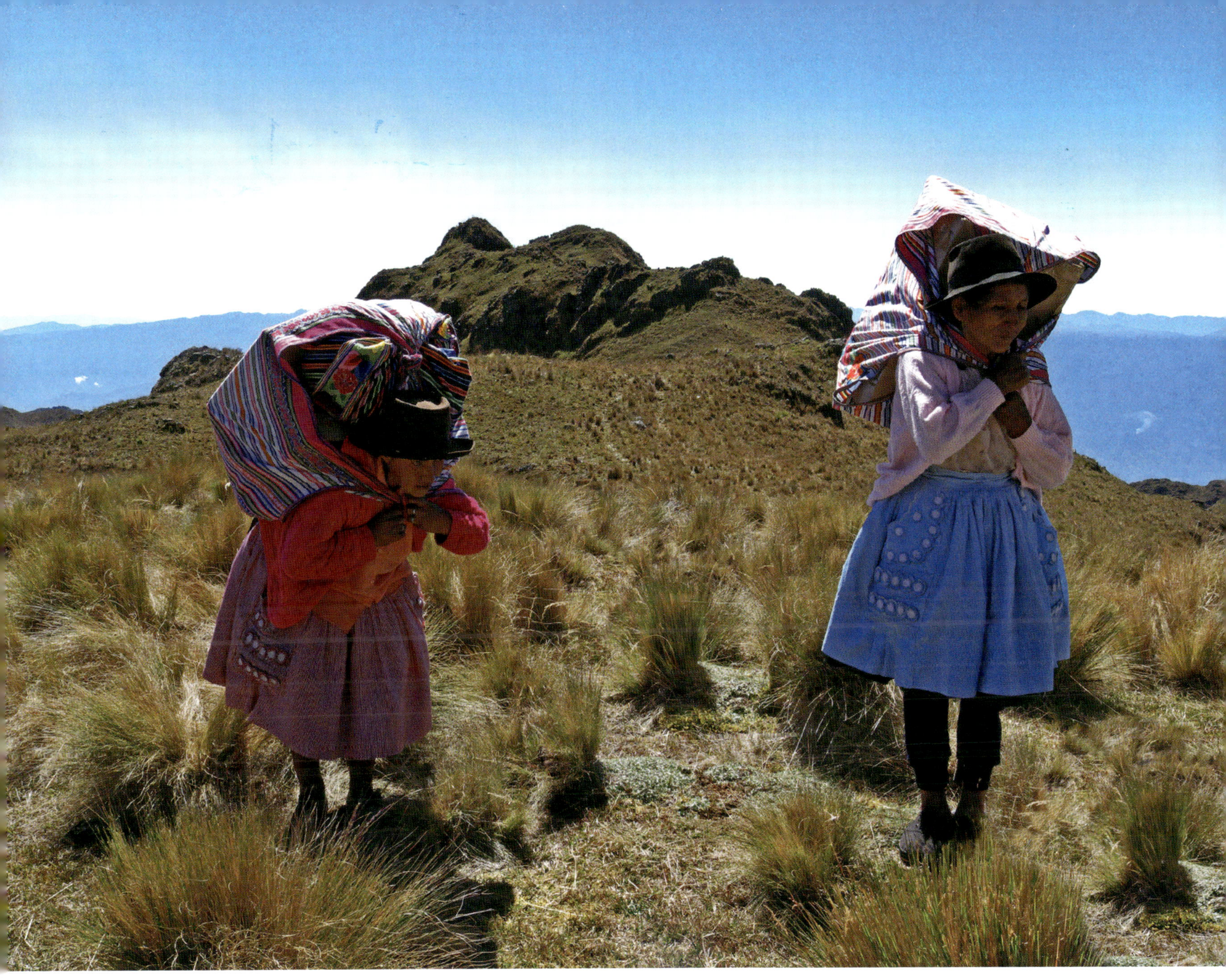

Two women on a six-hour hike from the tiny community of Pucamarca out to the nearest road, carrying the skeletal remains
of their relatives, two of the six men who were killed by Shining Path guerrillas in 1984 in Pucamarca. Ayacucho Region, Peru, 2012

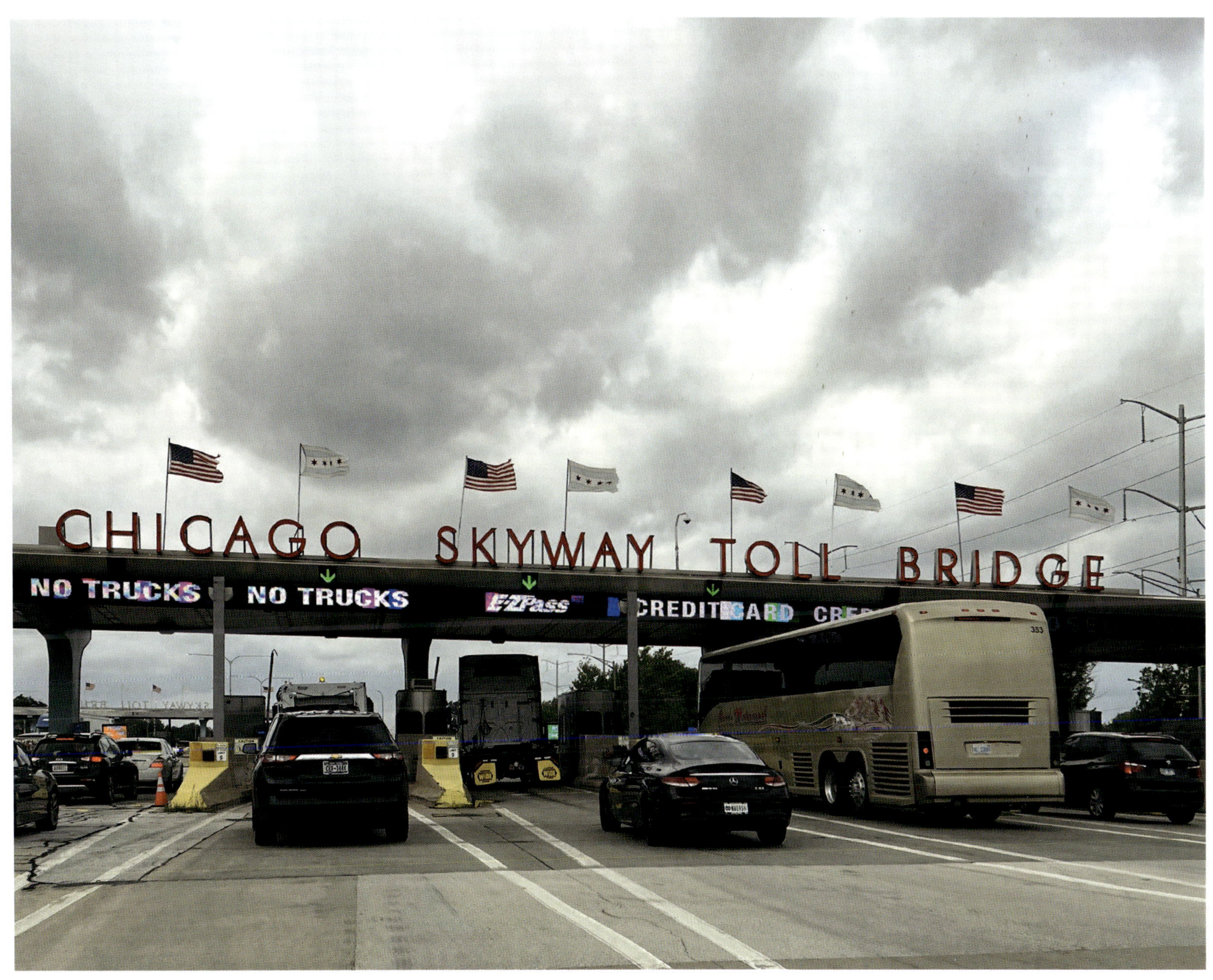

Boston to Denver road trip on Interstate 80 outside
of Chicago. Illinois, 2022

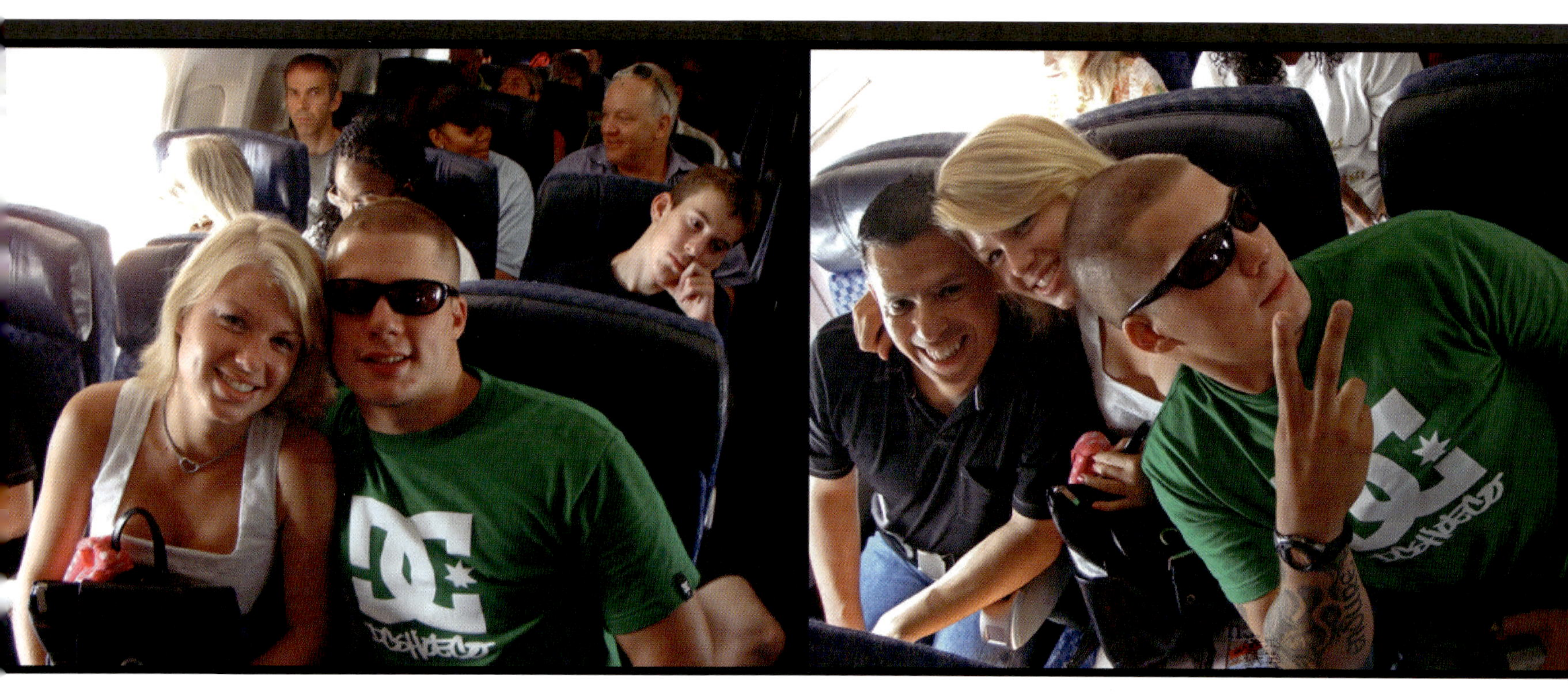

A US soldier returning from Iraq, on a flight from Newark, New Jersey,
to Denver, Colorado, 2007

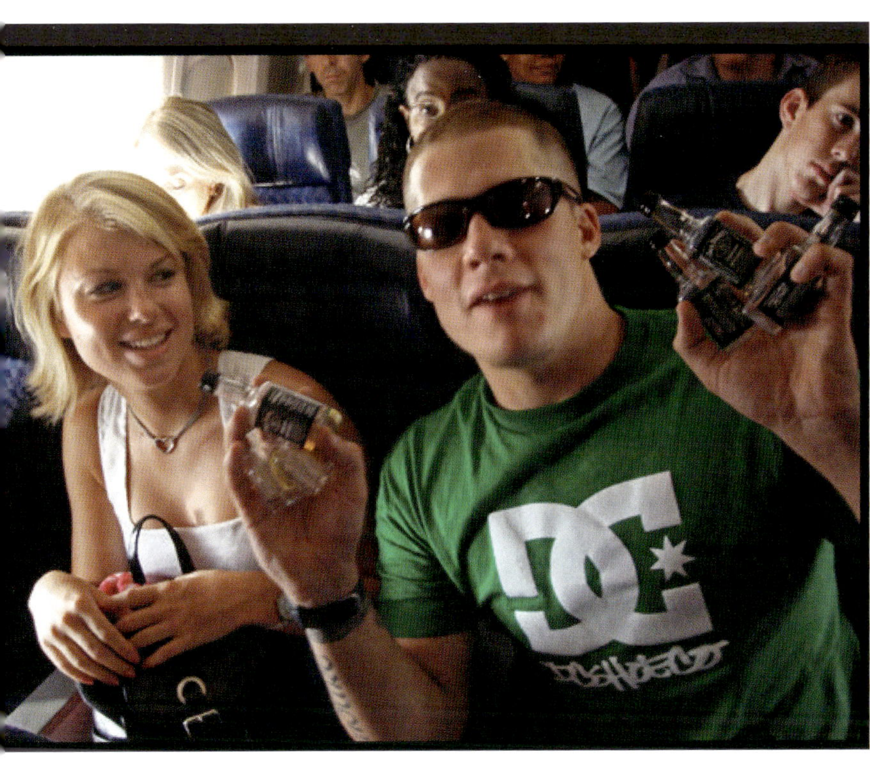

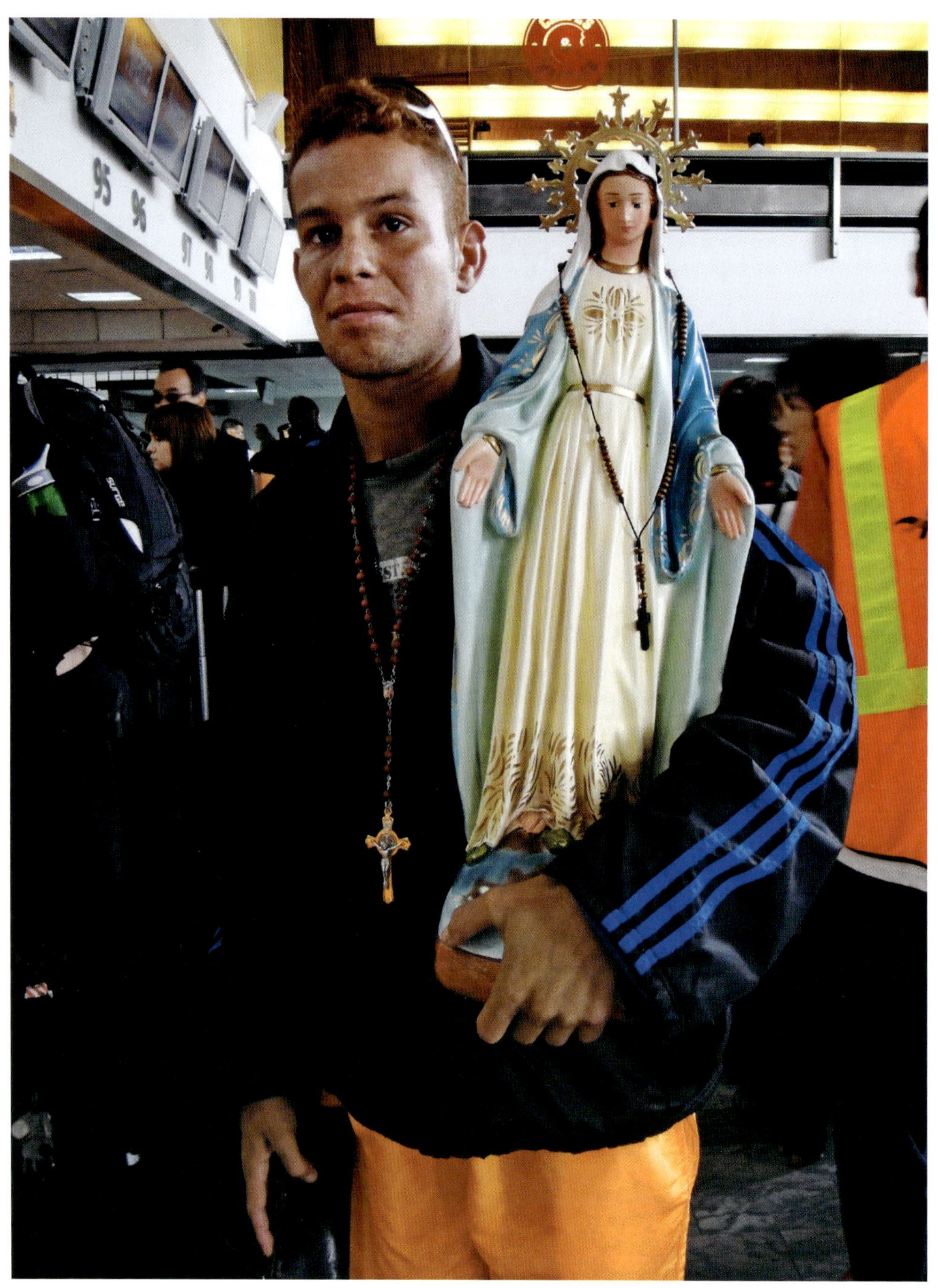

El Dorado International Airport.
Bogotá, Colombia, 2009

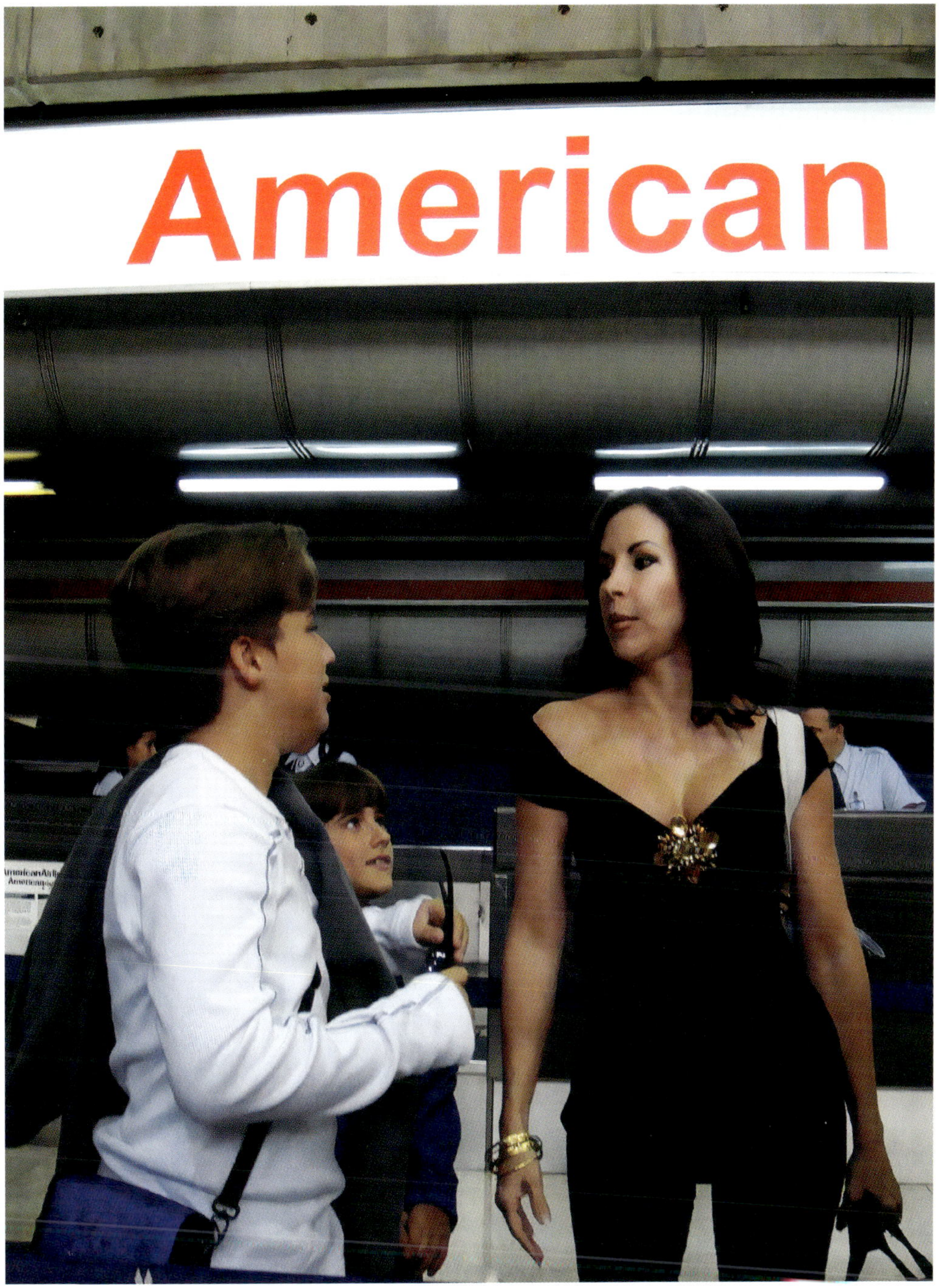

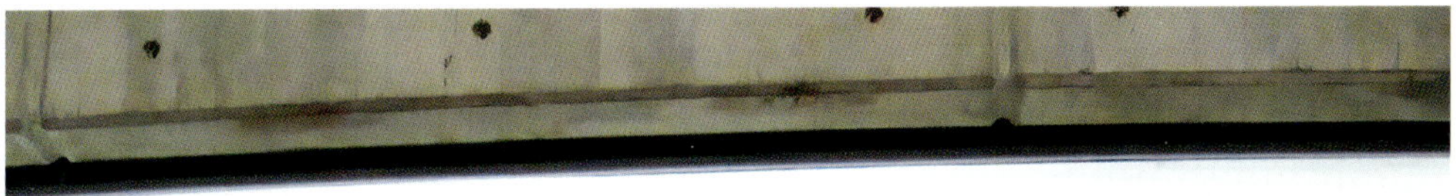

Simón Bolívar International Airport.
Maiquetía, Venezuela, 2007

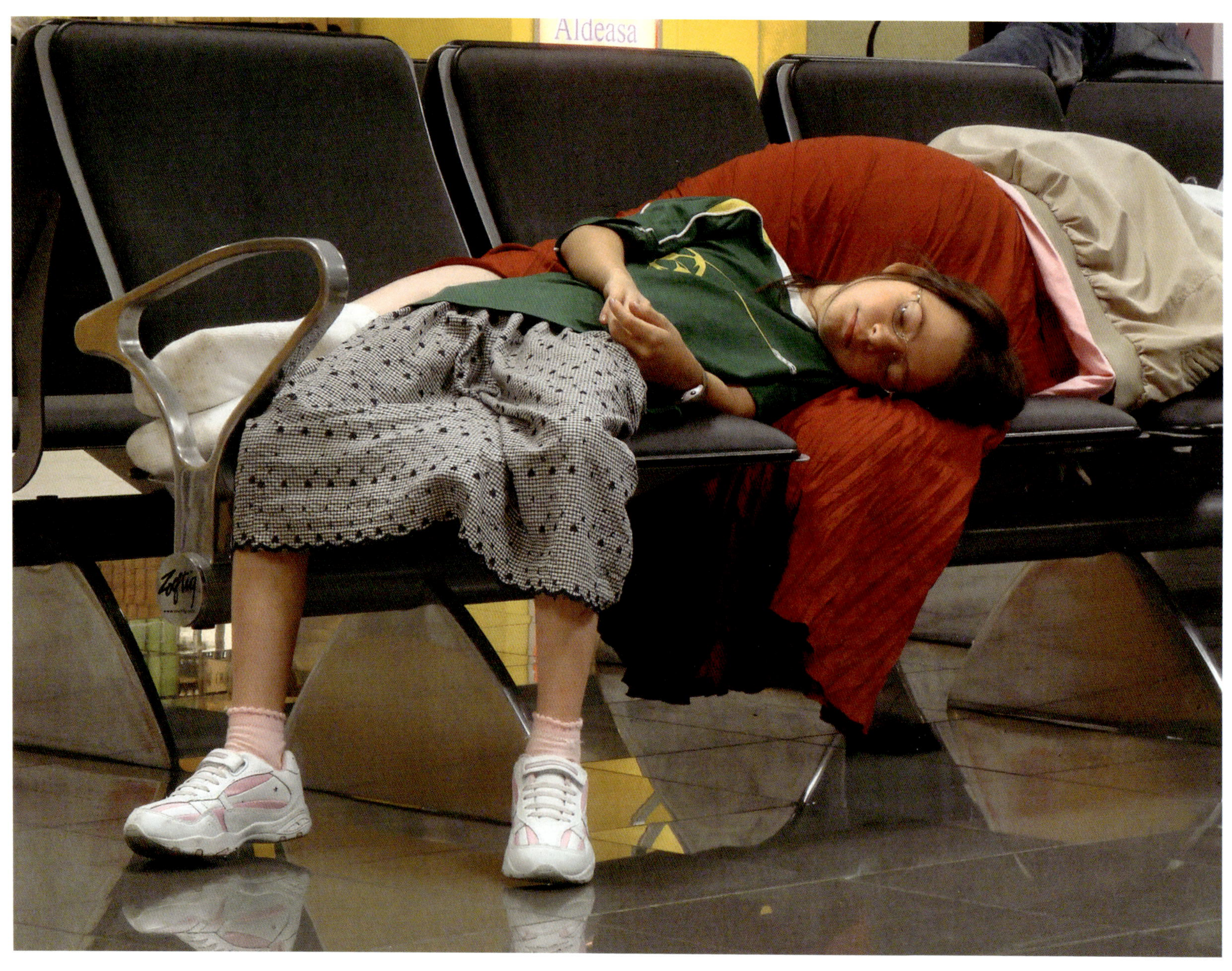

Jorge Chávez International Airport. Lima, Peru, 2007

Right: On a Lima to Cuzco flight. Peru, 2007

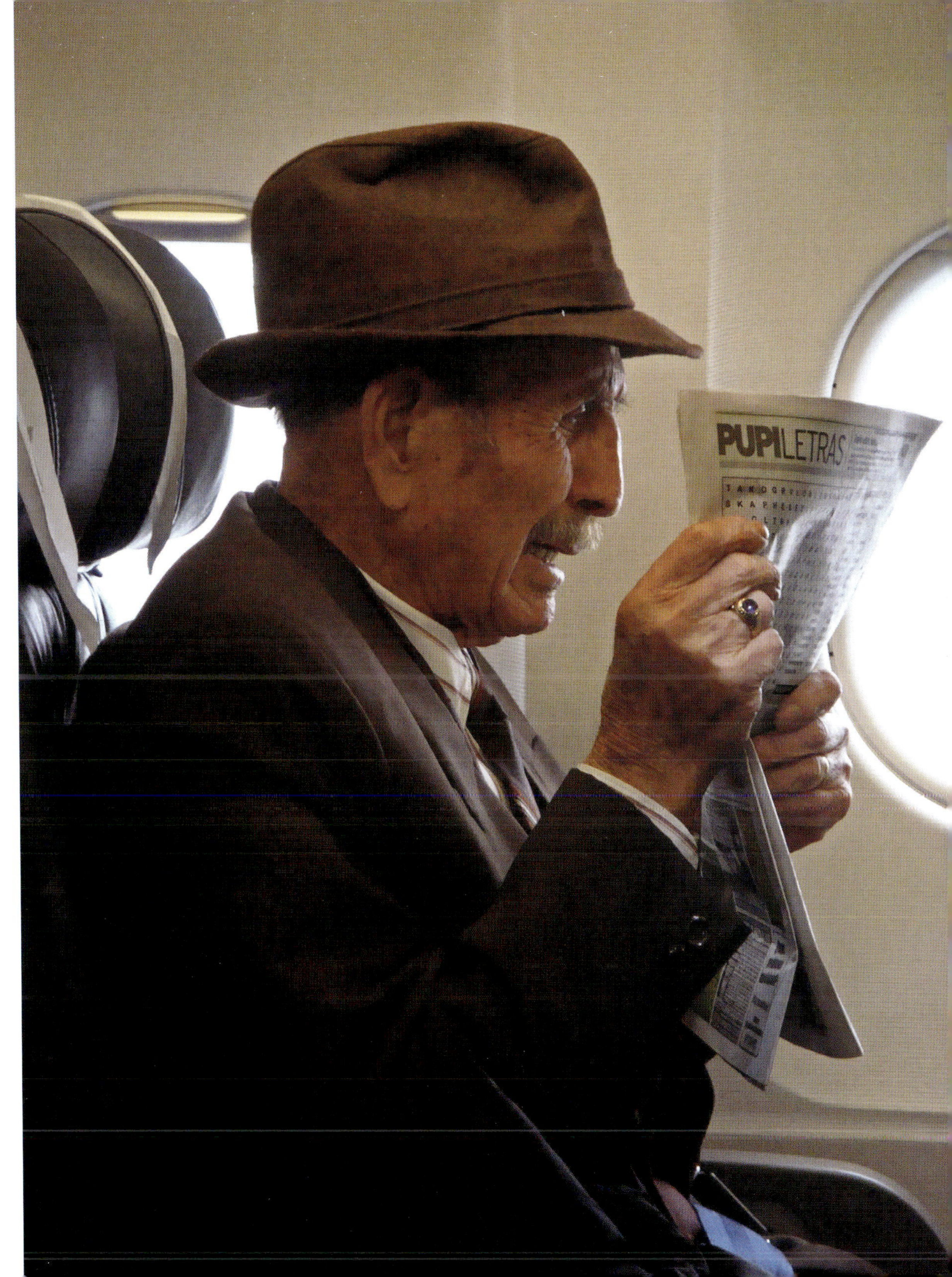

PUPILETRAS

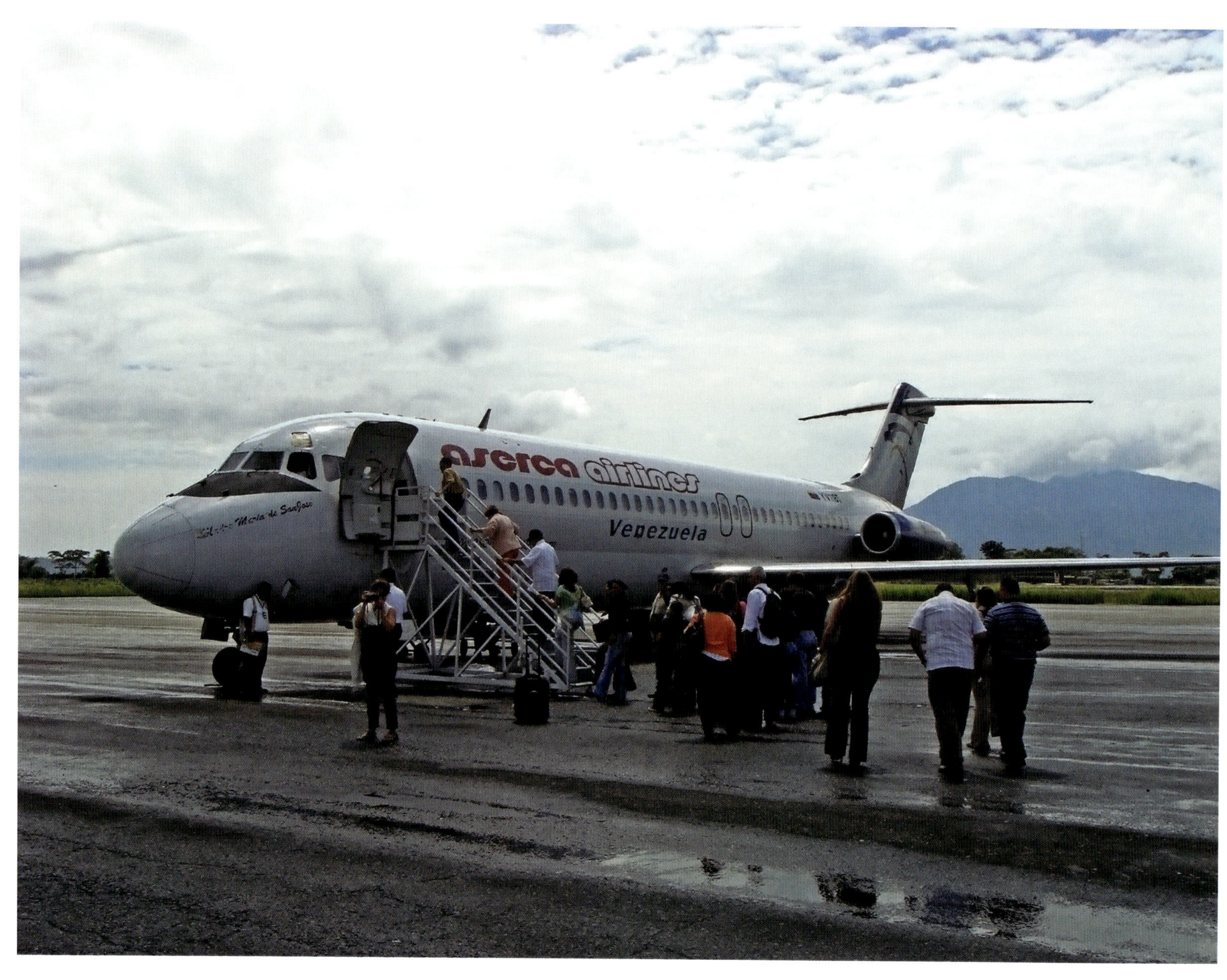

A flight from Santo Domingo, Táchira state
to Caracas. Venezuela, 2007

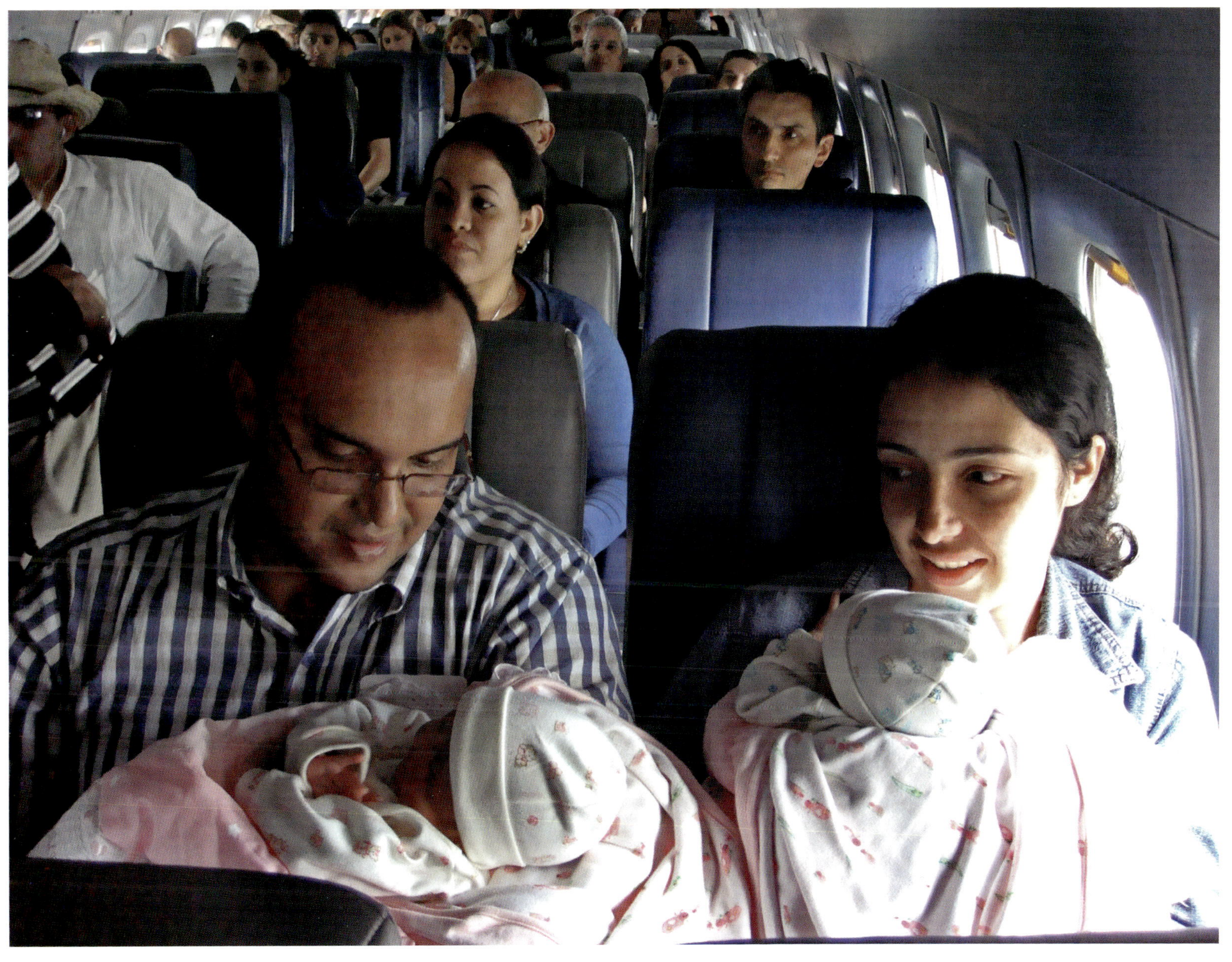

A flight from Santo Domingo, Táchira state
to Caracas. Venezuela, 2007

We all travel. We commute to school or work and back home. We go to the store or out for a meal or entertainment, or visit friends and family. Some flee violence and economic misery in their homelands in search of a better life elsewhere. For decades Jonathan Moller has photographed people in North and Central America, the Caribbean, South America, and Europe, making journeys by many different modes of transportation. There are people on all manner and sizes of boats, in cars, trucks, buses, subways, trains, and planes, and riding horses. There are people on foot carrying goods to or from market, with full sacks on their backs or baskets balanced atop their heads, and—in one instance—carrying backpacks filled with the bones of relatives murdered by guerillas trudging by foot through the desert.

Moller reminds us of the rich diversity of people and how they live in many different parts of the world. Perhaps we will understand others—and ourselves— better by engaging with these images.

Stephen Perloff
Editor
The Photo Review

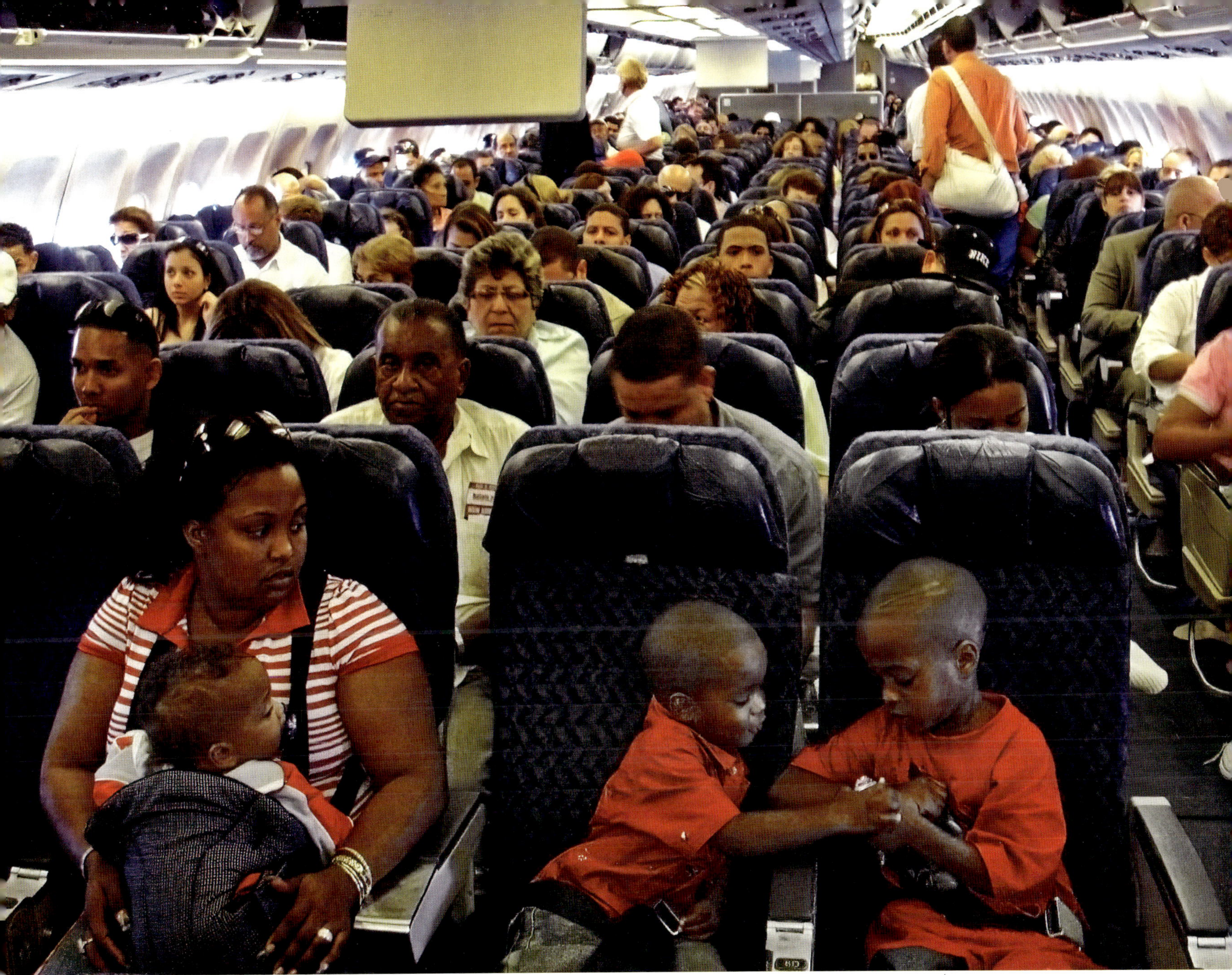

Boarding a flight from Santo Domingo, Dominican Republic
to San Juan, Puerto Rico, 2007

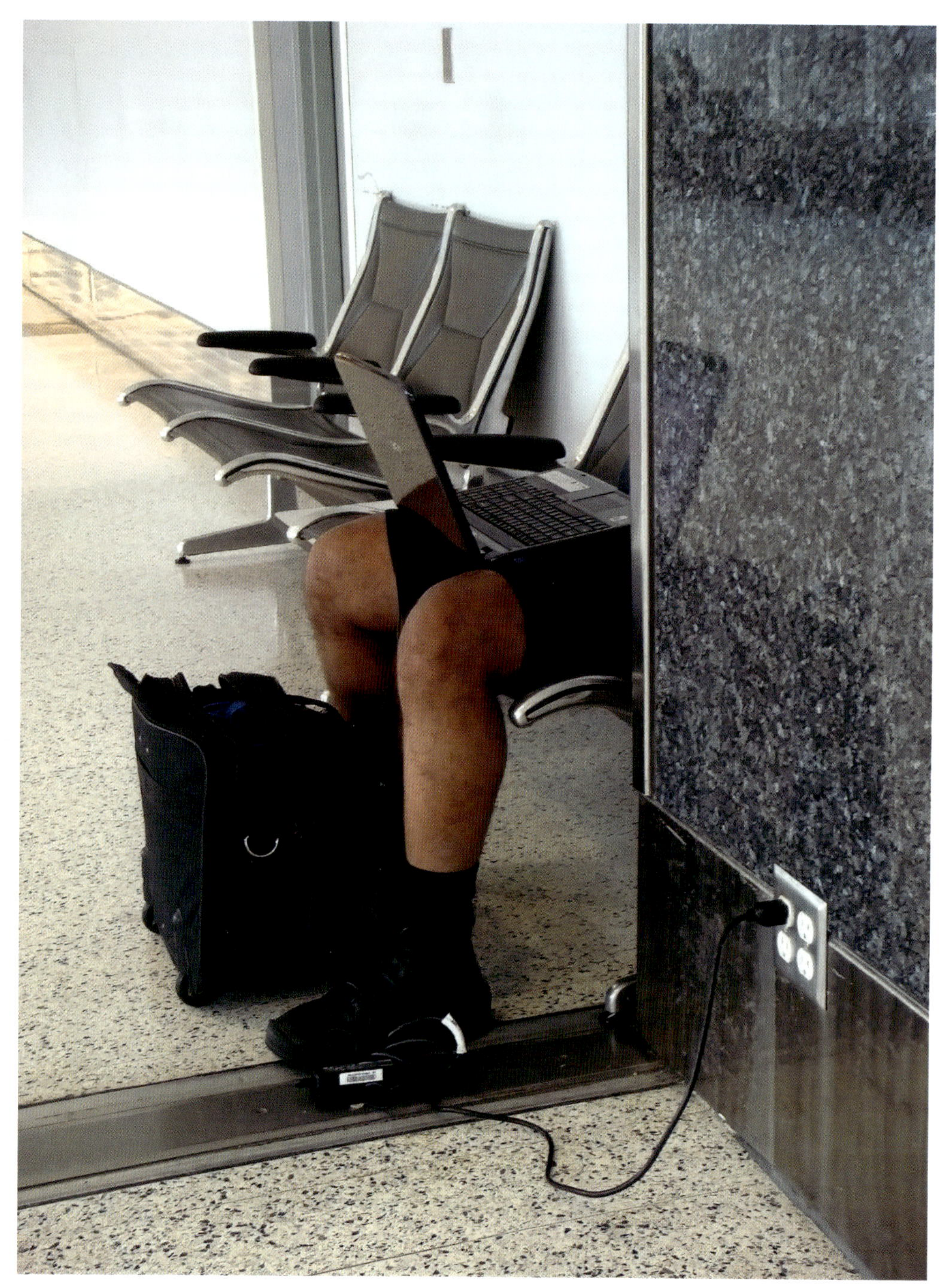

Texas International Airport. Houston, 2009

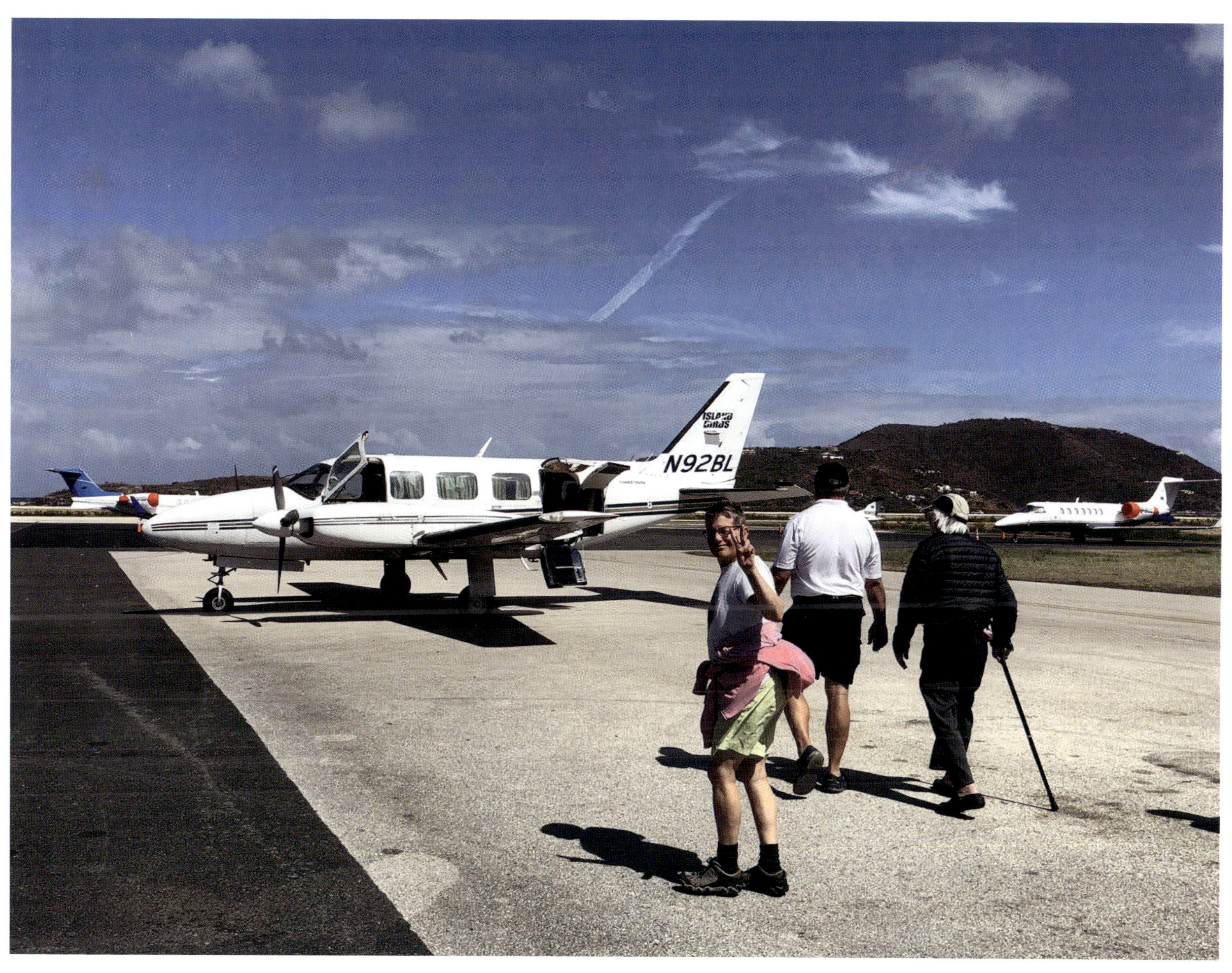

Terrance B. Lettsome International Airport.
Beef Island, British Virgin Islands, 2019

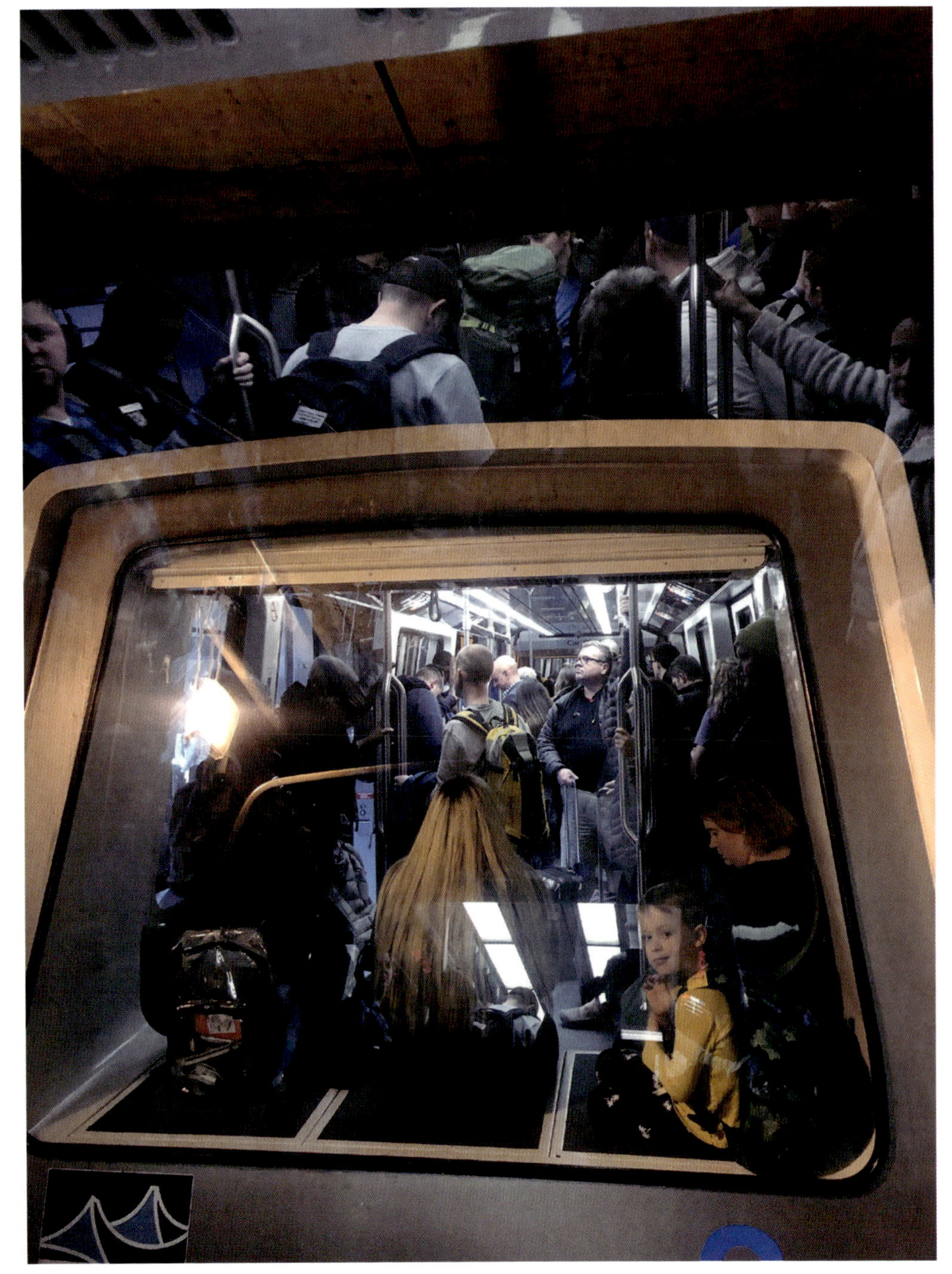

Denver International Airport. Colorado, 2019

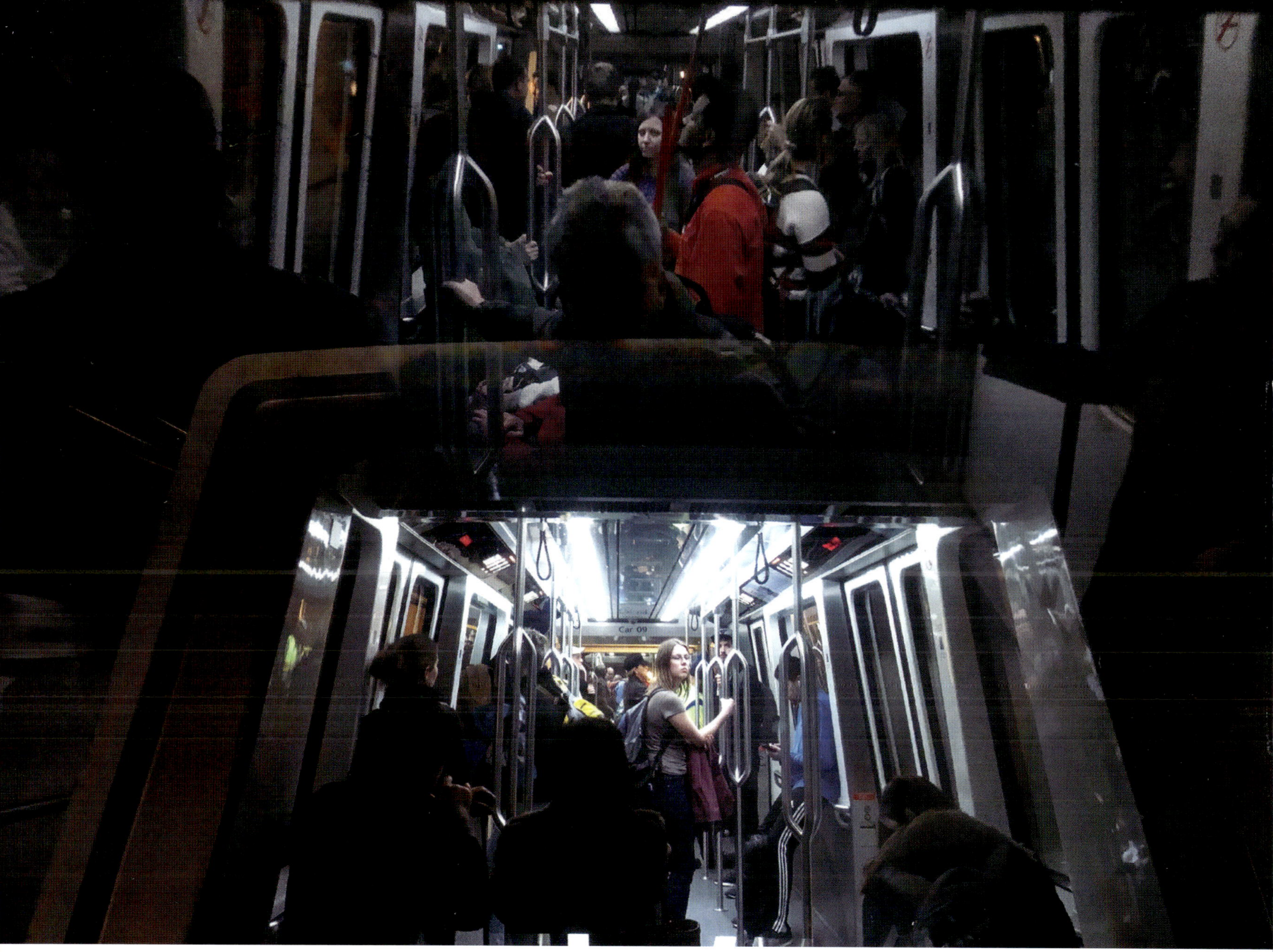

Denver International Airport. Colorado, 2019

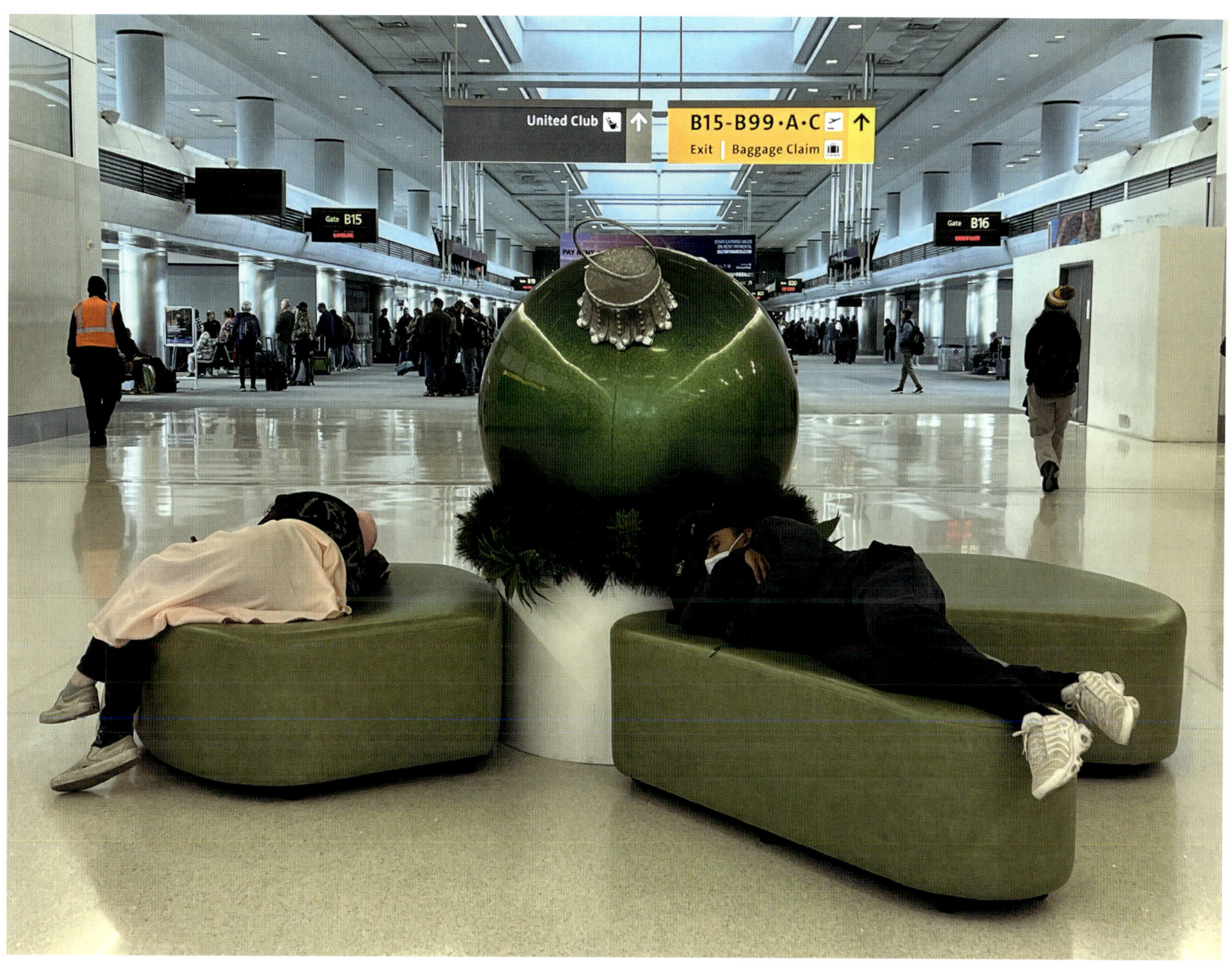

Denver International Airport. Colorado, 2023

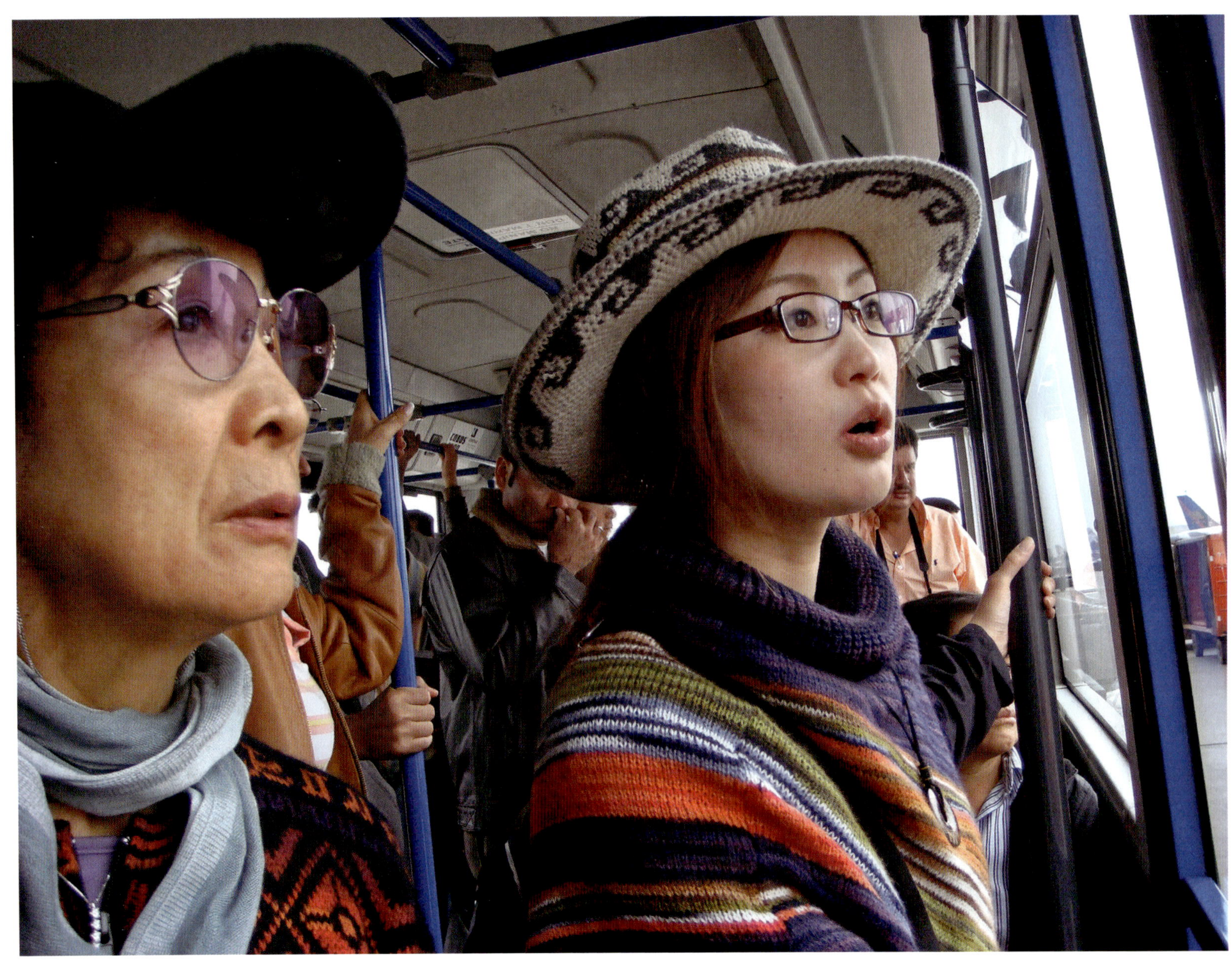

El Alto International Airport. Bolivia, 2007

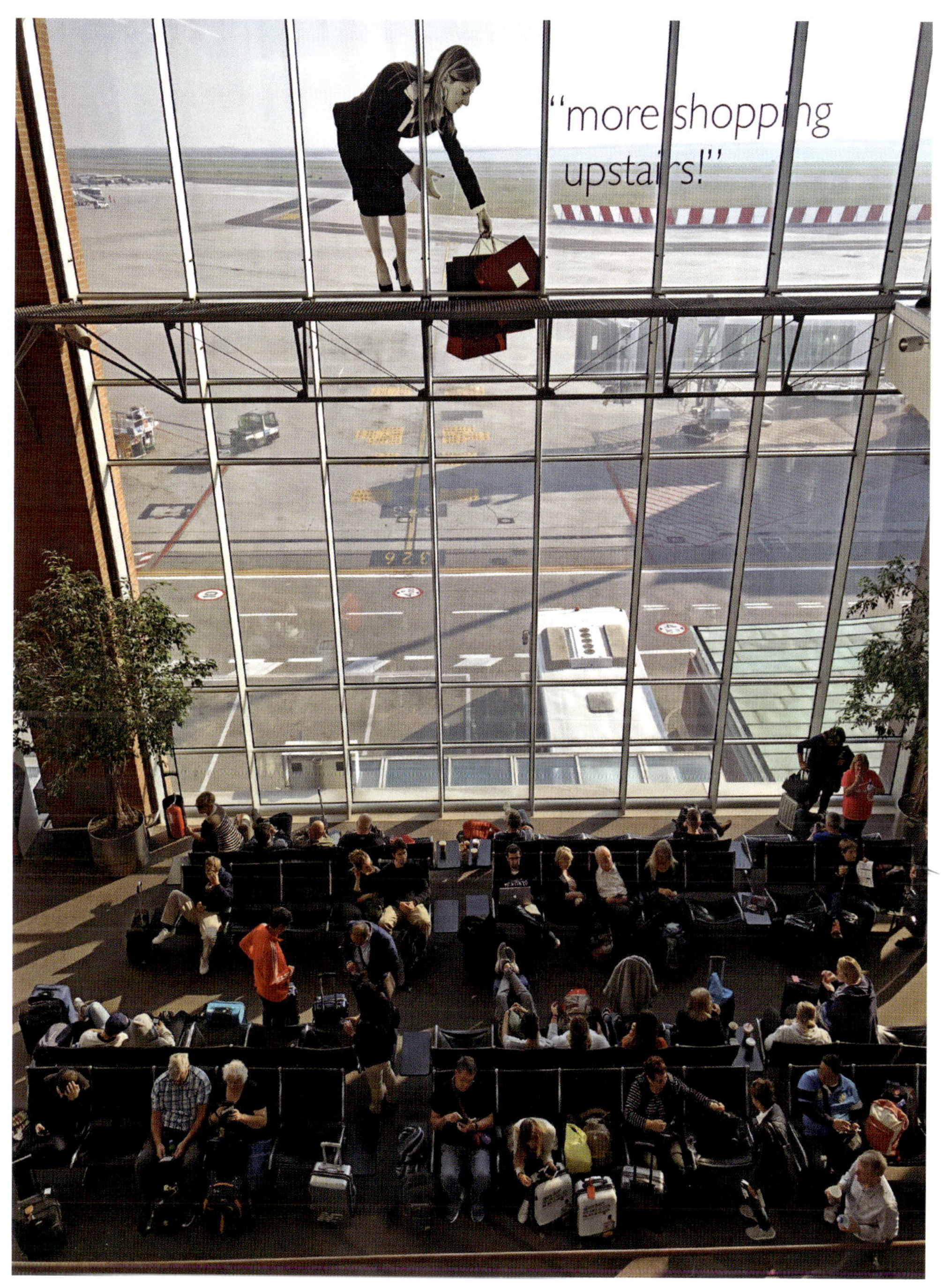

Marco Polo Airport. Venice, Italy, 2018

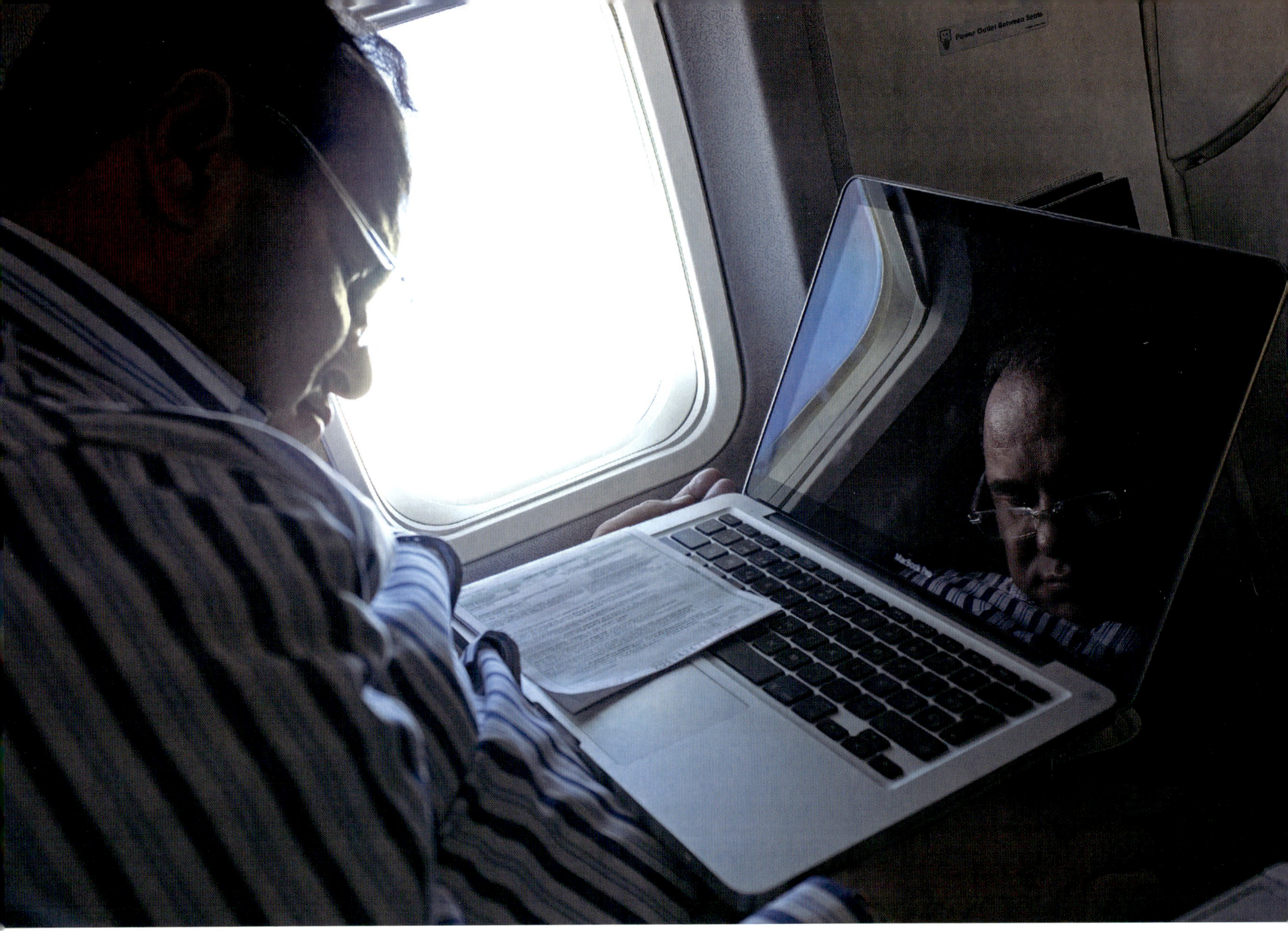

On a flight from Houston, Texas to Bogotá, Colombia, 2014

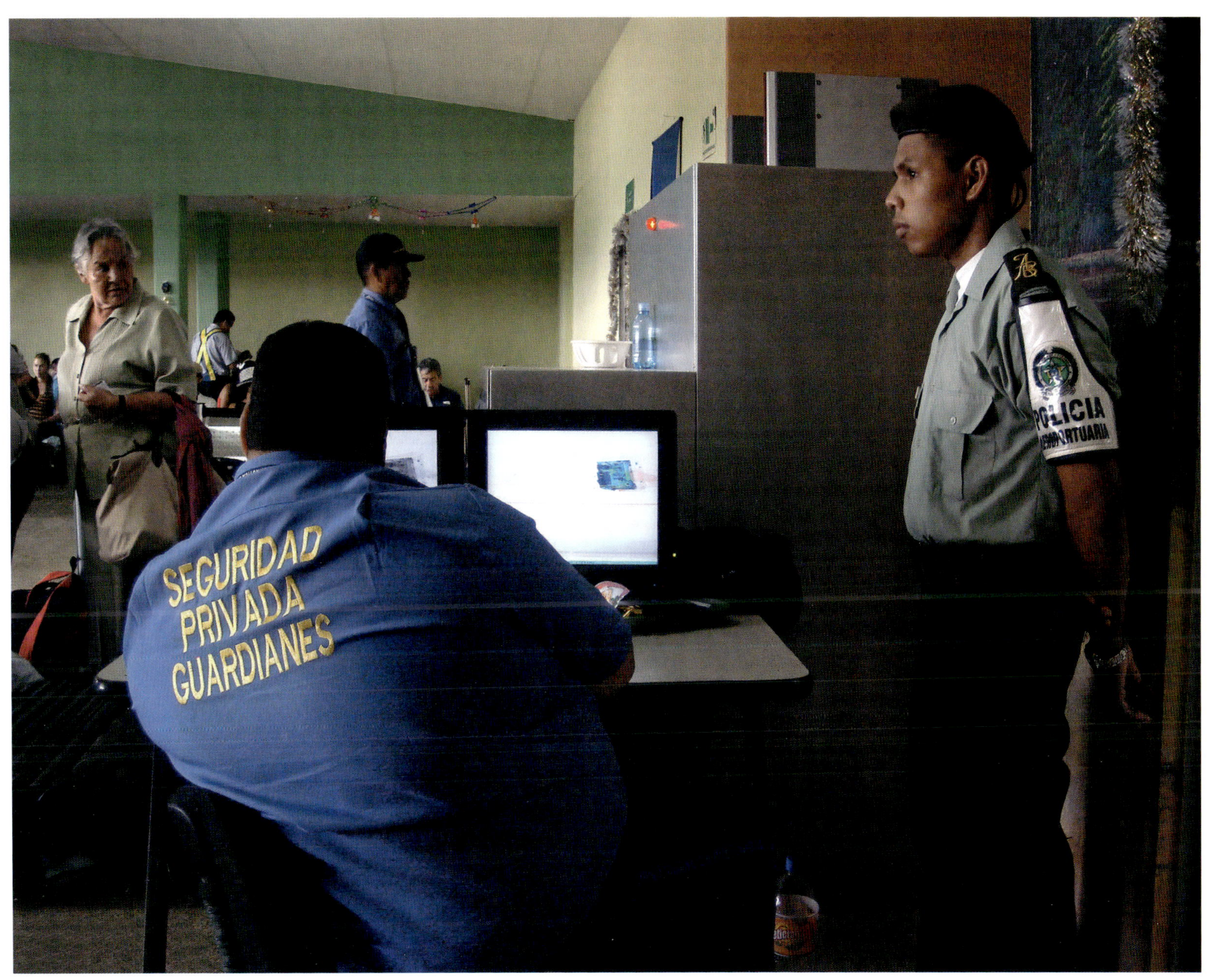

Leticia International Airport. Amazonas, Colombia, 2010

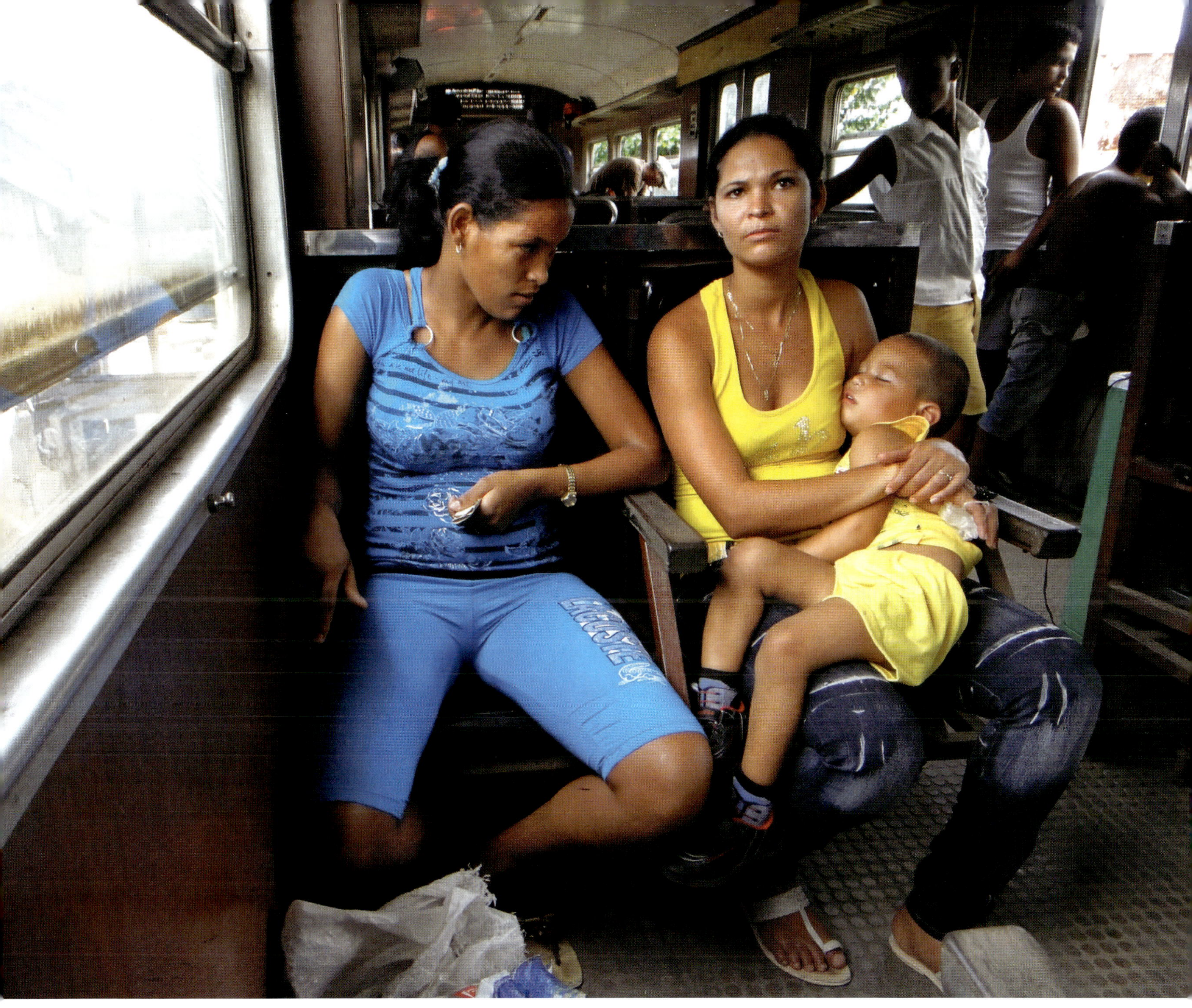

The electric Hershey train from Regla in Havana
to the city of Matanzas. Cuba, 2011

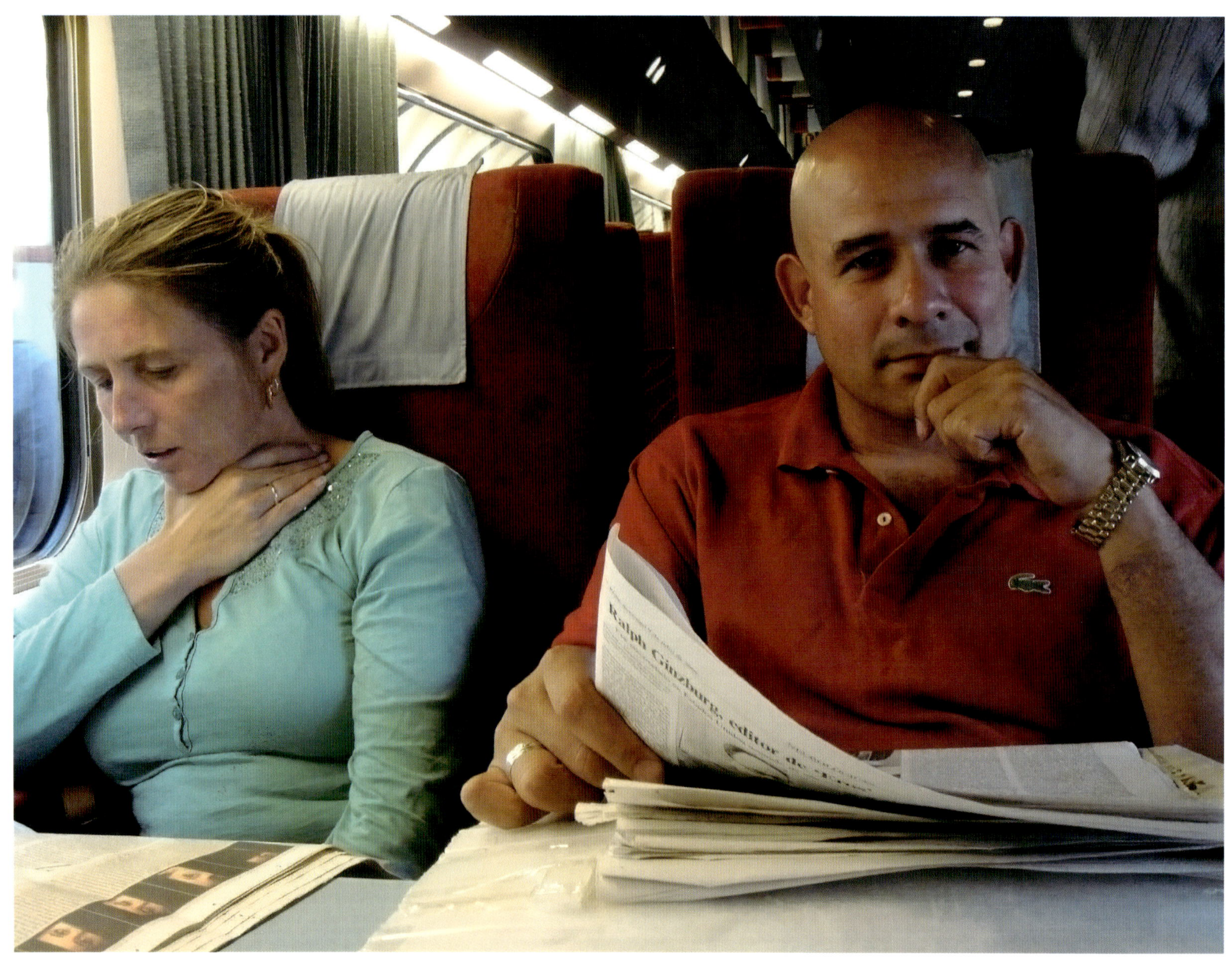

"El Cubano." Netherlands, 2006

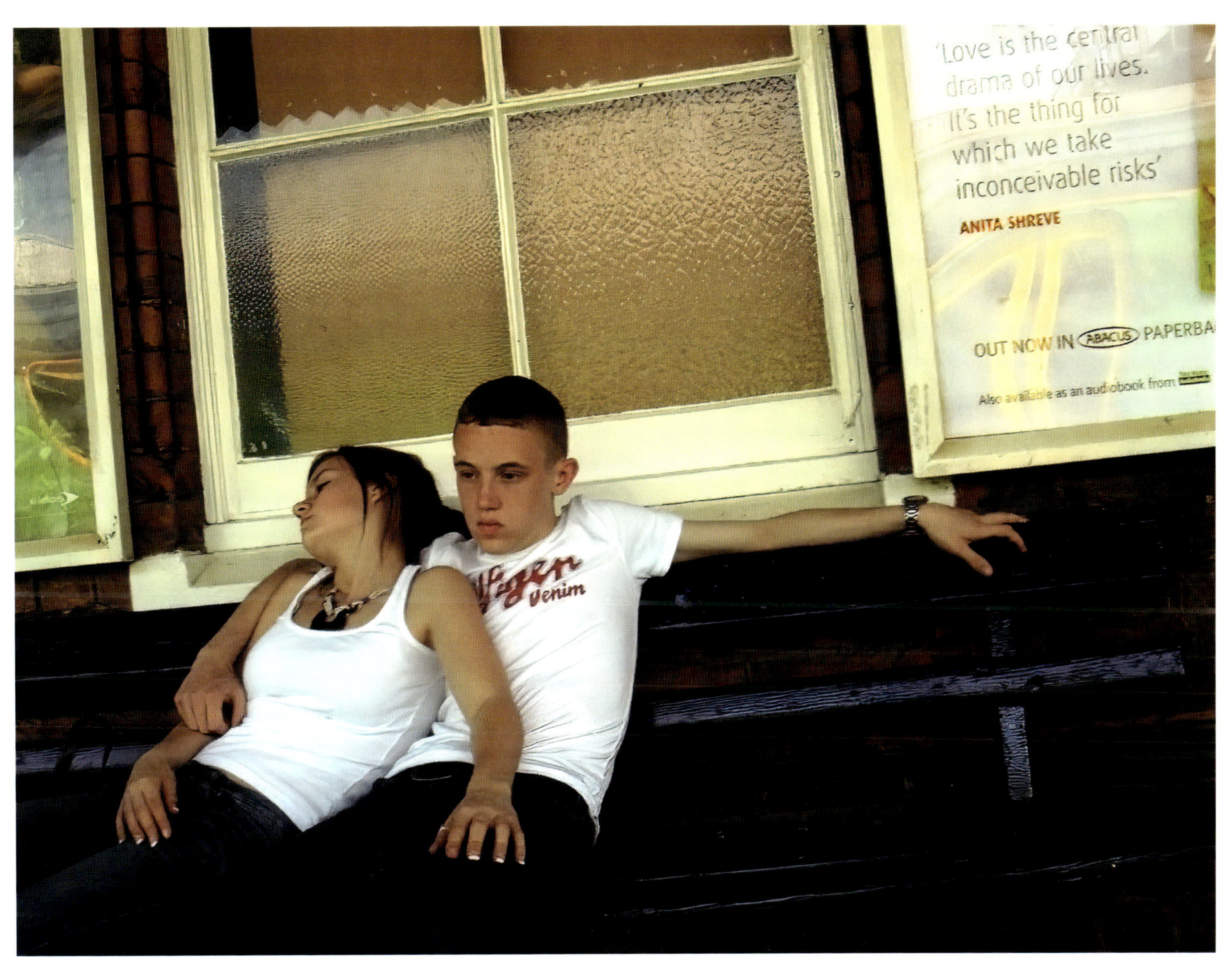

"Love is the central drama of our lives. It's the thing for which we take inconceivable risks"
Worcester Shrub Hill railway station. Worcestershire, England, 2006

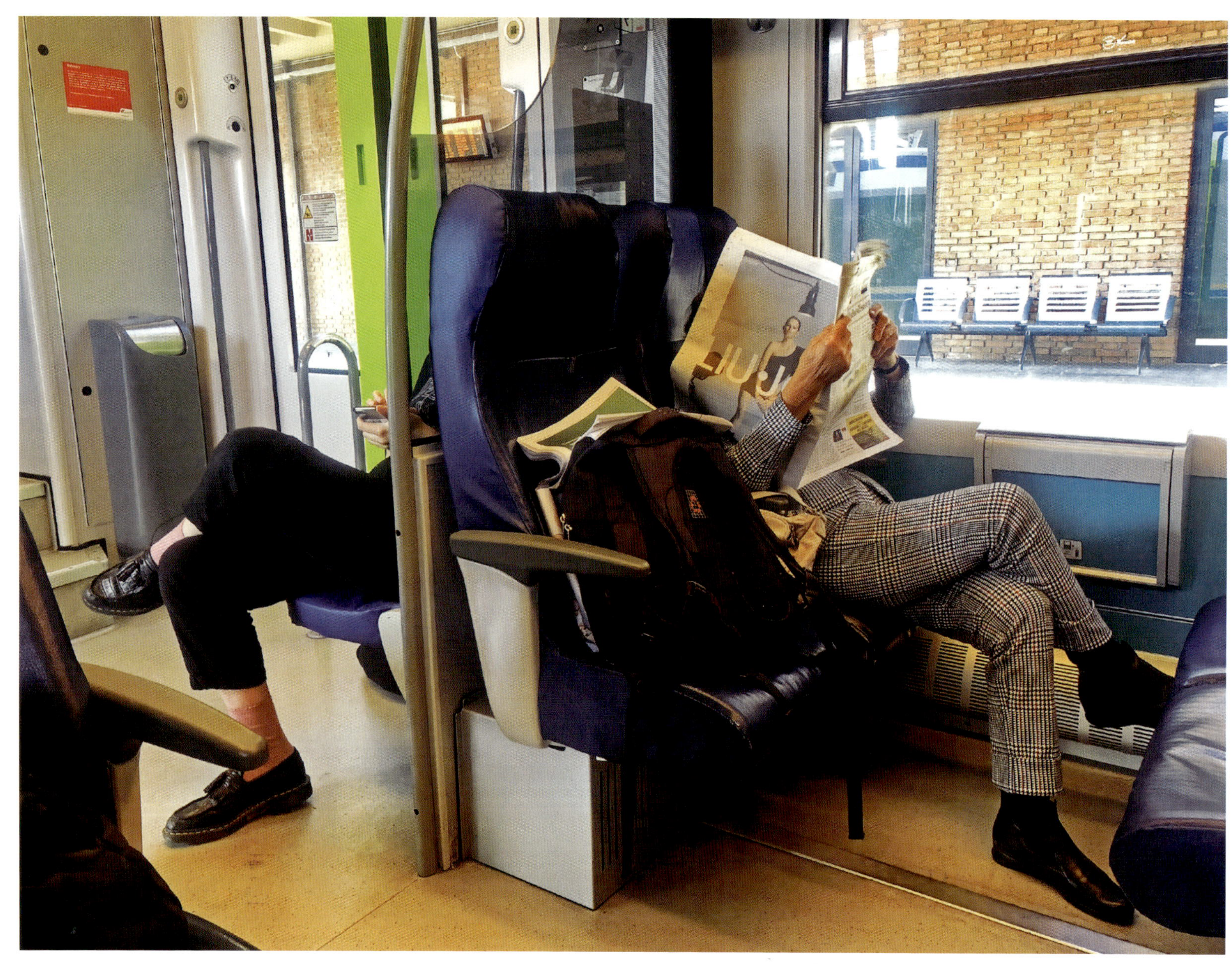

Chiusi, Italy, 2018

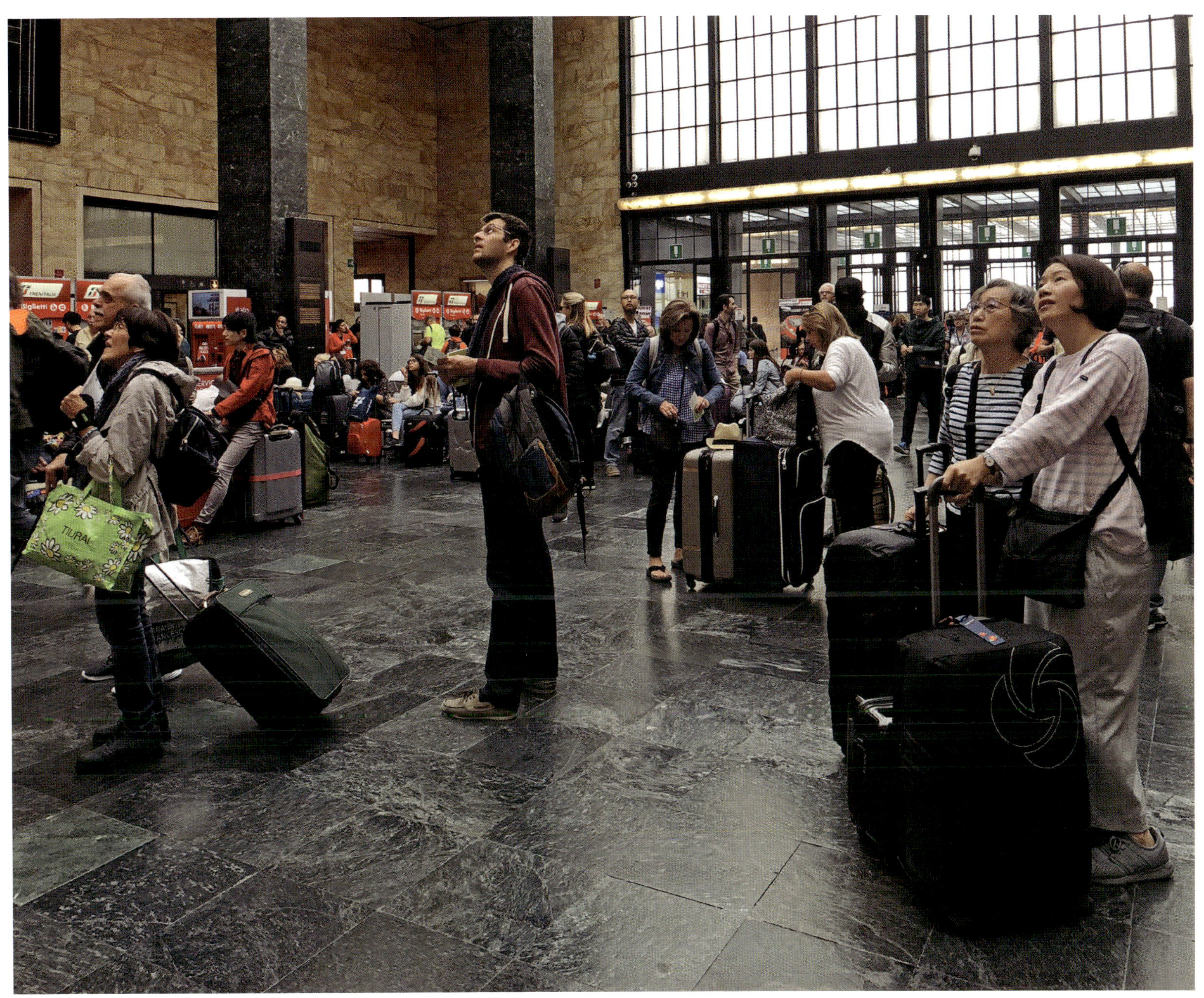

The Santa Maria Novella Train Station.
Florence, Italy, 2018

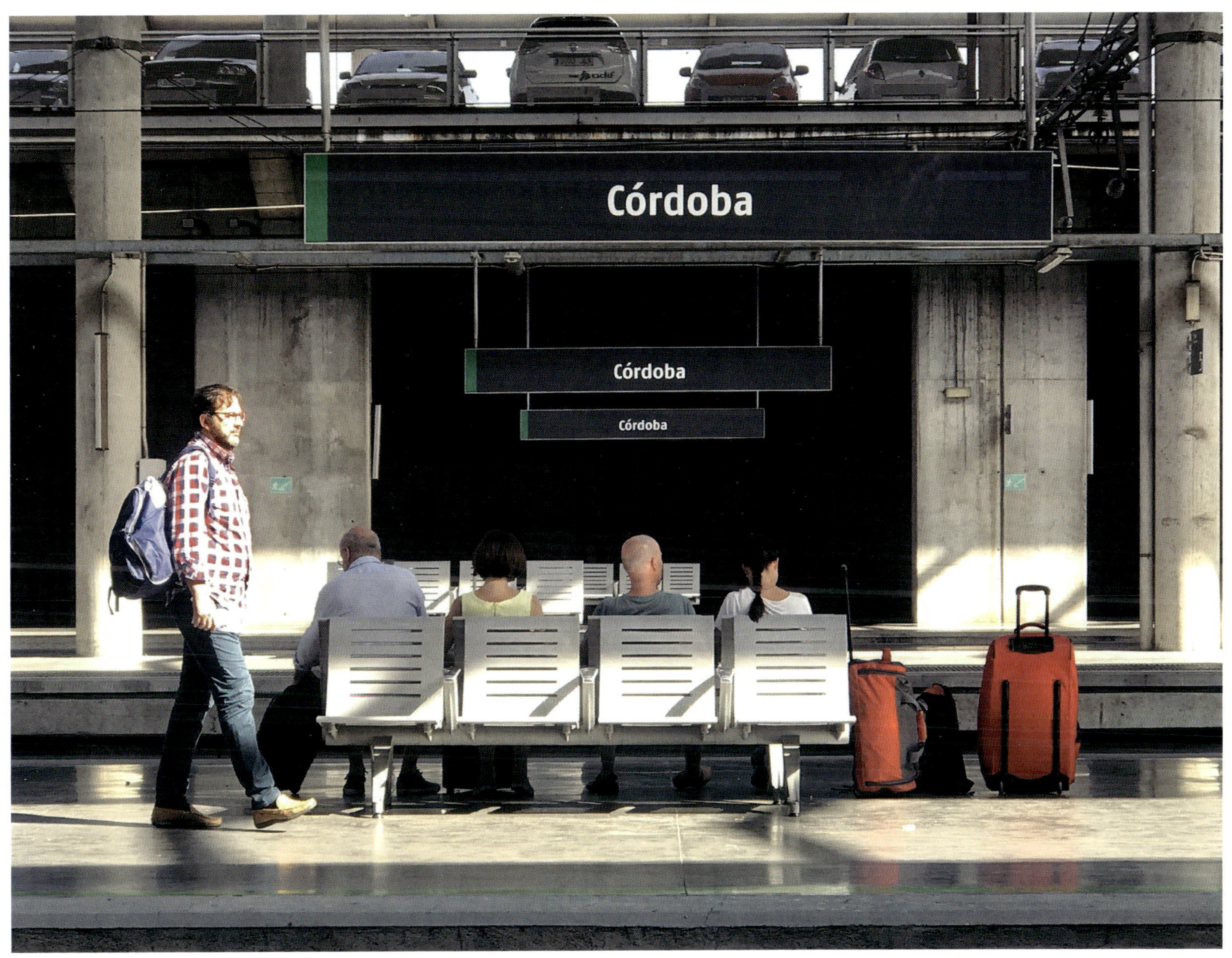

Córdoba, Spain, 2017

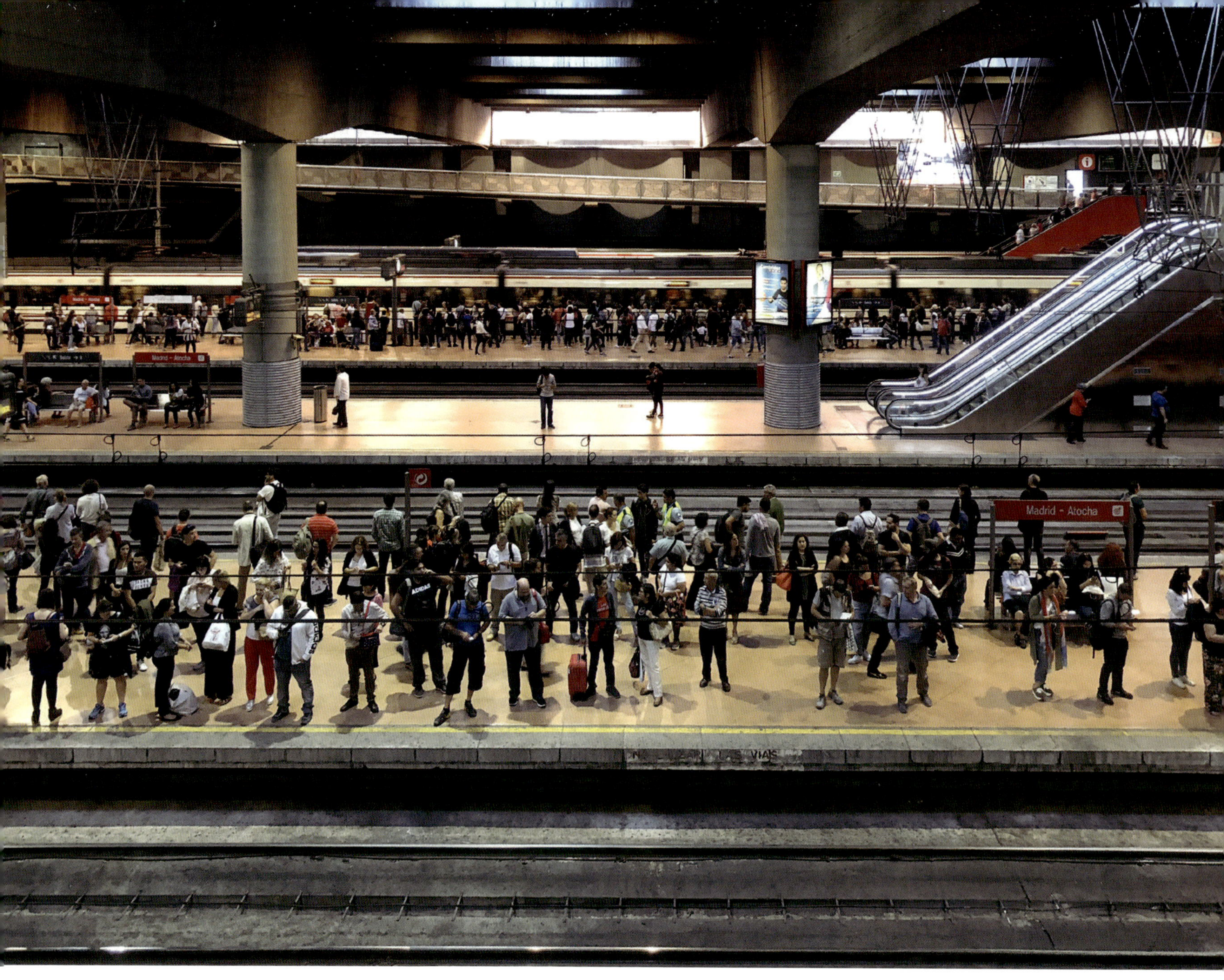

Puerta de Atocha Train Station.
Madrid, Spain, 2018

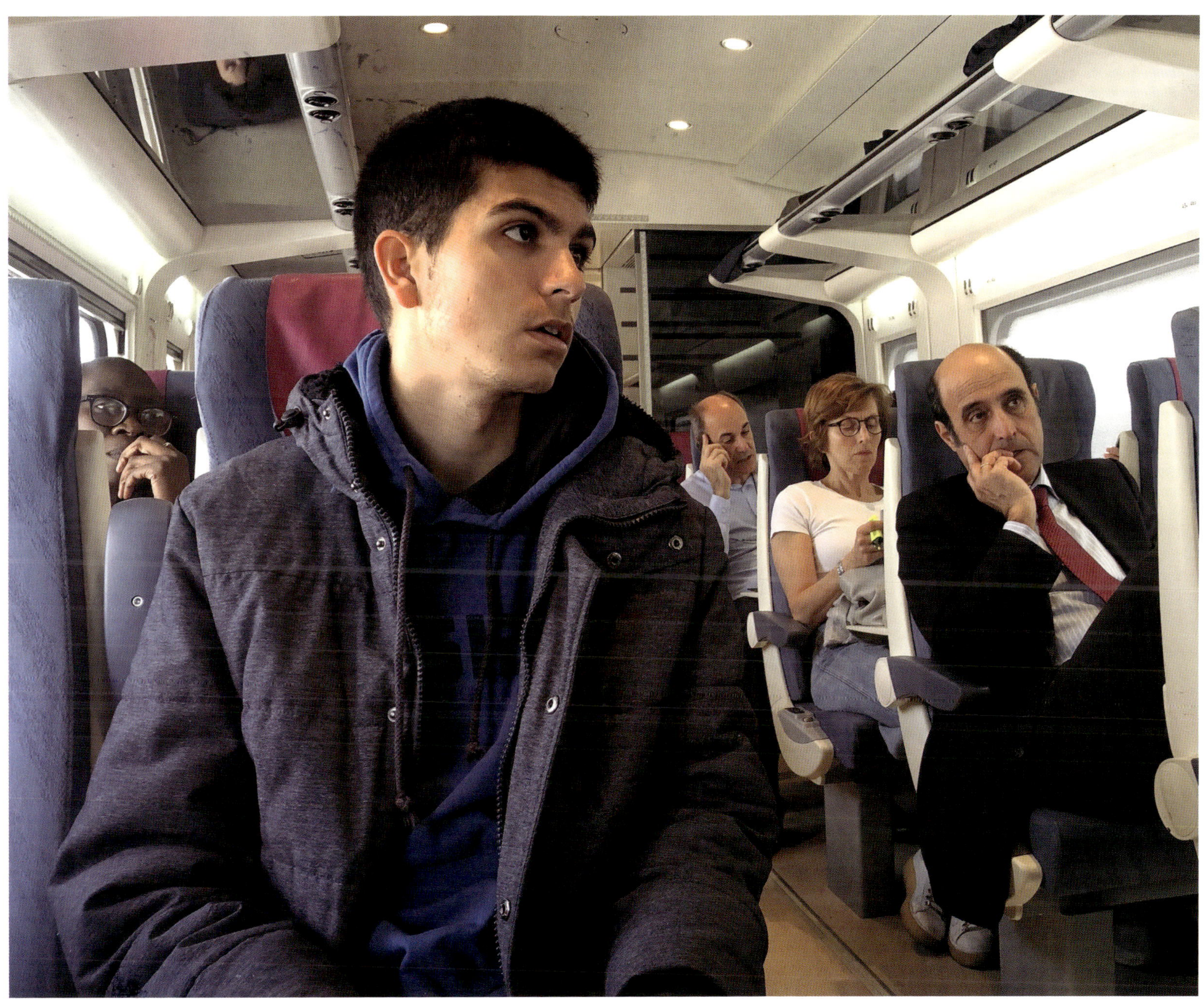

Train from Segovia to Madrid. Spain, 2019

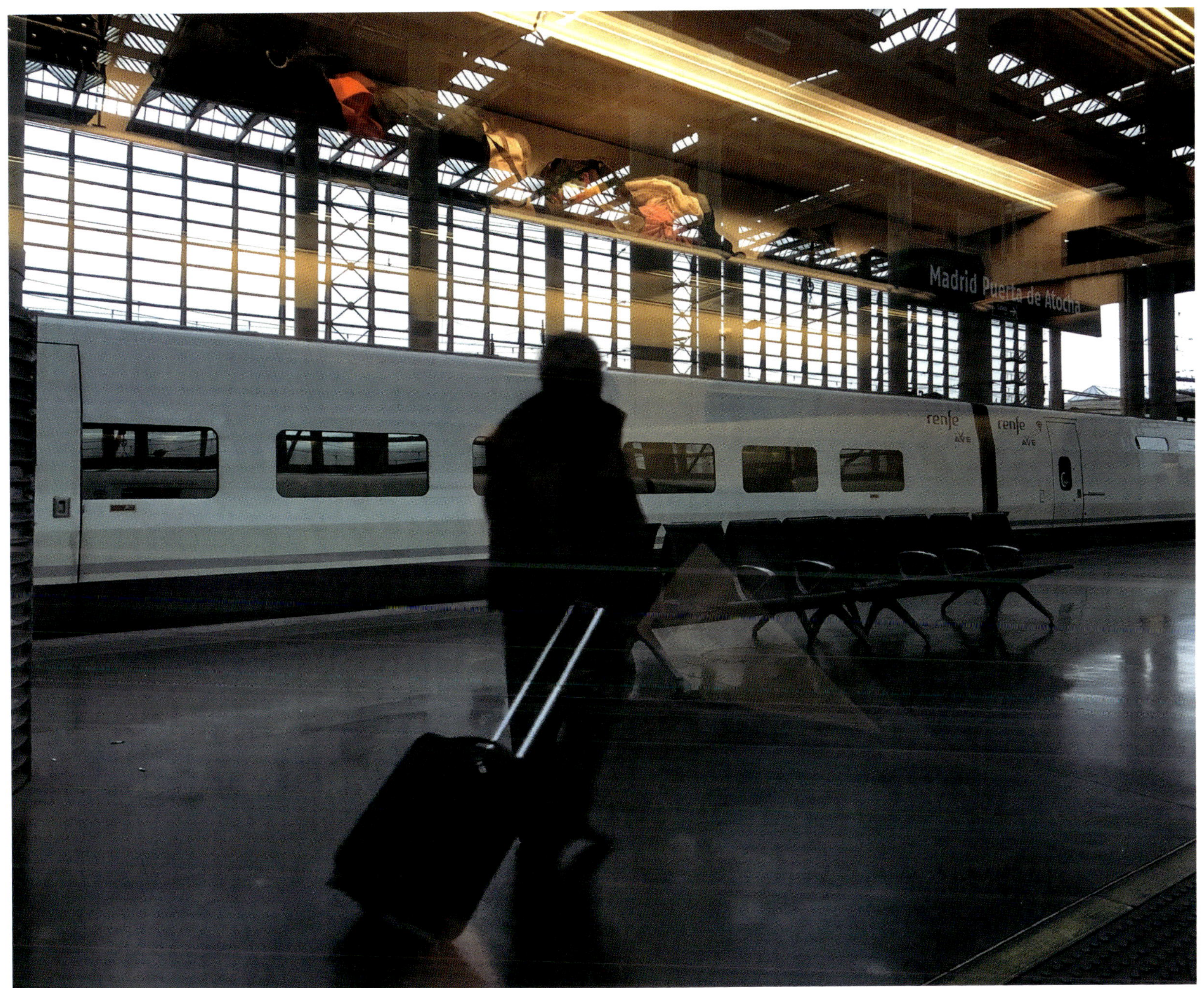

Madrid, Spain, 2019

The Passing Glance: The Transit Images of Jonathan Moller

As in thousands of desolate places across the world, a little boy awaits the passing of the train which will interrupt the monotony of a landscape that he finds perhaps too familiar, even if for us this landscape is that of the majestic Andean mountains. In the expert composition of the photo—the train splitting the mountains like an ascending, bright-blue band against the arid terrain, the child in the lower left corner dressed in red and blue, sitting on a grey rock, tenderly holding a red lollipop that echoes his bright sweater—what calls on our attention with a magnetic force—what Roland Barthes called the *punctum*—is the boy's gaze turned towards the camera—that is, towards us. The boy does not look at the train, the lollipop, or the mountains. He looks at us. Obviously, we know that the photo was taken in the past with respect to the moment in which we now look at it. However, the image shares with us an instant intimacy in an encounter between two people—the intimacy of passing glances between photographer and subject.

That encounter did not occur between the boy and us—the viewers of this book—but between the boy, Jonathan Moller, and his camera. Indeed, throughout this book, Moller shares with us passing moments where two people exchange looks or by contrast ignore each other's eyes. Those of us who look at this book may have experienced hundreds of such chance encounters within the last week, the last day, or even the last hour. In our lives of constant flux, these moments come and go without a trace. This book offers us a pause, a moment to look into those eyes, to reflect on other lives, and to think about the ways in which we connect, or not.

These 130 photographs capture moments throughout nearly forty years of world travel by Moller. Some of the photos were taken in Italy, Spain, and the United States; most of them come from Latin America: Brazil, Colombia, Cuba, Chile, El Salvador, Guatemala, Peru, and others. Moller's love for Latin America and its people is evident in these images of unknown people with whom the photographer has crossed paths during his many trips. We assume he did not necessarily become friends with the subjects of the images. However, they make us think about how we relate to others and the ways in which we sometimes avoid these connections. These images call attention to the fact that at times it can be a person in the forefront who despite being aware of the camera will avoid eye contact, while in other cases, a pair of eyes far from the foreground looks at us penetratingly.

In some cases, an image highlights an intimate connection within a crowd. On a boat in Nicaragua in 1991, three men rest on what looks like enormous mounds of trash bags. Three bodies share a space—one faces to the right; another faces the left. The third man, the one who is the furthest away, looks at the camera with his shiny dark eyes almost smiling. In 2019 on a train in Spain, all men and women mind their own business, from the businessman in a suit to the young man at the fore who refuses to engage with the camera. By contrast, the only dark-skinned man in the scene peers out from behind a row of seats—his chin resting on his longed-fingered hand adorned with a wedding band—looking inquisitively at the camera from behind his glasses.

Through these travel photographs, we see different landscapes, boarding gates, and diverse forms of transportation. However, what dominates is the possibility of encounter through crossing glances, of eyes that meet or avoid other eyes. Moller invites us to look at others and to see ourselves in a potential connection. Perhaps, after contemplating the photos in this book, we, too, will recognize others in the exchange of glances while waiting at the train station.

Margarita Saona
Professor of Latin American Literature and Cultural Studies
University of Illinois at Chicago

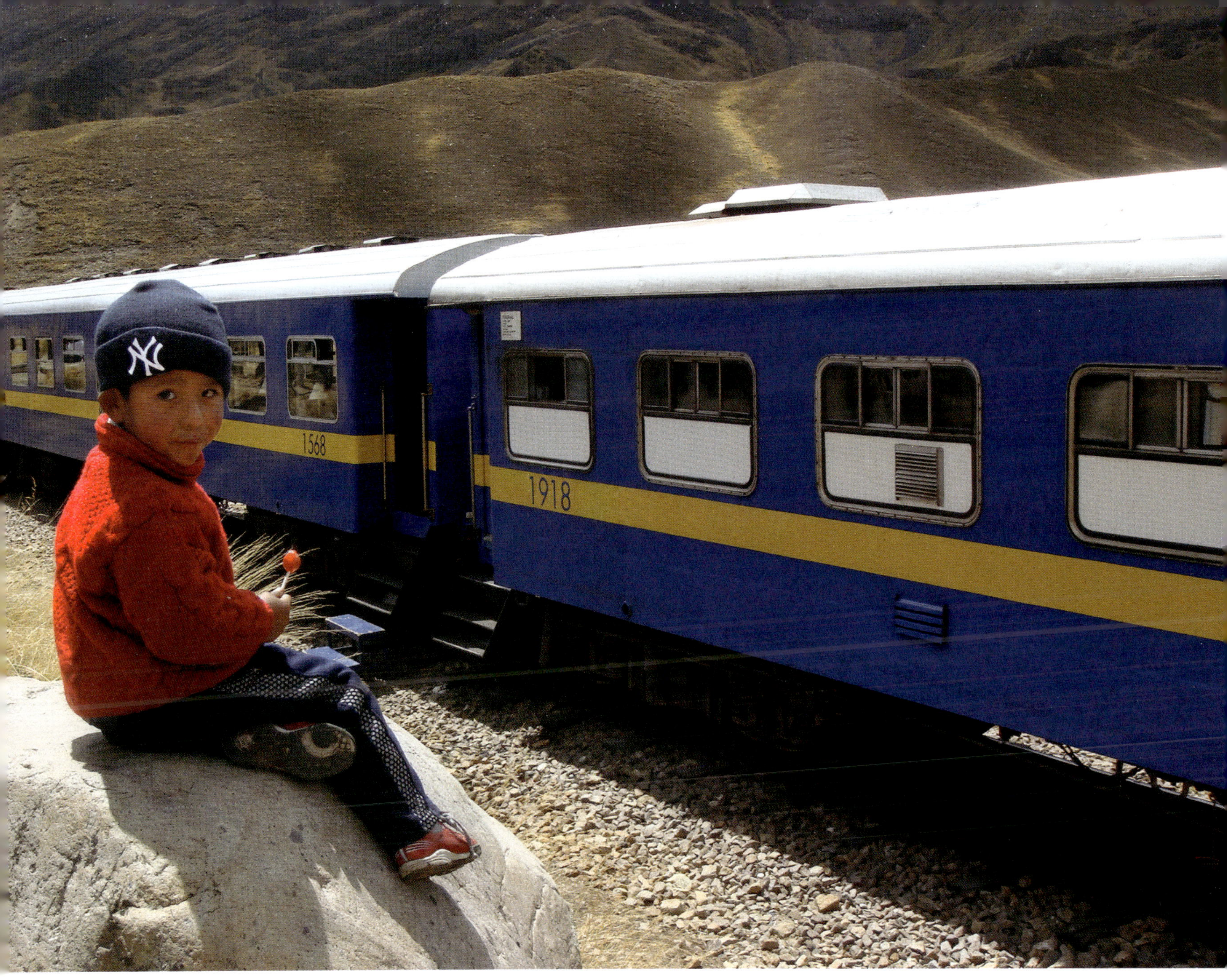

Cuzco to Puno train, Peru, 2007

Transit & Travel, Samuel Johnson & Jonathan Moller: An Appreciation

Dr. Samuel Johnson, the eighteenth century English lexicographer, essayist, and critic was greatly intrigued by travel. Most of his journeys, though, were in his mind.

> Let observation with extensive view,
> Survey mankind from China to Peru:
> Remark each anxious toil,
> Each eager strife,
> And watch the busy scenes of crowded life.[1]

Johnson never went to China or Peru, his furthest ramble being an 83-day trip through Scotland and the Outer Hebrides—no small feat in 1773. He thought and wrote about multiple aspects of travel and offered observations on the subject that might be useful in appreciation of Jonathan Moller's twentieth and twenty-first-century photography project, *In Transit: In the Company of Strangers*.

We know oftentimes eighteenth century travel was involuntary—as endured by captive peoples in slave ships; supposed criminals "transported" into exile in places far away; ship's crews made up of press gangs—all of which resonates with another Johnsonian observation.

> Being in a ship is being in a jail, with the chance
> of being drowned.[2]

Beyond the dangers of water, this quote readily applies to wider, more contemporary risks of being in an airplane, bus, train, or car—all of which appear as modes of travel here. Movement in general, whether across the street or around the globe, is not without peril. And now, more than two centuries after Johnson wrote those words, many of the travelers depicted in this book are also not in transit by their own volition—for pleasure or to "broaden" themselves, as they say. Even today, travel goals like these are afforded to a privileged few.

Instead, most of the people who appear in this marvelous sequence of photographs temporarily occupy places like the grimy, gritty "T"—Boston's benighted public transportation system—"chicken class" on busses; cramped airline seating whether big planes or small; scruffy waiting rooms or platforms; or scuttling up trails so skinny as to risk toppling down into the maw of canyons below. None of this looks particularly comfortable, and a mix of tension and boredom prevails. Most everyone is trying to get somewhere while bearing expressions that register resignation and stress. Displacement and coercion are implied. Buffeted by the forces of capitalism, politics, and climate, people are shunted from place to place in search of employment, opportunity, safety, and sometimes pleasure, even knowledge. In these photographs, there are no obvious selfies being taken.

To be sure, there are some smiles and a great deal of beautiful scenery! Paging through, I noted a man gazing out a bus window with evident pleasure; a slight grin from a ticket seller; a dude mugging for the camera while holding a bunch of tiny shot bottles of Jack Daniels; a smiling V sign from a passenger about to board a tiny jet; a couple seemingly entranced by the two babies they are holding; a quizzical but not hostile glance from a newspaper reader; a man with a twinkle in his eye playing with a child.

Some of the people we see may be headed to rewarding, fulfilling jobs. Others to nice hotels, maybe museums, or a delicious meal. But trying to read too closely to expressions, body language, and moods in the 130 images in this book can be a fool's errand and likely an injustice to the subjects. Many of the people depicted are wearing their "in transit" game face, offering little but speculation as to what they are really thinking, where they are going, what they are up to. The only certain thing is that each person could tell an interesting story, maybe multiple ones.

> In traveling, a man must carry knowledge with him, if he would bring home knowledge.[3]

Jonathan Moller has had the good fortune to travel often, to many different places and situations and, as Johnson suggests, to experience being in transit as an intriguing, creative process. The knowledge that Moller garners from each encounter is informed by what he has already experienced and seen. And what he brings home with him from these journeys continues to inform his ideas, his politics, his previous experiences, and certainly, his eye. We, the viewers, benefit from all that accumulated time he has spent cheek-to-jowl in lines, in waiting rooms, on ferries, with hundreds, maybe thousands of people, he doesn't know.

> The use of travelling is to regulate imagination by reality, and instead of thinking how things may be, to see them as they are.[4]

Since the advent of postmodernism in the latter part of the twentieth century, "realities" presented through photographic images have been consistently questioned. That said, a body of work as long-lived, broad, and well-considered as the pictures in this book offers a view of things "as they are," through pictorial and editing strategies such as framing, juxtaposition, sequencing, and other practiced tools and techniques. It is difficult, if not impossible to successfully read the individual pictures, but taken as a whole, it is impossible to avoid seeing things as they are through so much time spent in the company of strangers *in transit*.

Jim Dow
Professor of Photography, Histories of Photography and Contemporary Art, Emeritus
The School of the Museum of Fine Arts at Tufts University
Belmont, Massachusetts

1   Johnson, Samuel (1825), *The Works of Samuel Johnson, LL. D.* Vol. 2, Jones, p. 548.
2   Boswell, James (1829), *The Life of Samuel Johnson... With Copious Notes and Biographical Illustrations, by Malone, etc.* (entry for 16 March 1759), Jones & Company.
3   Boswell, James (1829), *The Life of Samuel Johnson... With Copious Notes and Biographical Illustrations, by Malone, etc.* Vol. 3, p. 302 (17 April 1778), Jones & Company.
4   Johnson, Samuel (1825), *The Works of Samuel Johnson, LL. D.* Vol. 2, Jones, p. 318.

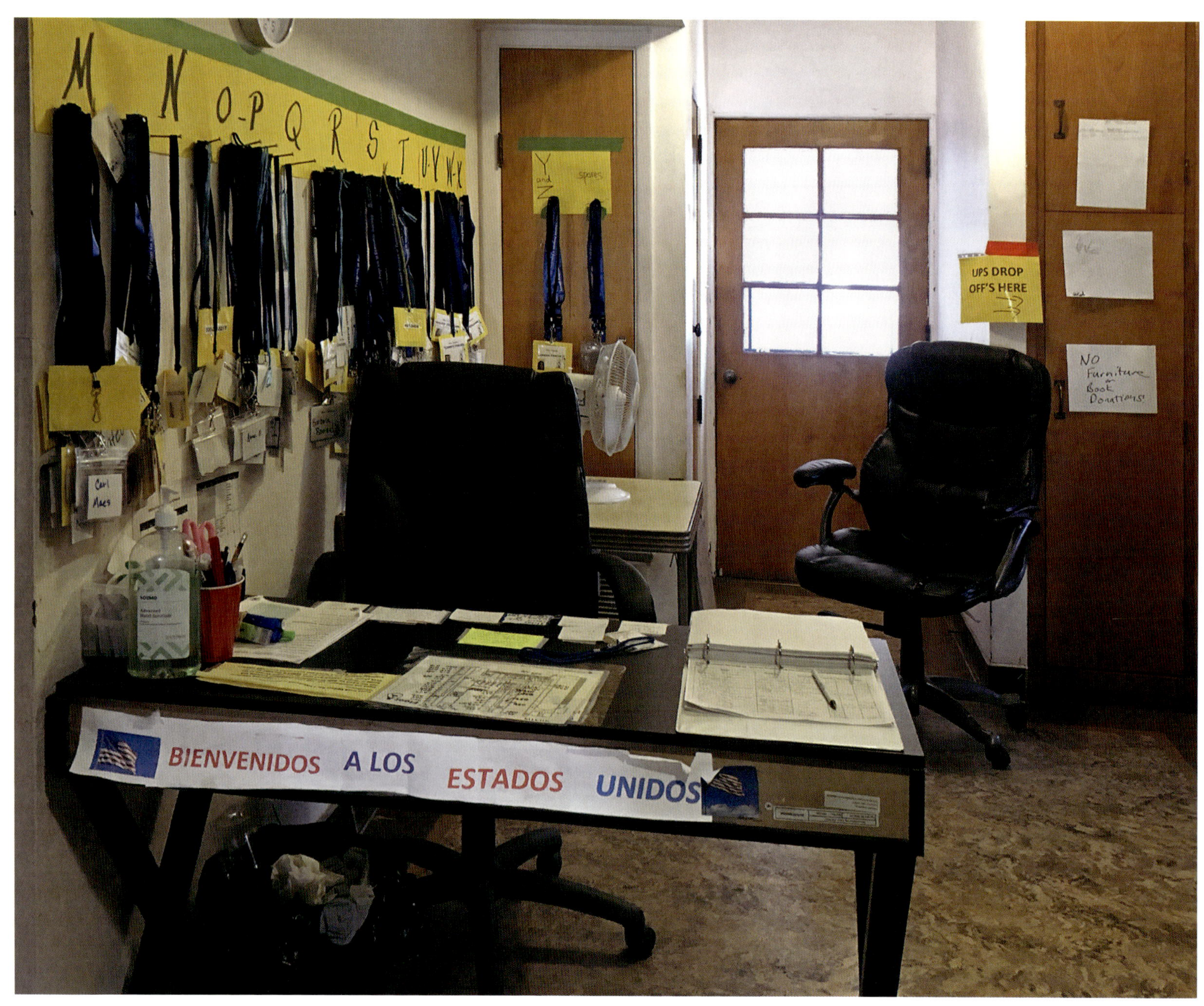

Migrant shelter in Tucson, Arizona, 2019

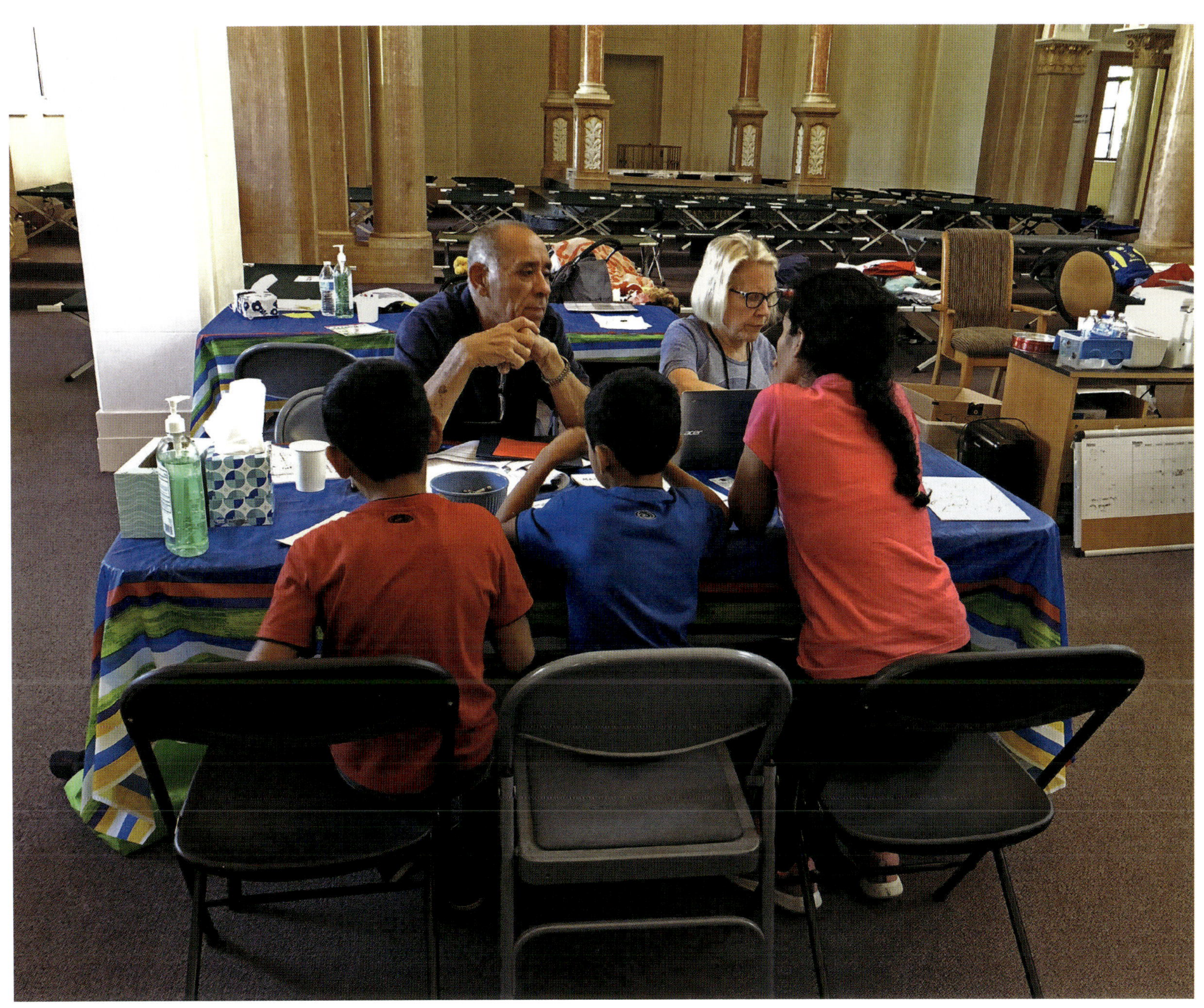

A mother and her two children from Honduras just arrived at a migrant shelter in Tucson, Arizona,
having traveled overland from Honduras, through Guatemala and Mexico to the US border, 2019

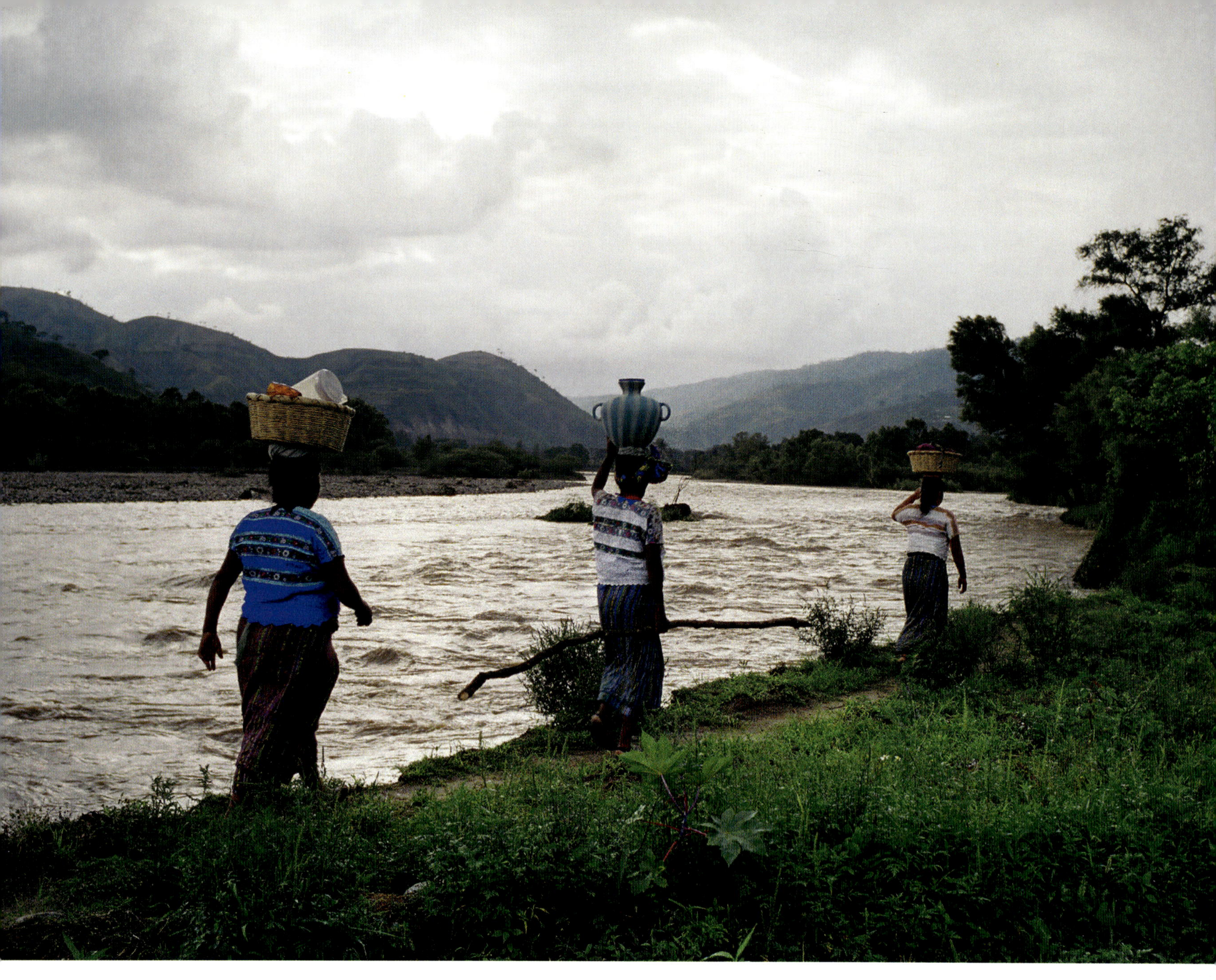

Three women walking back to their village from the main town
of Sacapulas. Quiché, Guatemala, 2001

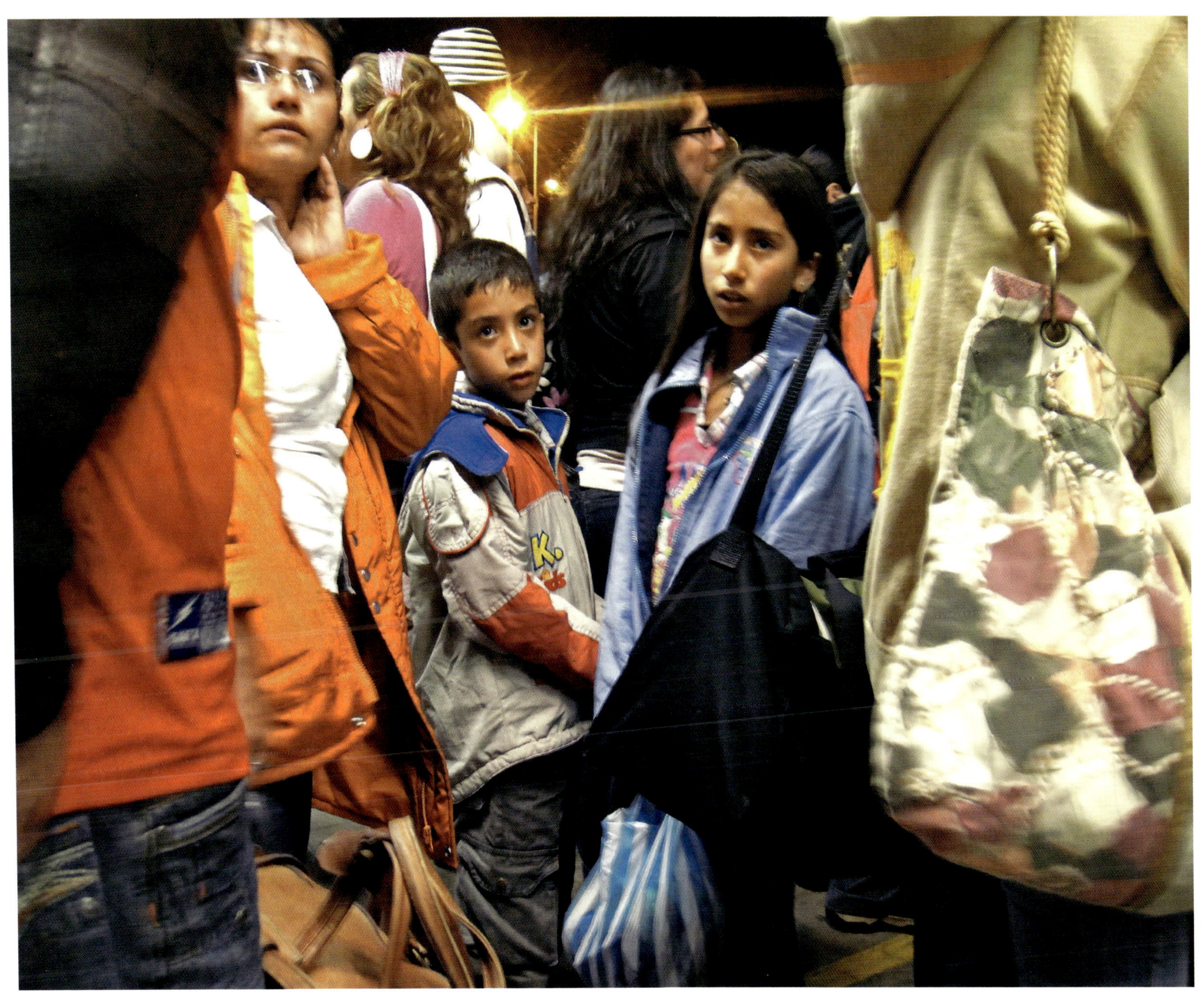

TransMilenio rapid transit bus system.
Bogotá, Colombia, 2009

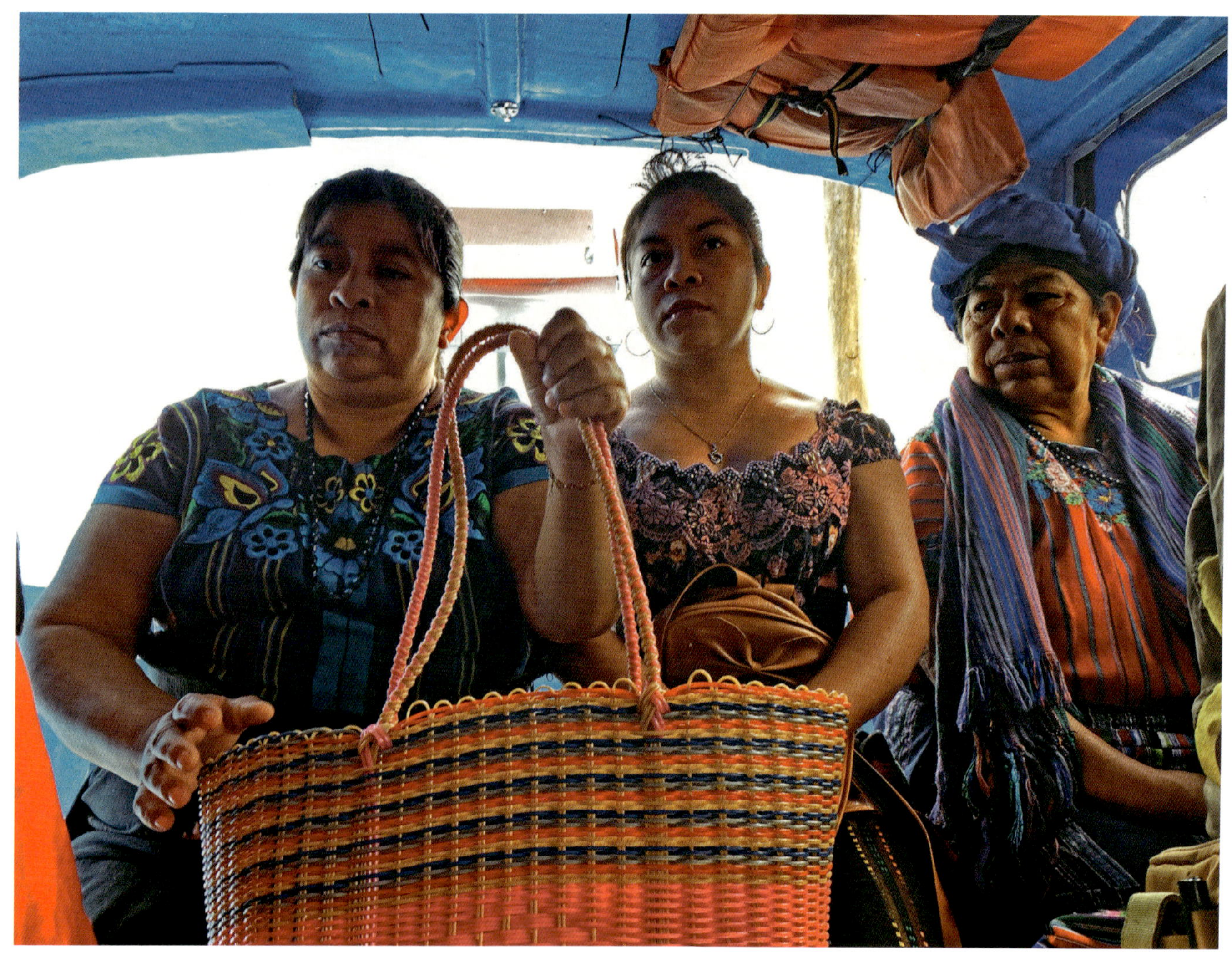

On a boat that takes passengers between the main town of Panajachel
and other small towns on the shores of Lake Atitlán. Guatemala, 2022

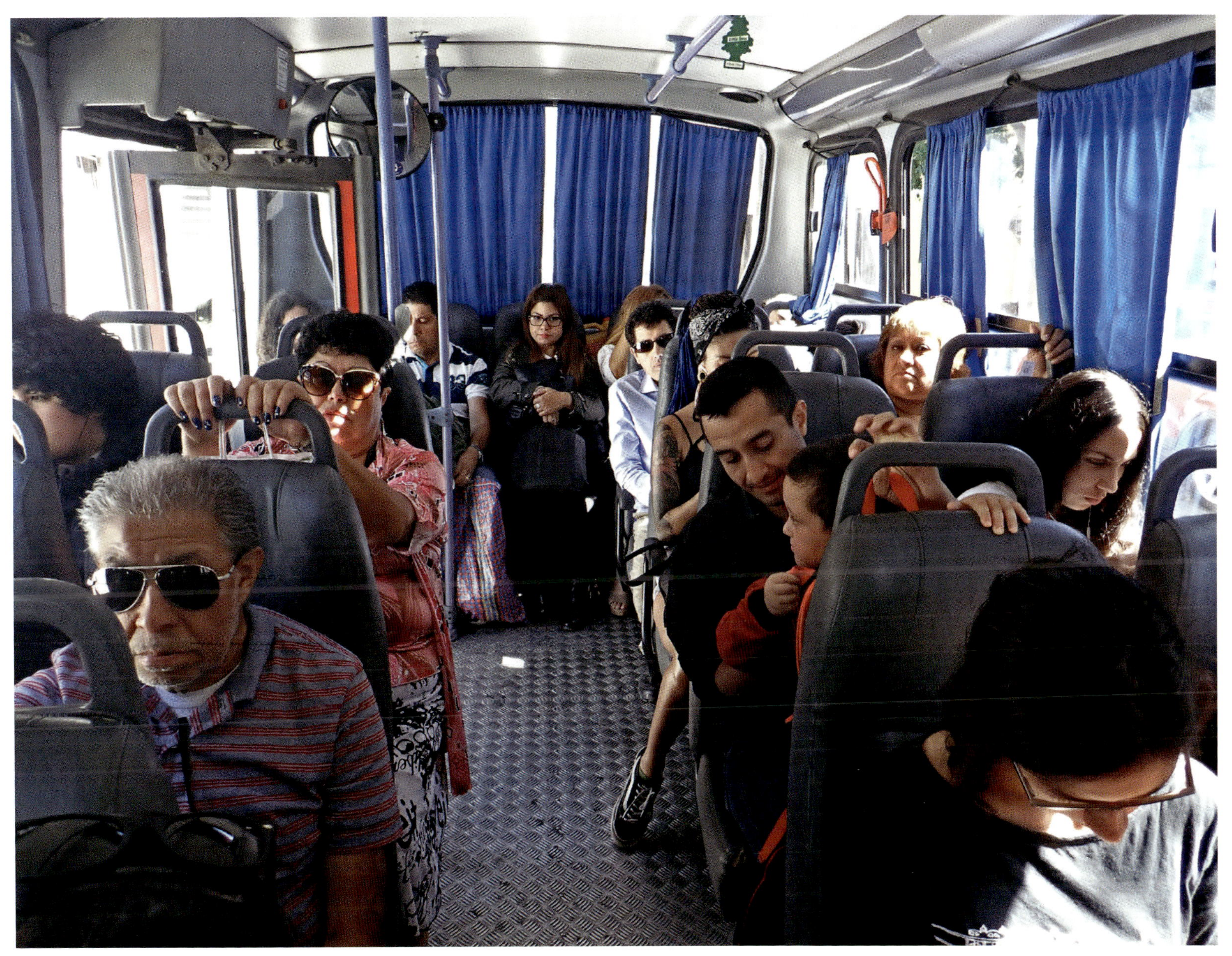

Valparaíso, Chile, 2018

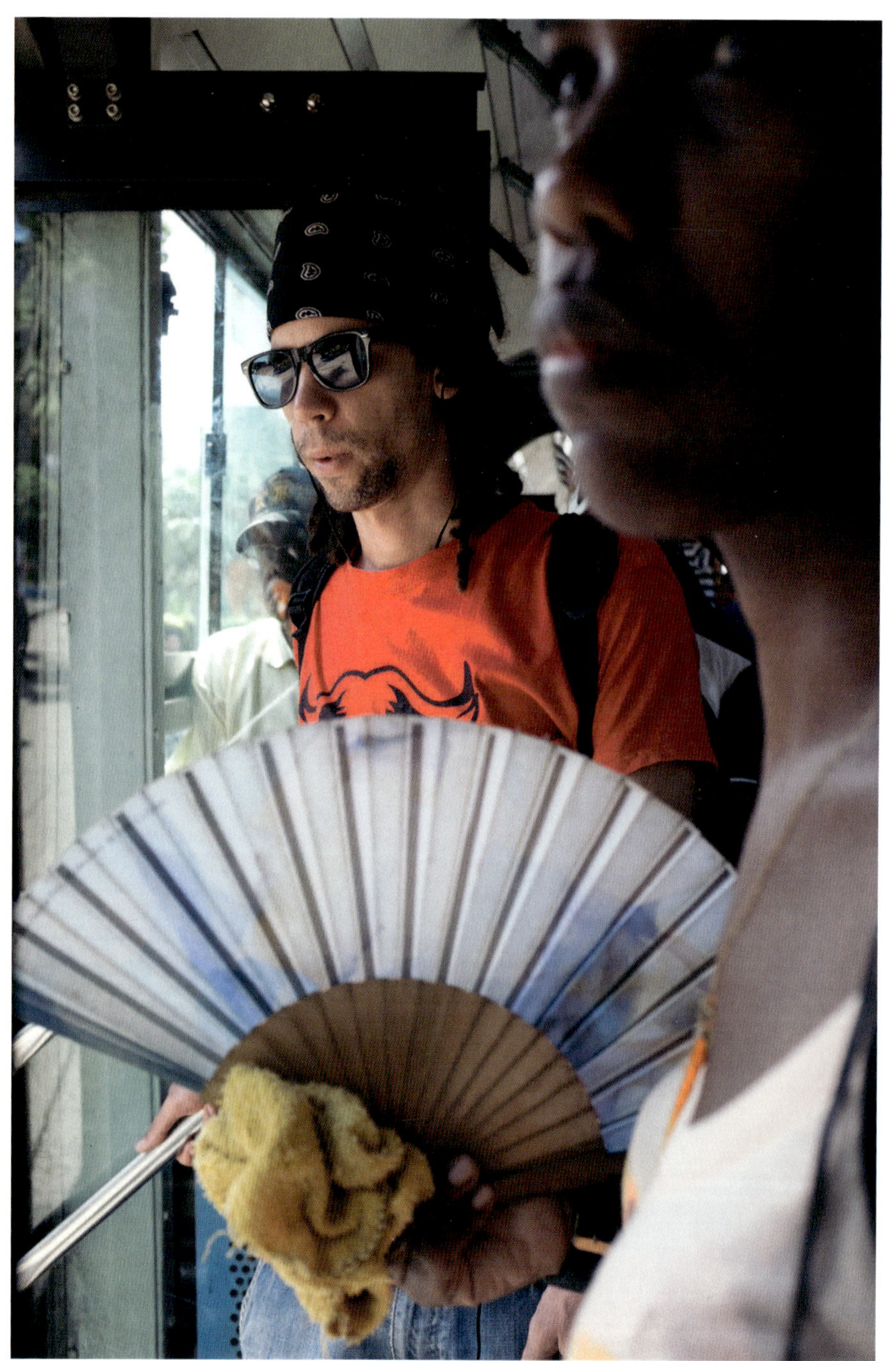

Havana, Cuba, 2015

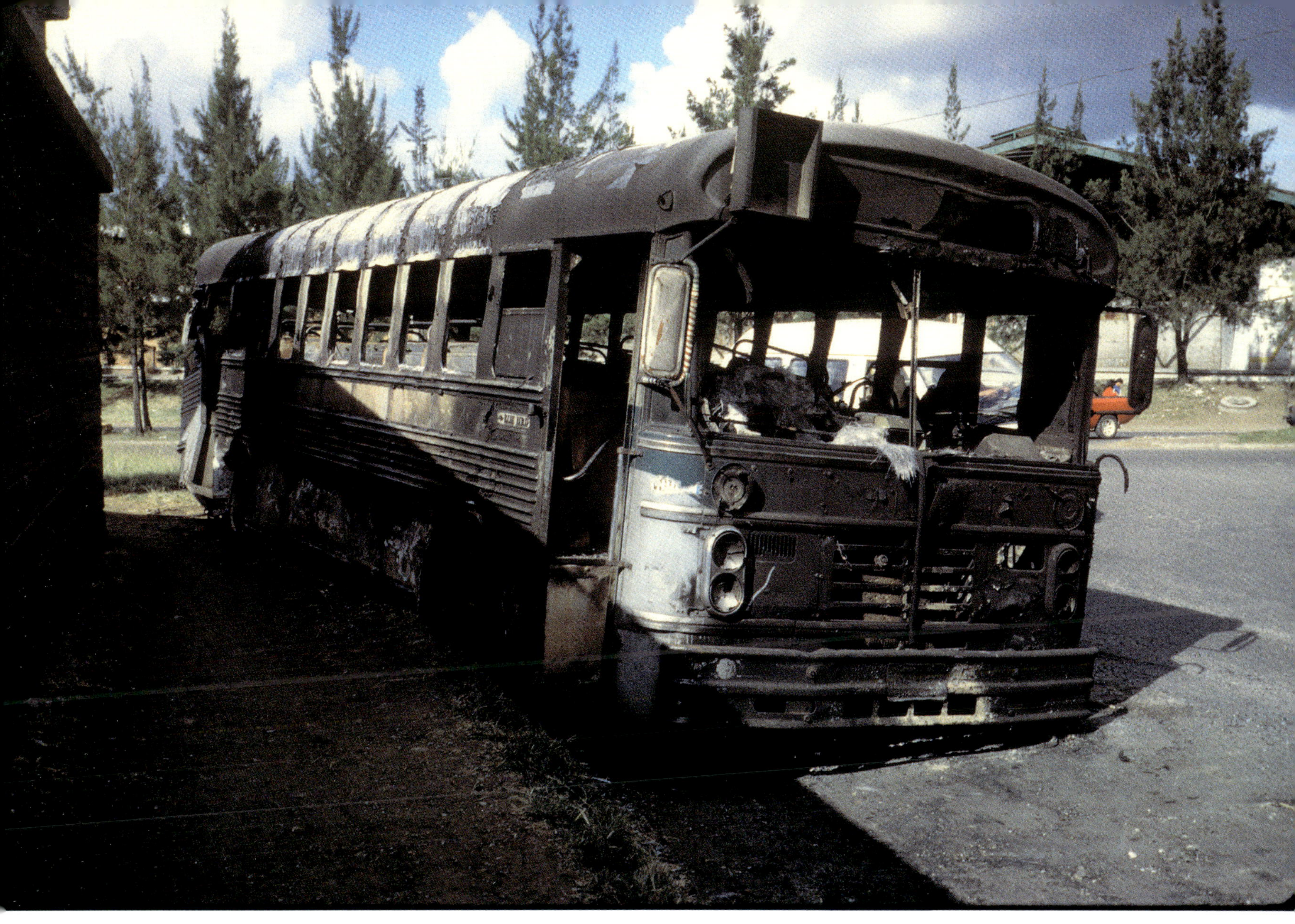

Outside of the San Carlos University, one of several city buses burned by people protesting bus fares that had just been raised by the government. Guatemala City, Guatemala, 1995

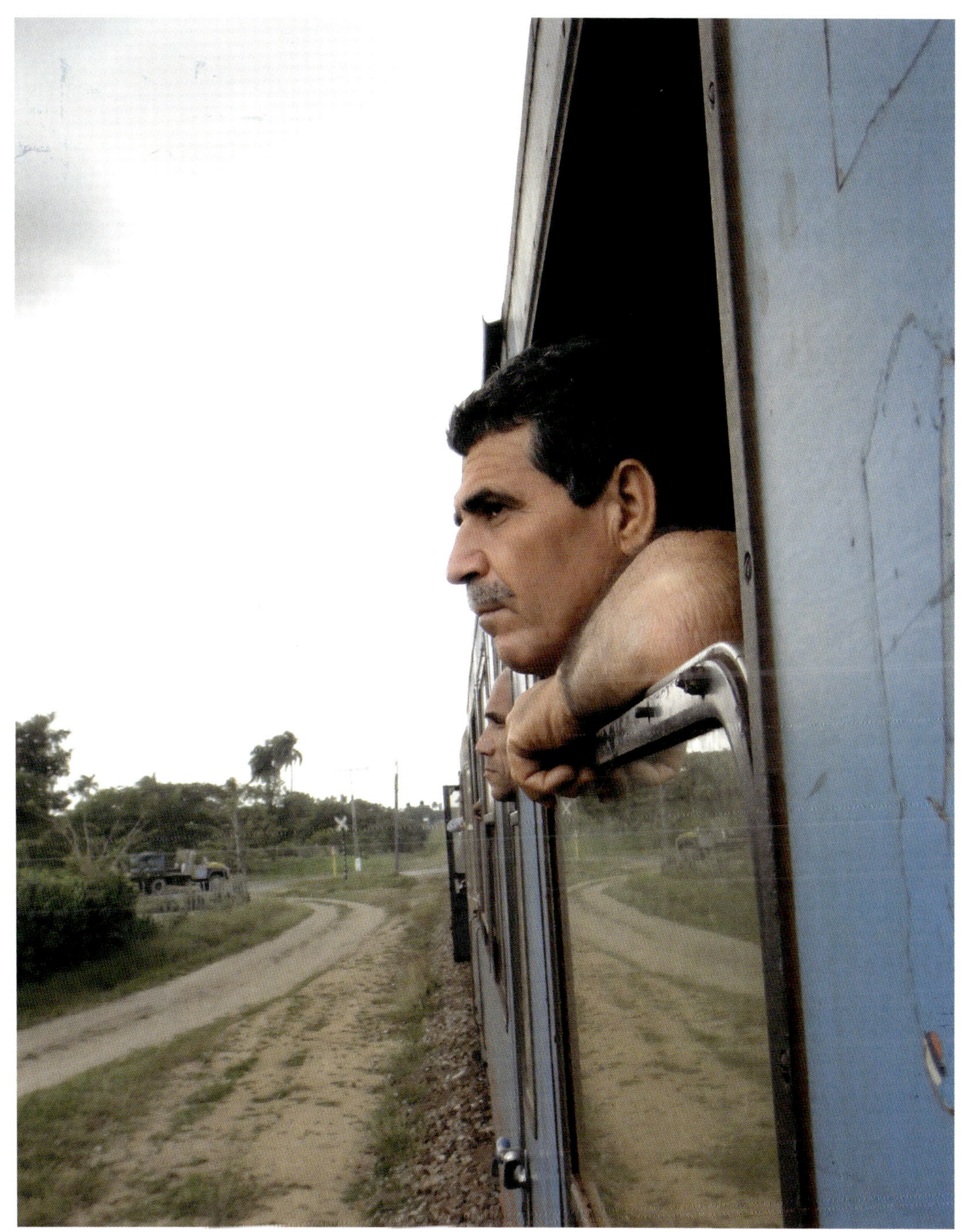

The train from Santiago to Santa Clara. Cuba, 2010

ACKNOWLEDGMENTS

Above all, I would like to express my profound gratitude to the people who contributed to this book with their writings and words: Harris Fogel, Margarita Saona, Jim Dow, Rudy Cotton, Guillermo Francisco Reyes González, Alpidio Alonso Grau, Stephen Perloff, Barbara Tannenbaum, Francisco Goldman and Brian Piper.

I am very grateful to Jim Dow and John Willis, who took the time to help me with the selection and sequence of images for this book. Special thanks also to the following people who shared their opinions with me about the photographs, possible titles for the book, and several other valuable thoughts and suggestions: Ann Morrow, Viviana Susa Parra, Lynn Sweezy, Kurt "Chico" Miron, Marsea Wynne, Francisco Goldman, and many others.

Thanks to Teresa Viera for facilitating the text by the Minister of Culture in Cuba. My thanks, also, to Harold Ober Associates, New York, for permission to include the poem "Subway Face" by Langston Hughes, and to the Wylie Agency for permission to include a quote by James Agee.

I am very grateful to Turner in Madrid for their excellent work editing, designing, and publishing this book—both this English edition and the edition in Spanish—; thanks especially to my editor, Laura Estévez, and also my new, second editor, Laura Badsey, and to the US copyeditor, Rees Storm; thanks also to the designer, Isabela Eseverri, as well as to María José Fresneda.

Finally, I wish to express my gratitude and respect for the people that appear in the photographs in this book, diverse examples of people in motion, in transit, our fellow humans on this planet who are working, traveling, commuting, struggling to survive, and all who are moving forward.

Thank you very much, everyone!

Jonathan "Jonás" Moller

JONATHAN MOLLER

Jonathan "Jonás" Moller is an award-winning documentary photographer and human rights activist. Since 1991 Moller has worked mostly in Central America (primarily Guatemala), as well as in Peru and in Cuba. He is the author of two books on Guatemala, *Our Culture Is Our Resistance* (powerHouse Books, New York, 2004) / *Nuestra cultura es nuestra resistencia* (Turner, Madrid, 2004) and *Rescatando nuestra memoria* (F&G Editores, Guatemala, 2009), a book about Peru, *The Past is Present / Paisajes ausentes* (Turner, Madrid, 2017), a book about the diversity of young Cubans, *Young Cuba / Cuba joven* (Turner, Madrid, 2018/2019), and the book *Black Lives Matter: Visualizing 2020* (Turner, Madrid, 2021).

Moller has exhibited and spoken widely in the United States, Latin America and Europe, in places as varied as the International Museum of Photography in Rochester, NY, McGill University in Montreal, the European Parliament in Brussels, the University of Granada, Spain, the Biblioteca Nacional del Perú, or the Memorial José Martí Museum in Havana. His photographs have been used by many NGOs in Latin America, the US and Europe for educational and advocacy purposes, from grassroots human rights and solidarity organizations to the Soros Foundation, Amnesty International and Human Rights Watch.

Moller's works are part of the permanent collections of more than twenty museums, including the San Francisco Museum of Modern Art, the Museum of Fine Arts Boston, the Museum of Fine Arts Houston, the Los Angeles County Museum of Art, the Brooklyn Museum of Art, the Museo Reina Sofía in Madrid, the Museo Nacional de Bellas Artes in Buenos Aires, the Casa de Las Americas in Havana, and the Museo de Arte in Lima.

www.jonathanmoller.org

PUBLISHER
TURNER

Coordination
Laura Estévez
Laura Badsey

Copyediting
Rees Storm

Design
Isabela Eseverri

Production
María José Fresneda

ISBN 978-84-19539-10-6
DL M-3459-2024